The information in this book is subject to change by catastrophic natural events, by the operators of restaurants, hotels and bars. There may also be errors on the part of the author and contributor.

First published in Italy in 1998 by
Tamari Montagna Edizioni
Viale S. Pertini 28, 35020 Maserà di Padova

Illustration and maps by Giuseppe Greco

Final English revision by Peter Barrow

ISBN 88-8043-052-1

THE ALPS OF TUSCANY

Selected hikes in the Apuane Alps, the Cinque Terre and Portofino

Francesco Greco
Illustration and Maps by Giuseppe Greco

TAMARI
Montagna
EDIZIONI

Acknowledgements

The idea for this book emerged after a group of hikers from the Mountaineers Club in Seattle visited Tuscany as part of an international exchange program with the Italian Alpine Club (CAI). I owe a deep debt of gratitude to members of both groups for their support, suggestions, and in some cases contribution of articles to this book. I would like particularly to thank:

USA (The Mountaineers): Helga Byhre, Clarence Elstad, Dianne Hoff (for the section on the Mountaineers, editing and suggestions), Jim Stiles (who has edited the Climbs section and given suggestions on Climbing equipment), Bev and Steve Johnson and Dave Coder (who has written the introduction to the Flora and edited all the Flora section);

Italy (CAI): Rolando Bandinelli, Pio Benedetti, Fabrizio and Francesca Broglia (for reviewing the description of all the hikes), Alberto Carmellini (the indefatigable organizer of the exchange program), Domenico Canino, Massimiliano Ferrini, Angelo Nerli (who has chosen and described the climbs), Carlo Jacob and Bruno Barsella (who have written the sections respectively on the trees and the flowers of the Apuane), Fabio Salomoni (for the section on the Italian Alpine Club, CAI), Alberto Bargagna, Walter Bencivelli, Piero Maestrini, Enzo Orlando, Maurizio Tronconi, Mauro Viegi and Lodo Gaetani (for the valuable contribution of the CAI section of Milano to the exchange program).

Special thanks go also to Peter and Johanna Barrow, Eric Ayrault and Cam Bradley for editing and considerably improving the manuscript. They first had to understand my Italian-English prose and then to convert the text into an understandable English and American-English respectively.

I am grateful to them all.

Contents

ILLUSTRATIONS

MAPS

Legend:

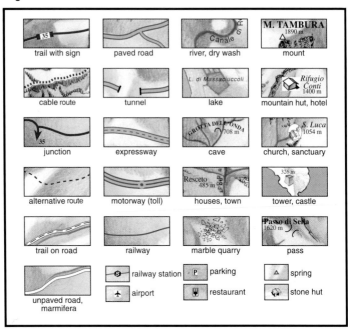

trail with sign	paved road
river, dry wash	mount
cable route	tunnel
lake	mountain hut, hotel
junction	expressway
cave	church, sanctuary
alternative route	motorway (toll)
houses, town	tower, castle
trail on road	railway
marble quarry	pass
unpaved road, marmifera	railway station
airport	parking
restaurant	spring
stone hut	

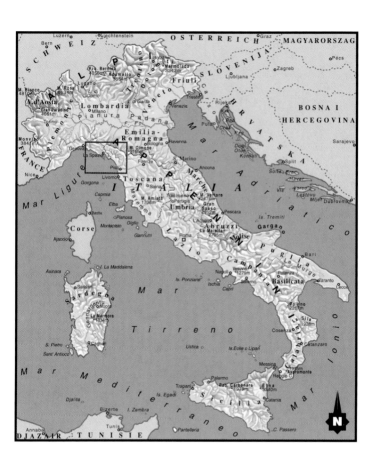

Map 1 - Italy, the Apuane Alps, The Cinque Terre and Portofino

Illustration 1 - The Apuane Alps

The hikes at a glance: a quick rating reference

Legend:

Diff	= difficulty (§)
Km	= length in kilometers
El	= elevation gain in meters
Time	= walking time in hours (§)
HiEl	= the highest elevation in meters

Rate: * a good walk

     ** a particularly good walk

     ***a walk that should not be missed

(§) Concerning classification of the hikes and walking time, see the chapter "Before Starting Your Hike".

Hikes in the Apuane Alps

Hike	Diff	Km	El	Time	HiEl	Rate	Comment
1-Procinto and M. Nona loop Start: Stazzema	S	12	850	5 ½	1297	*	One of the most interesting hikes in the southern part of the chain. Magnificent view from the summit. Visit the medieval town of Stazzema and its Romanesque church. The detour around the Cintura del Procinto is very enjoyable. Leave the climb of M. Procinto to well equipped and experienced hikers.
2-Pania della Croce Start: Levigliani	VS	14	1250	7	1859	***	This is the most popular hike and takes you to the summit of the most celebrated and frequently climbed mountain in the Apuane Alps. Some exposure along the west slope of the mountain.
3-M. Altissimo loop Start: Colle Cipollaio	M	9	700	4 ½	1589	***	One of the most panoramic hikes of the entire chain. It allows you to visit Michelangelo's marble quarries, follow a stretch of the Gothic Line and enjoy a 360° view of all the Apuane Alps.
4-Penna di Sumbra Start: Arni	S	13	900	6	1765	**	This hike traverses a lateral branch of the range, in Garfagnana. It is a long enjoyable hike along the south slope of M. Fiocca and the south ridge of Penna di Sumbra. Visit the old stone houses of Isola Santa.

Hike	Diff	Km	El	Time	HiEl	Rate	Comment
5-M. Sagro Start: Foce di Pianza	M	8	550	3 ½	1749	***	This hike has some of the best panoramic views in the Park. M. Sagro is very close to the sea and surrounded by marble quarries. Scenic drive from Carrara to Foce di Pianza.
6-Pizzo d' Uccello Start: Rifugio Donegani	M	8	700	4 ½	1781	***	Pizzo d' Uccello is the most northerly of the high mountains and one of the rockiest and boldest peaks in the Apuane. The scrambling to the top is exciting, some exposure. If the last stretch is omitted, the hike is still enjoyable and becomes easy.
7-M. Tambura, from Ametola Start: Ametola	S	8	1000	5	1890	***	M. Tambura is one of the highest mountains in the Apuane. The route follows the Garfagnana side of Via Vandelli and from Passo Tambura climbs up on marble scree and along the ridge to the top. Wide views of the coastline and the Apuane. Marble quarries.
8-M. Forato loop Start: Fornovolasco	M	10	800	5	1281	***	M. Forato is one of the most distinctive mountains of the Apuane Alps. The hike crosses stands of chestnut trees and climbs the south ridge up to the Arch with views of Versilia and Garfagnana. Enjoy the spectacular views from the Arch.

Hike	Diff	Km	El	Time	HiEl	Rate	Comment
9-M. Grondilice loop Start: Vinca	S	12	1000	6	1805	**	Along the route the environment changes dramatically: from the woods on the Vinca side to the rocky slopes of M. Grondilice, from the rocky Passo Grondilice to the grassy bucolic saddle of Foce di Giovo.
10-M. Tambura, from Resceto Start: Resceto	VS	15	1500	8	1890	***	The hike allows you to climb M. Tambura from the sea side. It crosses marble quarries, climbs along "via di lizza" and follows the most impressive stretch of Via Vandelli through dramatic scenery.
11-M. Sella Start: Resceto	S	12	1250	7	1739	**	M. Sella is one of the highest points on a long ridge in the central part of the chain. The hike climbs the wild Canale dei Piastriccioni and leads to the top along steep rocky slopes, with little vegetation, and along some "via di lizza".
Alternative hike: M. Sella loop	VS	16	1500	9	1739	**	Only those well equipped with climbing gear should attempt this interesting loop through Via Ferrata Vecchiacchi and along the most impressive stretch of Via Vandelli.
13-Pizzo d'Uccello loop Start: Rifugio Donegani	M	11	700	5½	1781	**	A little longer than Hike 6, this hike allows you to enjoy breathtaking views of the north wall of Pizzo d' Uccello. From Foce Siggioli to Giovetto the trail is steep and a little exposed.

15

Hike	Diff	Km	El	Time	HiEl	Rate	Comment
14-M. Pisanino Start: Rifúgio Donegani	S	12	1000	6 ½	1946	*	Monte Pisanino is the highest of the chain with very steep and grassy slopes all round. The first part of the trail through woodland is easy, it becomes steep and grassy after Foce Cardeto. Some exposure toward the summit.
15-M. Sagro loop, from Vinca Start: Vinca	VS	16	1300	8	1749	***	Monte Sagro has one of the best views in the Park. Starting from Vinca, on the Lunigiana side of the mountains, the hike passes through five interesting valleys and reaches the summit of the mountain.
16-M. Sagro loop, from Colonnata Start: Colonnata Start: Vergheto	VS	15	1400	8	1749	***	Almost the same itinerary as Hike 15, but starting from Colonnata, famous for "lardo" and its numerous marble quarries.
	S	12	1000	6	1749	***	From Case Vergheto the hike is shorter but still varied and very interesting.
17-M. Cavallo loop Start: Forno	VS	14	1400	7 ½	1752	**	This strenuous hike takes you through one of the wildest parts of the chain and passes some abandoned houses. Along the ridge the gradient is steep and the ground rough (some exposure). The trail passes close to the middle peak of M. Cavallo.

Hike	Diff	Km	El	Time	HiEl	Rate	Comment
18-Passo Uncini-M. Carchio Start: Pasquilio	M	10	700	5	1380	**	One of the most scenic routes in the south-west area of the Apuane, with wonderful views of the mountains and the coast. Some exposure from M. Focoraccia to Passo degli Uncini.
19-M. Matanna loop Start: Trescolli (Casoli)	M	10	850	5	1317	**	The hike is in the southern part of the Apuane. You walk across terraced fields on a hillside overlooking the sea and enjoy extensive views from the summit.
20-M. Croce loop Start: Palagnana	M	9	600	4	1314	**	From the summit of M. Croce you will enjoy one of the best views of Pania della Croce. The hike is in the southern part of the Apuane on the Garfagnana side. In May the mountain is full of narcissus and asphodels.
21-M. Gabberi loop Start: Farnocchia	E	8	500	3 ½	1108	*	This short and beautiful hike starts from the village of Farnocchia and passes first through chestnut and then beech woods near the top. From the summit there is a wide panorama of the coast and sea, lake Massaciuccoli, and the surrounding mountains.

Hike	Diff	Km	El	Time	HiEl	Rate	Comment
22-Pizzo delle Saette-Pania della Croce Start: Piglionico	S	12	950	6 ½	1859	***	A very enjoyable hike, strenuous but varied, which allows you to have a rest at the highest manned rifugio, to enjoy wide views of the entire group and descend Borra di Canala, one of the wildest canyons in the chain. There is some exposure in some parts of the hike. If you wish, you can have a shorter hike, without exposure and still very enjoyable.
23-M. Corchia loop Start: Passo Croce	M	10	700	5	1677	*	The hike is varied and panoramic, crosses grassy slopes, climbs rocky ridges and a steep couloir (a little exposure) and reaches the summit of M. Corchia. Rifugio Del Freo, with its red walls, is on the route.
24-M. Freddone loop Start: Tre Fiumi (Ami)	M	10	750	5	1487	**	An easy and exciting scramble along the north-east ridge of M. Freddone (some exposure). The hike passes through the beautiful village of Campanice with its ruined stone houses, a church and a bell tower, the last two are still intact.

Hike	Diff	Km	El	Time	HiEl	Rate	Comments
25-M. Fiocca Start: Ametola	S	11	850	5 ½	1711	*	The trail to Passo Sella is one of the most romantic in the Apuane Alps, for most of the way through a wood of beech trees. From the summit of M. Fiocca there are wonderful views of the mountains and of the Turrite Secca valley.
30-Solco di Equi and Via Ferrata to Foce Siggioli	S	8	1200	5 ½	1417	**	The first approach to climbing in the Apuane Alps. It allows you to climb the Via Ferrata to Foce Siggioli along a knife-edged ridge with wonderful views of the north wall of Pizzo d'Uccello.

Hikes along the Cinque Terre Riviera

Hike	Diff	Km	El	Time	HiEl	Rate	Comment
12-Cinque Terre Start: Monterosso	M	12	650	5	300	***	This is one of the most scenic coastal paths in Italy. Enjoy the five picturesque villages, terraced fields, olive groves, orange and lemon trees, agaves and cactuses, the Mediterranean bush, on steep slopes running down to the sea, and the complete absence of cars between the villages.
27-Camogli - Portofino Start: Camogli	S	15	600	5 ½	300	***	A delightful coastal hike around M. Portofino. The hike has splendid views of the high cliffs over the sea and most of the way one is surrounded by Mediterranean bush. Visit the ancient Abbey of San Fruttuoso and the picturesque villages of Camogli, Portofino and Santa Margherita.
28-Riomaggiore-Portovenere Start: Riomaggiore	M	10	700	5	511	***	Together with the Cinque Terre this is one of the finest coastal hikes in Italy. From the "Santuario di Montenero" there are spectacular views of the coast and villages from Portovenere to Punta Mesco. The last stretch has breathtaking views of the Bay of the Poets and of the islands of Palmaria and Tino. The hike eventually reaches the beautiful and picturesque village of Portovenere.

Hike	Diff	Km	El	Time	HiEl	Rate	Comment
29-Monterosso-Levanto Start: Monterosso	E	8	400	3	350	*	This short and easy hike gives you wide views of the coast from Monterosso to Portovenere to the south and from Levanto to Portofino to the north. Punta Mesco is a beautiful promontory covered in Mediterranean bush and stands of Umbrella Pine trees.

Planning a hiking holiday in the Apuane Alps

The first eight hikes in the Apuane Alps described in this book were selected in order that the Mountaineers two weeks in the Apuane Alps would give them as varied and complete a picture as possible of the area (see the chapter entitled "Hiking in the Apuane Alps: The Mountaineers-CAI program"). The purpose of this chapter is to help you plan either a shorter or a longer visit. Since none of the trailheads is more than two hours drive from virtually anywhere in the area, the following recommendations apply wherever you are staying.

If you have one day:
- *Pania della Croce, from Levigliani* (Hike 2), or
- *Pizzo delle Saette and Pania della Croce from Piglionico* (Hike 22), if you prefer a less strenuous hike and have no fear of heights.

If you have two days, in addition to the previous hike:
-*Monte Altissimo, from Colle del Cipollaio* (Hike 3).

For three days, in addition to the previous two hikes think about either
- *Monte Sagro from Foce di Pianza* (Hike 5), or
- *Monte Sagro loop from Vinca* (Hike 15), or
- *Monte Sagro loop from Colonnata* (Hike 16),
the latter two being both very strenuous and very rewarding.

For a four day visit, in addition to the previous hikes choose one of:
- *Pizzo d' Uccello* (Hike 6), if you have no fear of heights, otherwise
- *Monte Grondilice* (Hike 9).

With five days available: in addition to the previous hikes:
- *Monte Nona loop* (Hike 1).

For six days, in addition to the previous hikes:
- *Monte Forato loop from Fornovolasco* (Hike 8).

If you can spend seven days hiking then it is suggested that you add:
- *Penna di Sumbra* (Hike 4).

With eight days: you may follow the entire program of hikes in the Apuane Alps of The Mountaineers.

If you are going to spend more than eight days hiking, the "Quick

Rating Reference" section will help you choose additional hikes. But however many days you spend in the Apuane Alps you should do one of the two walks on the East Ligurian Coast, that is the
- *Cinque Terre* (Hike 12), or the
- *Camogli - San Fruttuoso - Portofino -*
  Santa Margherita Ligure (Hike 27).
You really must do one or the other of these two famous walks.

Introduction

Tuscany and the Apuane Alps

Have you ever been in Tuscany? Even if you have not, you assuredly will know something of this part of Italy which has been a favourite destination for tourists for centuries. If you are interested in art and architecture, and in their history, if you enjoy visiting medieval towns and exploring romantic countryside and certainly if you like to combine these pleasures with those of the table, then sooner or later you are sure to find yourself in Tuscany.

But have you ever been in the Apuane Alps? It is much less likely that you have visited the Apuane Alps, or indeed know a great deal about them. This is surprising in view of the fact that bits of these mountains are spread around the world. For these are mountains of marble, used by the Romans since the second century B.C., and by sculptors from Michelangelo to Henry Moore. When you have looked down at a perfectly smooth marble floor, been dazzled by the sun reflected by the white marble walls of a church or office block or been moved by the perfection of a Michelangelo statue you probably were looking at a piece of the Apuane Alps.

The mountains from which the marble has been taken contain magnificent peaks, deep canyons and a really wild environment only a few kilometers from the sea. And all this is close to the highly urbanized parts of Tuscany to the south and to the fashionable beaches of Versilia to the west. You can hike for hours, gaining thousands of meters of height and climbing walls up to seven hundred meters high. And when you reach the top the views are unforgettable. The whole coastline of Tuscany and the islands of the Tuscan archipelago, Capraia, Gorgona and Elba are spread out before you, to the east is the Apennine range and on particularly clear days you can see the mountains of Corsica and even the Maritime Alps.

The purpose of this book is to introduce you to some of the most enjoyable hikes in the Apuane Alps and at the same time to suggest places where to stay and especially, this being Italy, to eat. The book is organized to help you choose the hikes which will fit in with your schedule, your hiking experience and fitness. To this end, in addition to the detailed description of each of the thirty recommended hikes, comprehensive reference information is provided including a table of contents, lists of maps and illustrations and a reference table covering all the hikes to help in choosing the ones to do. There are several chapters with background information designed to enhance your enjoyment of the mountains; the areas covered include the trees and flowers of the Apuane, mountain huts, hiking clubs, climbing in the Apuane, Tuscan cuisine, driving in Italy and suggested local contacts.

All hikers would surely agree that any experience of the mountains is enhanced if it is shared with like minded mountain lovers. Readers of this book will soon realise that the author believes that when the experience is shared with local mountain lovers who know the mountains, the language, the culture, the history and the food and wine of the area then this enjoyment will be infinitely greater. In fact this book owes its genesis to a visit to the Apuane Alps in the context of an international exchange program which took place in 1995. The program and experiences of this two week program provide a great model for the intending visitor and therefore a little space is devoted to this subject here.

The exchange was organised between The Mountaineers of Seattle in Washington, USA and the Alpine Club of Italy (CAI). These two clubs, together with some friends from England who were already familiar with the Apuane Alps, organised a two week program. Included in the program were hikes in all parts of the Apuane, both the wilder and loftier central and northern sections, and the gentler slopes of the no less interesting southern part of the range. In addition sightseeing tours to Pisa, Lucca, Volterra, San Gimignano and Vico Pisano were included as was a hike along the coast through the Cinque Terre which, though it is not in the Apuane Alps, is close by - no walker should fail to include at least one day walking on this picturesque coast, so details of the best walks there are included in this book.

In October 1995 the visitors from America were immersed in local culture, food and wine as guests of CAI members, in Pisa and later in Milano. With the memories of this in mind, and following a return visit by CAI members to the Mountaineers in Washington State, this book has been conceived to encourage other English-speaking hikers to enjoy the beauty of these mountains. Walking, eating, drinking, singing and talking with local mountain lovers need not to be limited to special exchange programs of this sort because the local sections of CAI (their addresses are given) organize hikes, mainly at the weekend, for local members. They would be delighted to lead you on hikes in their beloved mountains; we can assure you of a warm welcome should you choose to join them.

Have a great time in Tuscany and enjoy your hikes in the Apuane!

The organization of this book

After the table of contents, illustrations and maps, a hike reference table is provided. This enables you to have a quick look at the hikes to see which ones best suit your schedule, fitness, etc. There follow several chapters of general introductory information including a description of the geography and climate of the Apuane Alps, transportation, trails and alpine huts.

Next comes the detailed description of some thirty hikes. The chapter with Selected Hikes contains the hikes which the Mountaineers did during their visit and, as these were selected to include a wide variety of hikes in all parts of the Apuane, they will give you a comprehensive picture of the mountains in the shortest possible time. The only hike which the Mountaineers did outside the confines of the Apuane Alps was the Cinque Terre; it can be done at any time, in fact it is recommended as a relaxing day following a strenuous day's hiking; the hike follows one of the most beautiful coastal paths in Italy. Included in this chapter are three additional hikes (*Monte Grondilice*, from Vinca, *Monte Tambura* and *Monte Sella*, both from the town of Resceto) which were not included in the Mountaineers' itinerary only because the time available precluded it and because they were a little more strenuous than the others. In a separate chapter are included another thirteen hikes. They give the hiker with sufficient time the opportunity to enjoy further wonderful views of these mountains. The next chapter covers some two day or longer hikes; for these you can either stay in a mountain hut (*rifugio*) or you can camp. There follows a chapter with a further three lovely hikes along the Cinque Terre Riviera.

The chapter covering "Climbs in the Apuane Alps" is of course dedicated to rock climbers; the climbs have been suggested and described by Angelo Nerli, President of the CAI section of Pisa, at the time of the exchange, and one of the authors of the most complete guide to these mountains, see References. To increase your enjoyment of other natural aspects of these mountains there is a chapter on the "Flora of the Apuane Alps", including a section on trees, written by Carlo Jacob, and on flowers by Bruno Barsella.

The most important information of all, for most hikers and climbers, is contained in the chapter "Where to stay, What to eat, Where to eat, Rifugio". Special care has therefore been devoted to its preparation, the details are based almost entirely on the personal experience of the author and his friends. A particular emphasis has been put on the kind of food that you, but also some Italians, might never have tasted or even read about, even in specialized publications about food and restaurants.

The appendices contain some of the material which was distributed to the participants in the International Exchange Program. This includes: a short presentation about the Alpine Club of Italy, written by Fabio Salomoni, the current president of the CAI section of Pisa; a description of the Mountaineers Club, by Dianne Hoff, at present Chair-person of the International Exchange Activity of The Mountaineers; and the program of the "CAI-The Mountaineers" exchange. More detailed are the chapters "Welcome to Italy" and "Driving in Italy", which could be of some interest to hikers and climbers, as well as to any tourist arriving in Italy. Further appendices cover the most common measurement units and conversion tables, a list of all the CAI Sections around the Apuane and Cinque Terre, a complete list of all the CAI trails in the Apuane Alps, and the main trails along the Cinque Terre and Monte Portofino. Finally you will find the bibliographical references and the index.

The Apuane Alps

The Geography of the Apuane Alps

The Apuane Alps are a chain of mountains located in Tuscany, between Carrara and Lucca. The main chain stretches about 60 km from the north-west to the south-east and is about 30 km wide. The entire group lies between a latitude of 44°13' and 43°45' north and a longitude of 9°52' and 10°27' east. The Apuane Alps are very close to the Tyrrhenian sea - Monte Altissimo and Monte Sagro being only about 10 km from the sea. Altissimo means "very high" and in fact, since it is so close to the sea, from the west the mountain does indeed seem to be one of the highest, even though the summit is only 1589 m. The northern part of the Apuane Alps, delimited by the Magra river, is called **Lunigiana**, of which Aulla is one of the main towns. In the east the Apuane Alps are separated from the nearby Apennines by the valley of the Aulella river, in the north part, and by the valley of the Serchio river, in the central and southern part. This region, between the Apuane Alps and the Apennines, is called **Garfagnana**. The principal town in Garfagnana is Castelnuovo (in the sixteenth century, between 1522 and 1525, Lodovico Ariosto, the author of the epic "Orlando Furioso", was Governor of this town). The narrow coastal plain to the west is called **Versilia**, it has many well-known summer beach resorts. The main towns here are Carrara, Massa, Forte dei Marmi, Pietrasanta and Viareggio.

The Apuane Alps are not very high; the highest mountain is Monte Pisanino, 1946 m. Nevertheless, since they are very close to the sea and the mountains appear much more "mountainous", especially from the sea side, and rockier than the Apennines, they have been called Alps. They are the **Alps of Tuscany**. They differ from the Apennines also from the geological point of view. While the Apennines are made of sedimentary rocks, the central nucleus of the Apuane Alps consists almost entirely of marble. The rocks, which originally were sedimentary (originating as sea bed) like the Apennines, were later transformed into crystal-like metamorphic rocks, through very strong pressure and high temperature during the corrugation phase.

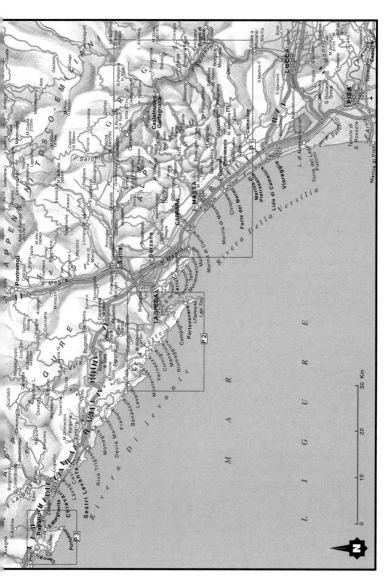

Map 2 - Portofino, Cinque Terre and Alpi Apuane

Climate, Best period, What to wear and What to take

Spring and autumn are the best seasons for hiking in the Apuane Alps. In spring, the mountains are covered with flowers, and in autumn, chestnuts and mushrooms are ready to be collected - there are local rules governing these activities. Summer is very hot for hiking, but the wild raspberries and blueberries which cover some of the slopes are a great temptation. If you do hike in the summer, you should plan for a swim at the end of your hike. The sea is just a few miles from the mountains. In winter the mountains are covered by snow and the hikes, easy in the other seasons, may become very dangerous and strenuous, and usually require the use of ice-axe and crampons. Hiking here in winter does provide you with the same sort of experience as hiking in very high mountains, but with quite different risks. Here in fact there is no risk of avalanches, but there is a very high risk of slipping on the ice. Ice often covers the snow, due to the very great difference between night and day temperatures. And, once you reach the top, you enjoy wonderful views of the sea and the islands. But you must have the necessary skills and equipment.

In spring and autumn in the Apuane Alps the weather may be warm and, on sunny days, hot. However at the top of the mountains it is often chilly, and if it is cloudy or windy it may even be cold. In the eastern slopes the weather may be a little cooler than in the west. Nights at a rifugio can be cold. Humidity is high in November and low in July and August. Rain is frequent since the rain-laden clouds from the sea meet this western-most range and also because there are often winds from the north-east. The rainiest months are usually October and December on the west slopes, and May on the east slopes. As the exception proving the rule, while hiking with The Mountaineers from October 17 to the beginning of November, we had only one day of rain. In any case, whichever the month, some rain protection, such as a light poncho or even better an umbrella, is essential. There should always be a pullover and a wind jacket in your rucksack. Extra clothes may be useful to have with you on higher hikes late in autumn and early in spring. And do not forget a flashlight, whistle and compass. From a less pessimistic point of view sun cream, sunglasses and a hat should always be carried. For all the hikes it is suggested that comfortable boots suitable for lightweight hiking should be worn. For the very strenuous hikes be sure to wear boots with good ankle support.

There are springs and other sources of fresh water, which is generally drinkable. Sometimes you find beside the fountain a glass for those passing by. Anyway you should have with you all the water you need for the day, it may be hot and you may not find a spring. In Italy, as usual everywhere in the Alps, you may carry with you all the wine you want. In the rucksack of Italian hikers is usually found a bottle of wine to be enjoyed at the summit of the mountains. Do not forget your corkscrew!

Roads around the Apuane Alps

The Apuane Alps are completely surrounded by roads:

- in Versilia, the western side from Viareggio to Sarzana, the motorway (*autostrada*) A12 from Genova to Livorno, and parallel to this the "Aurelia" State road # 1. The Via Aurelia was the road made by the Romans to connect Rome to Gallia (France) through Ventimiglia;

- on the northern side, from Sarzana to Aulla, the State road #62 "della Cisa", and the motorway A15 "Parma-La Spezia";

- in Garfagnana, the eastern side, the road connecting Lucca with Castelnuovo Garfagnana, and from here to Aulla through Minucciano;

- on the southern side, the road from Viareggio to Camaiore and from Camaiore to Lucca, and the new motorway A11 "Viareggio-Lucca".

In the past crossing this mountain barrier was not at all easy. Only footpaths connected the towns on opposite sides of the mountains. Along the paths there are still very small stone huts, called *marginette* in Versilia and *maesta'* in Garfagnana, built long ago to provide a shelter and a spot for praying for the walkers. Nowadays the Apuane Alps are crossed by the narrow and winding road from Querceta to Castelnuovo Garfagnana (41.5 km long) through the tunnel *Galleria del Cipollaio*, at a height of 799 m. The road is also known as *La Strada del Cipollaio*. A more recent road, connecting Massa to Garfagnana directly, also crosses the main divide of these mountains, at an elevation of a little more than 1000 m, through the tunnel of *Monte Pelato*. But a couple of kilometers after the tunnel it joins (km 23.5 from Massa) the previous road to

Castelnuovo Garfagnana. This road is called *La Strada di Pian della Fioba*. Both the roads are very panoramic and we suggest that you drive them in any case.

La Strada del Cipollaio: from Querceta to Castelnuovo Garfagnana

To reach Querceta, from the motorway *Genova-Livorno* take the exit *Versilia* and follow the signs to "Castelnuovo G.", where G. stands for Garfagnana. After Querceta the road passes through the towns of Corvaia and Seravezza (50 m elevation), here on the right of the road is a beautiful *Medici* villa, 1561-1565, lately used as the City Hall (in Italian *il Comune*); the road then winds along the valley of the river Vezza. After passing the town of Ruosina (102 m elevation) and passing the fork to Ponte Stazzemese and Stazzema, the road starts climbing the steep slopes of the mountain up to a long and narrow tunnel, *Galleria del Cipollaio*, at a height of 799 m. Before the tunnel and on the way up, there is a view of *Pizzo Falcovaia*, now an open-air marble quarry. The peak has been literally cut off and along the side there is a talus slope of marble debris.

Illustration 2 - Pizzo delle Saette (1720 m), from Isola Santa in the valley of Turrite Secca

After the tunnel the road enters Garfagnana and descends along a narrow valley, named *Canale del Freddone*, and reaches the *Turrite Secca valley*, one of the wildest in the Apuane, in the area called *Tre Fiumi* (Three Rivers, about 750 m elevation). The Turrite Secca is a creek along a deep and narrow valley almost all the way running underground, so the name *secca*, which means dry. Here there is an intersection with the road to Arni (916 m) which has recently been extended to Massa (*La Strada di Pian della Fioba*). Very soon after the intersection, along the main road, at the *Bar Trattoria La Romana*, you can try the tasty *Focaccia con il lardo di Colonnata* (a flat and round home-made bread filled with lardo from Colonnata, another small town very close to Carrara and famous also for its numerous marble quarries; in off-season, available weekends only). Along this part of the road there are wonderful views: on the left are *Monte Fiocca* and the almost vertical marble wall of *Penna di Sumbra* and, on the right, *Pizzo delle Saette, Pania della Croce* and *Pania Secca*. The road passes through the village of Isola Santa (550 m, which means Holy Island, since in the past centuries there was a hotel for the pilgrims crossing the valley) and after about 41.5 Km from the start the road enters Castelnuovo Garfagnana (elevation 270 m).

At the beginning of the twentieth century the part of the road from the sea to the mountains was a railway used mainly for transporting marble from the quarries of *Monte Altissimo* and *Monte Corchia* to the coast. There are interesting old pictures of this railway at the Hotel Raffaello in Levigliani (one of the hosts, Raffaella Barsottini or Lido Poli, will be very happy to show them to you).

La Strada di Pian della Fioba: from Massa to Tre Fiumi

To reach Massa, take the exit *Massa* from the autostrada *Genova-Livorno*. From Massa (64 m elevation) the road climbs and after several switchbacks in 4 km reaches the small spa village of San Carlo Po (294 m). While driving, you may have glimpses of the old Castle of Malaspina and, when in San Carlo Po, from the parking lot, like a balcony over the sea, you have wonderful views of the coast and the Gulf of La Spezia and *Bocca di Magra* (mouth of the Magra River). After San Carlo Po the road passes through the town of Antona (10 km from Massa, 402 m elevation) and, with several switchbacks, in 6 km reaches the pass *Pian della Fioba* (860 m), from which you have breathtaking views of the main divide of the Apuane Alps. Very close by there is an Alpine Botanical Garden and the *Rifugio Citta' di Massa* (900 m). The road runs now along the slope of the mountain, through five short tunnels and finally enters Garfagnana through the tunnel of *Monte Pelato*, 21 km from Massa, about 1050 m elevation. Shortly after the tunnel you find the restaurant-hotel *Le Gobbie*, 1037 m elevation. From here the road slowly descends, past some marble quarries, through the town of Arni, and reaches the road from Querceta to Castelnuovo Garfagnana, in the area called *Tre Fiumi*, 2.5 km from the tunnel.

Railroads and Busses

The Apuane Alps are also surrounded by State Railroads (*Ferrovie dello Stato - FS*). Trains connect Lucca to Aulla, Aulla to Viareggio and Pisa, Viareggio or Pisa to Lucca. The trains are not expensive. Unfortunately, almost all the train stations are far from the trailheads. In some cases you may take a bus, in other cases you have to walk to the trailhead (a lift would of course be useful but is very unlikely that you will find anybody going to your trailhead).

From **Pietrasanta** busses leave for:

- *Stazzema, Levigliani, Galleria del Cipollaio, Tre Fiumi, Arni*: four times on weekdays, once on Sundays and holidays; it takes about 1½ h from Pietrasanta to Arni;

- *Isola Santa, Castelnuovo Garfagnana*: twice on weekdays and once on Sundays and holidays; from Pietrasanta to Isola Santa the ride takes about 1½ h, and ½ h from Isola Santa to Castelnuovo.

From **Castelnuovo Garfagnana** busses leave for:

- *Isola Santa, Tre Fiumi, Arni*: three times on weekdays and once on Sundays and holidays; from Castelnuovo to Arni it takes about ½ h;

- *Galleria del Cipollaio, Levigliani, Seravezza*: twice on weekdays and once on Sundays and holidays; from Castelnuovo to Seravezza it takes 1½ h;

- *Gramolazzo, Gorfigliano and Minucciano*: three times on weekdays; it takes about 1¼ h from Castelnuovo to Minucciano;

- *Vagli di Sotto, Vagli di Sopra*: twice on weekdays; it takes about 50 minutes from Castelnuovo to Vagli di Sopra.

From **Piazza al Serchio** busses leave for:

- *Gramolazzo, Gorfigliano, Minucciano:* three times on weekdays; it takes 35 minutes from Piazza al Serchio to Minucciano.

From **Gallicano**, with railway connections, the station is "Barga-Gallicano", busses leave for:

- *Fornovolasco*: twice on weekdays; 30 minutes.

From **Lucca** busses leave for:

- *Fabbriche di Vallico, Gragliana* (5 km from Palagnana): three on weekdays; the ride takes about 1¼ h from Lucca to Gragliana.

Weekdays are from Monday to Saturday. In Italian, weekday is referred as *giorno feriale,* while Sunday or holiday as *giorno festivo.*

For information, bus stops and schedules, call:

-CLAP:	Pietrasanta	0584	792107
	Castelnuovo G.	0583	62039
	Lucca	0583	587897
-Autolinee Donati-Gallicano		0583	74028
-FS Stations:	Aulla	0187	420491
	Carrara Avenza	0585	858124
	Castelnuovo G.	0583	62364
	Lucca	0583	47013
	Massa	0585	790791
	Piazza al Serchio	0583	60021
	Pisa	050	41385
	Viareggio	0584	44350

About trails and trailheads

There is a convenient numbering system for the ubiquitous trails in the Apuane Alps. The numbers guiding you are on rocks along the side of the trail, signs at junctions or displayed on marginetta, the covered shelters maintained for travellers in need of rest. Trail numbers are usually painted on small rectangular signs, called *segnavia*. The sign will have three bands, white in the middle with red on either side. Summit routes, however, are usually signed with blue marks. Full numbered labels are usually present at the start and at significant stops. Simpler red marks are used as blazes on the path. Look for them on rocks, trees, and walls. For a complete list of the trail numbers go to the chapter "The CAI trails in the Apuane Alps".

Hikers' maps at 1:25000 and 1:50000 (see References) are available in news-stands and bookstores. Unfortunately they have not recently been updated. There are no official park entrances and at the beginning of the trails there may not be any posted information about the Park. There are no toilets along the trails, except for natural ones in the open air. In Tuscany, as in the rest of Italy and Europe, regional or national parks include both wild and more developed areas. The extent of civilization here is such that it is difficult to escape from the impact of people. In fact, the charm of these areas lies in their balance between nature and civilization.

In Parks like the Apuane Alps paths, trails and roads may have been in existence for centuries. These routes were established for the use of local villagers, workers in the marble quarries, and religious pilgrims. Originally the trails started directly from town centers. If you start your excursion in the center of small towns like Levigliani or Stazzema, or others in the Versilia or Garfagnana areas, you will see the local routes on a large notice-board. There will be a diagram or map of the trail system with trail numbers and walking times, sometimes sculptured in the marble. The red blazes on stone walls and houses will become familiar as they lead you on your way. In recent times, development and new roads have altered many of the routes. Trailheads have occasionally been moved from the center of town. Today there may or may not be a fixed trailhead. Therefore sometimes it is difficult for the directions for finding the trailhead to be precise and clear, since you may start from different locations along the way. Be patient! You may find red marks and trail signs before reaching the actual start of the hike (mainly because of new roads) or you may find that the trail you have started after a while takes you to a new road and from there it may be difficult to find the next red mark. Please keep this in mind as you navigate. As a general rule, follow the directions outlined in the description of the hikes and, if the information proves inadequate, please feel free to ask local people: they will be very happy to help you and this could be an opportunity for you also to get acquainted with local people and who knows...? The directions to the trailheads have been given on the assumption that you have a car. For the hikes along the Ligurian coast, we recommend that you take the train. In this case not only can you enjoy a ride by train, but also you can plan interesting loops.

Via Ferrata and Sentiero Attrezzato (cable route)

Via Ferrata and *Sentiero Attrezzato* (literally: Equipped Trail) are rock-climbing routes secured with metal cables, iron ladders, iron pitons, and/or steps cut in the rock. The way up is then easier and safer for climbers without any fear of heights. A Sentiero Attrezzato is usually shorter and less difficult than a Via Ferrata. To climb a Via Ferrata you must have your climbing harness, a helmet, a sling and a carabiner for self-belay on the cable and along the ladder. In the Apuane Alps there are several Vie Ferrate (plural of Via Ferrata):

- the *Via Ferrata di Foce Siggioli*, made in 1971 by the CAI section of Pisa, see the first climbing route in the Climbs;

-the *Via Ferrata del Procinto*, the oldest one, made in 1893 by the CAI section of Firenze, see "Hike 1- Procinto and Monte Nona loop";

- the *Via Ferrata Vecchiacchi*, made in 1977 by the CAI section of Lucca, see "Hike 11- Monte Sella";

- the *Via Ferrata Salvadori* along the crest of Monte Forato, made in 1978 by the CAI sections of Versilia, see "Hike 8 - Monte Forato loop";

- the *Via Ferrata Piotti* from Vinca to Foce di Giovo;

- and finally, the *Via Ferrata Zaccagna* from Solco di Equi to Vinca through the Cresta Nattapiana, at Foce dei Lizzari.

Rifugio (Mountain hut)

A *rifugio* is an alpine hut which provides a shelter in the mountains to hikers and climbers. In the Apuane Alps there are several rifugio. You will find a complete list of the rifugio, CAI and private, in the Apuane Alps in the chapter "Where to eat, What to eat, Where to stay, Rifugio".

Some rifugio are manned, and in this case they provide meals. Others are unmanned but have bunks and outhouses for overnight visitors. Many require reservations for overnight stays, though you can always stop in for lunch. While each rifugio may have a different schedule, they are all normally open during summer weekends, and many are open all summer long. In the winter, most rifugio are not open, but they often have a room or a section open, called *locale invernale*, where you can come in for shelter, but there will be no meals. Most of the rifugio in the Apuane are owned by CAI, and special rates for food and accommodation are available for CAI members and members of other Clubs which are in turn members of UIAA (*Union Internationale des Associations d'Alpinisme*).

I strongly encourage you to take advantage of the rifugio system, at least for a meal if not for overnight. The rifugio are friendly gathering places for mountaineers and hikers, and provide a wonderful opportunity to share a meal and conversation with other hikers, typically Italians from the area. In this way you can see the remote beauty of the Italian mountains without missing the warmth, culture, and wine of the Italian people.

The Natural Park of the Apuane Alps and Visitor Centers

From 1985 the whole chain of mountains has been included in the Natural Park of the Apuane Alps. The area of the Park is about 543 square kilometers, of which only 121 are protected as a "natural reserve". The park also includes 22 municipalities, among them Castelnuovo Garfagnana, Carrara, Massa, Stazzema, Pietrasanta and Camaiore. For information and material about the Park visit one of the visitor centers (Centro Accoglienza):

- Castelnuovo G., Piazza Erbe 1,   0583   644242
- Seravezza, Via C. Del Greco 11,   0584   756144
- Seravezza Ufficio promozione parco   0584   75821
- Forno di Massa, c/o ex Filanda,   0585   315300

Before Starting Your Hike

Classification of the hikes and walking time

Easy (E)	up to 8 km, up to 500 m elevation gain
Moderate (M)	up to 10 km, up to 800 m elevation gain
Strenuous (S)	up to 14 km, up to 1200 m elevation gain
Very Strenuous (VS)	over 14 km, over 1200 m elevation gain

The hiking time is for an average hiker, taking an hour to cover 4 to 5 km plus an hour for each 300 to 350 m of ascent.

Maps

We suggest that you have with you a map of the area at a scale 1:50,000 or greater, see References below. To our knowledge, the maps of the Apuane Alps at 1:50,000 have not been recently updated. From a hiking point of view, the sketch maps in this book are more accurate, but they are only meant to give a general idea of the area. News-stands and bookstores may have a selection of trail maps. You may find maps also at the local sections of CAI (addresses and hours in the chapter: "The local CAI Sections").

Names of Mountains, Valleys and other geographic features: in English or Italian?

Mountains, valleys, passes and other geographical features are identified by their Italian names. Sometimes when translation is possible an English translation is given in brackets. Obviously if you are looking for a mountain on a map, or, if you need to ask local people directions about a valley or a pass, it is better if you know the Italian name than a necessarily imprecise and frequently absurd translation. So you will find *Monte Altissimo* and not Mount Very High, *Pizzo d' Uccello* and not Bird's Peak. Even the name of the chain, Apuane, has been left untranslated since the name does not have an English transliteration and there is no point in creating another useless neologism.

International standard signals

While in the mountains, you should have with you a flashlight and a whistle. In case you need help the standard request for help is 6 long signals in a minute repeated at one minute intervals. If you intercept a help signal, the standard answer is three signals in a minute again repeated at one minute intervals.

Rescue Corps (Soccorso Alpino)

Rescue Corps are managed all over Italy by the Alpine Club in cooperation with the Carabinieri. Scattered all over Italy, but mainly around the mountains, there are 220 stations of the National Alpine & Speleological Rescue Corps, with over 6,800 volunteers. Some are in Tuscany and many of them around the Apuane Alps. The *Soccorso Alpino* can be contacted anywhere in Italy by telephoning the Carabinieri on 112. In case of medical emergency dial 118, anywhere in Italy. CAI membership includes alpine rescue insurance.

When you meet other people

"Hi!", "Hello!", "How are you doing?" will sound very nice to Italians, but if you want to use local terms then try to say: *Salve!, Ciao!, Buon giorno!*, or *Buona Sera!*

Where to end your hike

An old companion of mine during our hikes in the Apuane Alps, Norino Tognocchi, used to say: *a hike is never over, until your legs are under a table.* In order to follow Norino's wise adage, after each hike we give you a suggestion where to put your legs under the table, and *Buon appetito!*

Local Terms

Bivacco	Bivouac
Buca	Cave, hole, pit

Callare	Pass
Canal, canale	Valley, ravine
Canalone	Couloir
Capanna, like *Rifugio*	Hut
Cava	Quarry
Cima	Summit, top
Costa, costola	Ridge
Cresta	Crest, ridge
Edicola	Shrine
Finestra	Pass, literally window
Fiume	River
Foce, Focola	Pass
Guglia	Needle
Lago	Lake
Lizza, Via di lizza	Steep rocky path for sliding down blocks of marble (originally lizza was a rudimentary sledge for carrying down the blocks)
Marginetta, maesta'	A stone hut to provide shelter and a place of worship for the walkers
Marmifera	a dirt road built for transporting marble from the quarries
Marmo	Marble
Montagna	Mountain
Monte	Mount
Paleo	A long and resistant grass in the Apuane
Pania	Peak; from penna (pen) = feather, probably the same origin as for the Apennines (the backbone of Italy) and Pennines (a range of hills in England)
Parete	Wall, cliff
Passo (or Foce, Focola)	Pass
Penna	Peak (see Pania)
Picco, Pizzo	Peak

Piro	Piece of wood, planted in the ground, around which ropes were wrapped to hold and give direction to the blocks of marble on their way down the lizza; sometimes, instead of wood, piro is made of marble: a marble piro is visible along the lizza from Cave Cervaiole to the town of Azzano.
Punta	Point, peak
Ravaneto	Marble scree (discharged or natural), talus
Rifugio, Capanna	Mountain hut
Segnavia	Sign with the number of the trail
Sella	Saddle
Sentiero	Trail, path
Solco	Narrow and deep valley, literally Furrow
Tabernacolo, Teca	Shrine
Torre, torrione	Tower
Valico	Pass
Via di lizza	see Lizza
Voltolina	Hairpin bend, switchback, zigzag
Zucco	Peak

Selected Hikes in the Apuane Alps

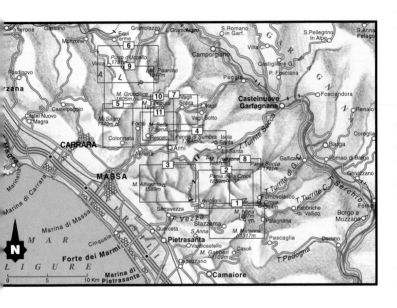

Map 3 - "Selected Hikes in the Apuane Alps" Reference Map

Illustration 3 - Procinto (1177 m) and "i Bimbi" (the Children), from trail #5 towards Callare Matanna

Hike 1 - Procinto and Monte Nona loop

Difficulty	*Strenuous*
Length	*12 km*
Elevation gain	*850 m*
Walking time	*5 ½ h*
Highest elevation	*1297 m (Monte Nona)*
Trailhead	*Stazzema (439 m)*
Trails	*#5 from the trailhead to Rifugio Forte dei Marmi (865 m), Callare Matanna (1130 m) and Albergo Alto Matanna (1037 m);*
	#109 from Albergo Alto Matanna to Foce delle Porchette (982 m);
	#8 from Foce delle Porchette to Fonte Moscoso (about 800 m);
	#6 from Fonte Moscoso to the trailhead.
Points of interest	*Loop of the Cintura del Procinto*
	Monte Procinto (1177 m)
	View from the summit of Monte Nona
	The town of Stazzema

This hike is one of the most interesting in the southern part of the Apuane Alps. Stazzema, a small, beautiful, medieval village, is well worth visiting. The town has a long narrow street with old houses with flower-filled terraces on both sides, the Medici tower with an *a palle* clock (palle means balls, a reference to the mechanism), and the beautiful twelfth century Romanesque church of *Pieve di Santa Maria Assunta*, just before you enter the town. Procinto is one of the most distinctive mountains in the Apuane Alps. It is a tower of rock, not very high (1177 m), shaped like a volcanic "plug" with almost vertical walls (from 100 to 150 m high). This plug is standing on another large cylinder of rock, also with vertical walls (over 100 m high). In between these two blocks, with cliffs above and below, along the so-called *la Cintura del Procinto* (the "belt" of Procinto), runs a very enjoyable trail, a nearly level path at about 1000 m elevation.

How to reach the trailhead

Take the *Strada del Cipollaio* from Querceta for 8.5 km to the junction for Ponte Stazzemese, cross the town and in 7.5 km from the junction reach Stazzema (elevation 439 m). Just before you reach the town, in a very picturesque location, you will see the "Pieve di Santa Maria Assunta". You may park your car in the parking lot close to the church and start your hike from here, walking toward the center of town. In the past, in fact, the trail used to start from the center of town. You will pass through the entire town, enjoying the view of the old stone houses and their flowers, and continue along a steep narrow road until you reach a paved road, in about 15 minutes. Turn left and follow the road going up. The first few hundred meters is paved, after which it becomes a dirt surface. Before the paved surface ends, on the right you will find the trailhead for both trails #5 and #6. A marginetta is very close, on the right of the trail. You may reach the trailhead directly by car. In this case drive back from the church to the first switchback. Take the uphill road on your left just in the middle of the curve and you will reach the trailhead in a couple of kilometers. In this case, do not fail to visit Stazzema and the Pieve before or after the hike.

The hike

Trail #5 climbs gently toward the Rifugio Forte dei Marmi, located at Alpe della Grotta (elevation 865 m). Almost all the way up you are walking through chestnut woods. In Autumn the chestnuts are ready, so collect them off the ground, peel them, including the brown husk, and eat them raw, if they are tender. Just before you reach the rifugio, you will see a marginetta and beside it a fountain of fresh spring water (1½ h from Stazzema). Turn right toward the rifugio, and in about 50 meters, trail #5 climbs up in the rocks to your left. If the rifugio is open, though, go straight for another 50 meters and stop there for a coffee, a cappuccino or a sandwich. Why not lunch? They prepare a wonderful *panigacci* and *testaroli al pesto* it is said, all homemade (see "Where to stay, What to eat, Where to eat, Rifugio"). While relaxing in the rifugio, you enjoy fine views of Procinto, i Bimbi (the children), the West Wall of Monte Nona (300 m over your head) and the small towns in the green valley.

Once you are ready, go back 50 meters to trail #5 and continue your hike. From here, the trail, designed by Aristide Bruni and cut in the rocks more than 100 years ago, climbs up the overhanging rocks (slight exposure) and soon reaches the base of the west wall of Monte Nona. Here on the left a narrow path starts (red marks) and goes towards Procinto (see detour description below), trail #5 continues straight ahead. It

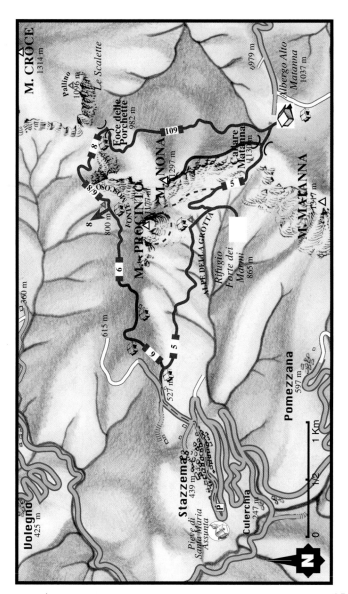

M. CROCE
1314 m

Pallino
1006 m

Le Scalette

Foce delle
Porchette
982 m

109

M. NONA
1297 m

Carraie
Matanna
1131 m

Albergo Alto
Matanna
1037 m

979 m

8

M.te CORCHIA

8

800 m

FONTE

6

8-9

615 m

FONTE

9

5

527 m

M.te PROCINTO
1177 m

5

ALPE DELLA GROTTA

Rifugio
Forte dei
Marmi
865 m

M. MATANNA
1347 m

360 m

Uolegno
425 m

Stazzema
439 m

Pieve di
Santa Maria
Assunta

P

Culerchia
247 m

Pomezzana
597 m

N

0   1/2   1 Km

47

ascends moderately through a beech grove first, and then in short switchbacks (along the way you will find a natural arch in the rocks with views of Procinto) it reaches Callare Matanna, elevation 1130 m, in 1 hour from the Rifugio. Close to the pass is one of the few shrines to be found in the Apuane, it is visible even from Stazzema and from the Pieve. At the

Illustration 4 - Procinto (1177 m), from trail #5 towards Rifugio Forte dei Marmi

pass go left on the path which climbs gently along the south ridge of Monte Nona up to the summit (½ h), from where there are magnificent views of Procinto (from the top, this time), the coastline, the islands of Gorgona, Capraia and Elba, the huge massif of Pania della Croce, and on the other side, Garfagnana and the Apennines. If the weather is particularly clear, you can even see the island of Corsica and the Maritime Alps on the border between France and Italy.

From the summit go back to Callare Matanna (15 minutes from the summit) by the same route. Then go down towards the *Albergo Alto Matanna* (1037 m) and a few meters before you reach the Albergo on the left is trail #109 (a red mark is visible on an electricity pylon). Trail #109 goes up and down along the east slopes of Monte Nona, on the Garfagnana side, and reaches Foce delle Porchette (982 m), a pass with lovely views and a small marginetta (1 h from Callare Matanna). Several trails converge at Foce delle Porchette: trail #8 a very old path connecting Cardoso and Palagnana; trail #108, which goes from the pass toward Monte Croce; and trail #109, the one we have taken from the Albergo Alto Matanna which goes to Foce di Petrosciana. Follow trail #8, which is the only one crossing the pass on the left and going down on the Versilia side. After several short switchbacks the trail reaches Fonte Moscoso (fountain) (½ h, about 800 m elevation). From here leave trail #8, which goes down toward Cardoso, a town badly damaged during the last flood in June 1996, and follow trail #6, which goes slightly up toward the town of Stazzema. The trail, winding through chestnut woods, quickly descends to the trailhead (45 minutes from Fonte Moscoso).

An enjoyable detour: Cintura del Procinto.

From trail #5 at the bottom of the Monte Nona wall, take the narrow path (red marks) on the left which follows the bottom of the wall and reaches a narrow pass and then goes over a small bridge to the Cintura del Procinto. The path is almost level as it continues around (360 degrees) the Cintura del Procinto, with wonderful views. This detour takes about 1 hour.

Illustration 5 - Procinto (1177 m), east and south walls

A climb: Procinto (1177 m) along the via ferrata

While walking the path around the Cintura del Procinto, you will find on the south face of Procinto the start of the *Via Ferrata* (cable route, see "Before Starting Your Hike"). You can climb to the summit by way of the via ferrata provided that you have brought your climbing harness, a sling, a carabiner for your self-belay on the cable, a helmet and no fear of heights. The via ferrata starts with a short iron ladder. It continues along a very exposed climbing route with steps cut in the rock and a metal cable to assist your ascent. On top of the Procinto (about 150 meters above the Cintura) you will find an area with dense vegetation of small trees and bushes called *il Giardino* (the garden). Just before you reach the summit, there is a fresh spring in a low cave, called the *antro di Budden*, in memory of Richard Henry Budden, President of the CAI section of Firenze, from 1874 to 1895, the year of his death. The climb takes about 1 h, from the Cintura and back.

Where to end your hike

You might still be full from your lunch at the Rifugio Forte dei Marmi. Nonetheless if, after a long day in the mountains, you want to try fish go to the Restaurant *Da Piero* in Pietrasanta. The address is Via Traversagna 3, Pietrasanta (telephone 0584 790031). All the food is excellent, and inexpensive, but the fish dishes, in particular, are very tasty. In case you want either a traditional *minestra di farro* (a soup of *triticum spelta* grain), or fresh homemade pasta, and a dish of *polenta e funghi* (polenta, which is a kind of porridge of maize, and mushrooms), then stop at the first town after Stazzema, Mulina di Stazzema, and go to the Restaurant *Luciana* (0584 777008, closed on Monday). But if you prefer barbecued meat and do not care about the cost, then there is no doubt at all: drive directly to Pietrasanta and once there continue towards Lucca along the State road #439. A few hundred meters after Pietrasanta turn left on the road to Valdicastello (the birthplace of a famous poet of the last century, Giosue Carducci). Just after the junction on the left you can see the ancient and beautiful chapel *Pieve di San Giovanni e Santa Felicita*, mentioned since 855. Across the road is the Restaurant *Da Beppino* (tel. 0584 790400). They also serve homemade *tordelli* and *farro*.

Hike 2 - Pania della Croce

Difficulty	*Very strenuous*
Length	*14 km*
Elevation gain	*1250 m*
Walking time	*7 h*
Highest elevation	*1859 m (Pania della Croce)*
Trailhead	*Levigliani (600 m)*
Trails	*#9 from Levigliani to Rifugio del Freo (1180 m); #126 from Rifugio del Freo to Pania della Croce (1859 m).*

Illustration 6 - Pania della Croce (1859 m) and Pizzo delle Saette (1720 m), Mosceta and Rifugio del Freo

Points of interest   *A via di lizza*
Passo dell' Alpino (view)
Mosceta
Rifugio del Freo
Pania della Croce

Pania della Croce is the most celebrated and most frequently climbed mountain in the Apuane Alps. It is also known as the Queen of the Apuane Alps, and Dante Alighieri referred to it as *Pietrapana* in The Divine Comedy (Dante, Inferno, Canto XXXII, 29). The town of Levigliani is well worth visiting, it is located on the south slope of Monte Corchia (1677 m) and is many centuries old. A pre-Roman necropolis was discovered in the last century. The town is also the base for exploring the *Antro del Corchia*, a 1210 meters deep cave with 60 km of galleries. It is one of the deepest caves in Italy and in the world.

How to reach the trailhead

Take the road *Strada del Cipollaio* for 15.5 km from Querceta always following the signs to Castelnuovo G. Ignore the first sign at a junction where Levigliani is shown on both roads. Continue on the main road toward Castelnuovo and after 1 km, turn right at the second junction signposted to Levigliani, this is the old road. Continue through Levigliani and, 100 m after the Hotel Raffaello on your right, park in a small parking lot. If you are staying at the Hotel Raffaello, you can start the walk from the hotel.

The hike

From the parking lot, continue on the steep road on your left for about 20 m and then cross the bridge on your right. Here there are signs, at present - they are prone to disappear, for trail #9 and the Rifugio del Freo. Walk along the paved road for a little more than ½ km and then continue on the dirt road. This road is mainly used by trucks bringing marble from the quarries of Monte Corchia. On the way up you will see a *via di lizza*; this is a very steep route, made of pieces of marble, used in the past for sliding big blocks of marble down to the main road. Follow the road, which climbs up in long switchbacks, for a couple of km. Finally, when the road splits in two, follow the left fork for about 80 m, then take

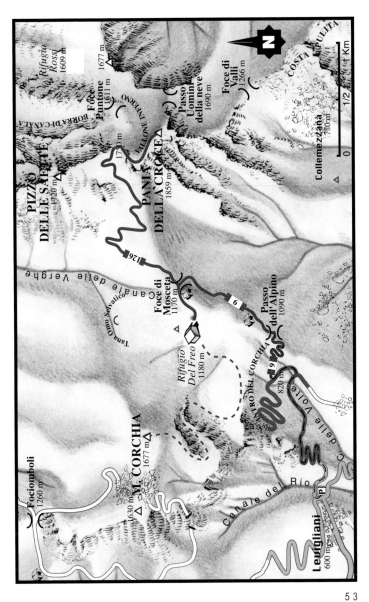

PIZZO
DELLE SAETTE
1720 m △

BORRA DI CANALA

Foce
Puntone
1611 m

Rifugio
Rossi
1609 m

1677 m △

VALLONE D'INFERNO

PANIA
DELLA CROCE
1859 m

1731 m

Passo
Uomini
della neve
1690 m

Foce di
Valli
1266 m

COSTA PULITA

Collemezzana
1700 m ▽

0   1/2   1 Km

N

Canale delle Vergne

126

Canale Selvatico

Foce di
Moсeta
1170 m

6

Passo
dell'Alpino
1090 m

Tana Omo

Rifugio
Del Freo
1180 m

M. CORCHIA
1677 m △

Fociomboli
1260 m

1630 m △

RETRO DEL CORCHIA

820 m

delle Volte

Canale del Rio

Leugliani
600 m

P

an old stone footpath on the right (45 minutes from Levigliani). Near the beginning of the stone path, after a few switchbacks, along a steep and narrow couloir, there is an entrance to Corchia Cave (*Antro del Corchia*), which is called *Buca del Serpente* (Snake Pit); at present it is closed. The trail, in little more than twenty short switchbacks, leads you to Passo dell' Alpino (1090 m) (1½ h from Levigliani). From Passo dell' Alpino you get the first broad views of Procinto and Monte Nona (Hike 1), and the valley stretching below you. From here the trail continues on the left along the ridge and after another short zigzag over the pass. All of a sudden there is a "surprise view", Pania della Croce rises above you in all its majesty. Here on the left is a small *marginetta* (a stone hut, see "Local Terms" in the chapter "Before Starting Your Hike"). The trail gently climbs toward the Rifugio and passes through a short stretch of fir trees to reach a second marginetta (½ h). Here you are in Mosceta (1170 m), a large flat area of meadows and raspberry bushes. From the marginetta you will see the Rifugio Del Freo with its red walls and the Italian flag. Be sure to take a break here to enjoy the view of Pania della Croce and Pizzo delle Saette.

After visiting the Rifugio, go back to Mosceta and take trail #126 for a long, steep walk along the west slope of Pania della Croce. In a little more than 1½ h, you reach the north ridge of the mountain at an elevation a little lower than 1750 m, with extensive views of the wild, rocky and narrow valley of Borra di Canala below. Continue up on the right, just below the ridge, until you reach the crest (*Collo della Pania*). From here leave the trail, which descends toward Rifugio Rossi, and go right along the round, almost flat, crest. A footpath leads you quickly to the summit (2 h from Mosceta). In Italy, on the top of almost every mountain, you find either a Cross or a statue of the Madonna (in the Apuane made of marble, of course); here on top of Pania della Croce, as one would expect from the name, there is a big Cross. From the top of the mountain there are magnificent views of the entire Apuane Alps, the sea, Garfagnana and the Apennines.

From the summit, return to Levigliani following the same route, in about 3 h.

Less Strenuous Alternatives

There are some excellent alternative routes if you do not wish to walk to the summit of Pania della Croce.

- You can stroll around the Rifugio, there is a cave (the "Tana dell' Omo Selvatico" - be careful: do not go too far in), and explore the woods close by;

- or visit the abandoned houses in one of the villages, Puntato (987 m elevation, trail #128) or Col di Favilla (elevation 940 m, trail #9) (allow two hours per village, round trip from the rifugio); the level of difficulty for the complete hike from Levigliani is M;

- or climb Monte Corchia (2 ½ h round trip from the rifugio). The level of difficulty for the complete hike from Levigliani is S. Follow the trail almost directly in front of the rifugio (a bit to the right), which leads you to the south-east ridge of Monte Corchia, facing Levigliani. Once there, follow the path which closely follows the ridge up to the summit. Return to the rifugio by the same route.

Where to end your hike

You cannot miss a dinner at the *Hotel Raffaello*, in Levigliani. The food is excellent; do not miss their speciality (make an advanced reservation): *spalla di capretto* (roast shoulder of kid); see the chapter "Where to stay, What to eat, Where to eat, Rifugio". Here, also, you can see pictures of the old railway from Galleria del Cipollaio to the sea (ask the hosts, either Raffaella Barsottini or Lido Poli).

Illustration 7 - A view from Pania della Croce

Hike 3 - Monte Altissimo loop

Difficulty	*Moderate*
Length	*9 km*
Elevation gain	*700 m*
Walking time	*4 ½ h*
Highest elevation	*1589 m (Monte Altissimo)*
Trailhead	*Colle Cipollaio (990 m)*

Illustration 8 - On trail #142, from Vaso Tondo (1380 m) to Cave Fondone (about 1200 m)

Trails	*#141 from Colle Cipollaio to the junction with trail #31 (paved road);* *#31 from the junction to Cave Cervaiole (about 1150 m) (paved road);* *#142 from Cave Cervaiole to Passo del Vaso Tondo (1380 m);* *#143 from Passo del Vaso Tondo to Monte Altissimo (1589 m);* *#142 from Passo del Vaso Tondo to Cave Fondone (Fondone quarries) (about 1200 m);* *#31 from Cave Fondone to the paved road and trail #141 from the junction to Colle Cipollaio.*
Points of interest	*Cave Cervaiole and Cave Fondone, marble quarries* *Linea Gotica (Gothic Line) from Picco Falcovaia to Monte Altissimo* *Monte Altissimo, the marble mountain of Michelangelo*

This hike gives one some of the most panoramic views in the Apuane Alps. Monte Altissimo (*altissimo* means very high) is not the highest mountain in the Apuane Alps, but it appears to dominate the other peaks when viewed from the coast because it is so close to the sea. Tradition says that Michelangelo used to come here to select the best marble for his statues.

How to reach the trailhead

Take the road *Strada del Cipollaio* from Querceta for 21.5 km to the entrance of the tunnel *Galleria del Cipollaio*. Just before the tunnel, take the private road on the left; it climbs up a couple of kilometers to Colle Cipollaio, elevation 990 m. Park the car off the road near the barrier, which prevents public traffic continuing along the road. The private road is used by the trucks carrying big blocks of marble from the *Cervaiole* and *Fondone* quarries.

The hike

The first part of the hike is along the road beyond the barrier. The road soon reaches the junction with a marmifera on the right, along which trail #31 comes from Arni. Join this trail, #31, as it continues along the paved road, which winds steadily upward. From the road there are extensive views of the Strada del Cipollaio which traverses the steep west slope of Monte Corchia high above the narrow valley. After a little more than ½ h the road takes you to an impressive open air marble quarry, the Cervaiole. A visit to the quarry is highly recommended. There are no restrictions on access to the quarry, but it is private property so if you encounter workers, ask them for permission to visit the area. At the quarry leave trail #31, which goes towards the town of Azzano through the quarry, and follow the road. From the quarry the road surface becomes dirt (marble debris) and climbs, on the right, to the top of the quarry. Follow the red marks of trail #142 to reach a building used in the past as a cafeteria and dormitory for the workers. The trail passes to the left of the building and follows a long stretch of the *Linea Gotica* (the Gothic Line, an imaginary line drawn by the Germans in World War II to divide Italy in two parts; they intended to leave the part of Italy to the south to the Allies). Along the trail, you can see military artifacts, trenches and fortifications. After 45 minutes you reach a pass, from which there is a good view of the summit of Monte Altissimo. From the pass, the trail drops about 30 m (moderate exposure), crosses an old marble quarry and ascends to *Passo del Vaso Tondo*, so-called for its shape (Round Vase Pass, 1380 m). Three trails converge here: the one, #142, you have been walking on, which from here goes towards the marble quarry at the base (your return route to the car); another trail coming from the direction of the coast, exposed and vertiginous, called *il sentiero della Tacca Bianca*, the White Track Path, because of the white marble debris coming from the quarries above it; and finally trail #143, which goes from the pass to the top of Monte Altissimo. Take trail #143 up along the ridge line. From the west, the mountain looks like a high, huge stone wall. The views are breathtaking as you peer down from the notches in the ridge on your way up to the summit of Monte Altissimo, elevation 1589 meters, 2 ½ h from Colle Cipollaio.

From the summit you have a 360° view of all the main mountains of the Apuane Alps, the sea and Lake Massaciuccoli and the town of Torre del Lago Puccini, the home of Giacomo Puccini (1858-1924), composer of such famous operas as *La Boheme*, *Tosca* and *Madame Butterfly*. The return trip follows the same route down to Passo del Vaso Tondo. From there take trail #142, a very enjoyable path with marble steps leading

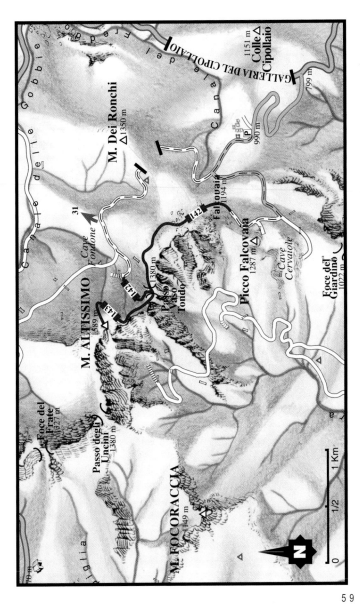

GALLERIA DEL CIPOLLAIO

Colle △ Cipollaio
1151 m

799 m

990 m

P

Canale del freddo

Canale delle Gobbie

M. Dei Ronchi
△ 1350 m

Cave Fondone

31

Falquaia
1194 m

142

Picco Falcovaia
△ 1287 m

Cave Cervaiole

31

M. ALTISSIMO
1589 m

143

143

1380 m

Passo Vaso Tondo

Foce del Giardino
1022 m

Foce del Frate
1327 m

Passo degli Uncini
1380 m

M. FOCORACCIA
1149 m

riglia

70 m

N

0   1/2   1 Km

Illustration 9 - The marmifera from Cave Fondone (about 1200 m) towards Colle del Cipollaio (990 m)

to the marble quarry, Cave Fondone, famous for the quality of its white statuary marble. The trail continues along a dirt road (a marmifera) on your right, goes through a short tunnel, and leads you quickly back to the paved road and the cars at Colle Cipollaio (about 2 h from the summit).

Where to end the hike

This time it may be too early to have dinner immediately after the hike, but do not fail to have a *focaccia con lardo di Colonnata* a flat homemade bread, toasted and filled with lardo from Colonnata (in off-season, available weekends only), with a glass of local wine at the *Trattoria La Romana* (0584 789023). You will find the trattoria a couple of kilometers past the tunnel Galleria del Cipollaio on the Garfagnana side, on the right of the main road to Castelnuovo Garfagnana. If you prefer a pizza this time, drive back to the main road, "Strada del Cipollaio", turn right toward Querceta, go 4.5 km and turn right again at the junction with the road to Terrinca, where you will find the *Trattoria da Tassιlone* (0584 778140) which serves excellent wine and pizza.

Hike 4 - Penna di Sumbra

Difficulty	*Strenuous*
Length	*13 km*
Elevation gain	*900 m*
Walking time	*6 h*
Highest elevation	*1765 m (Penna di Sumbra)*
Trailhead	*Arni (916 m)*
Trails	*#144 from Arni to Passo Fiocca (1560 m);*
	#145 from Passo Fiocca a blazed trail leads to the summit of Penna di Sumbra (1765 m) and from there to Capanne di Careggine (840 m). The stretch from Passo Fiocca to the summit is a little exposed (metal cable).
Points of interest	*Il Fatonero wood*
	Passo Fiocca, a perfect marble saddle
	Penna di Sumbra
	The town of Capanne di Careggine
	The abandoned town (except for a few houses) of Isola Santa, on the artificial lake

Illustration 10 - Penna di Sumbra (1765 m), south slope, from trail #145 towards Capanne di Careggine (840 m)

This hike traverses a lateral branch of the Apuane Alps range, on the Garfagnana side. It is long, but very enjoyable because of its variety and because of the wonderful views of the Turrite Secca valley and the surrounding mountains. An added attraction is a drink or, better still, a meal at *La Ceragetta*, the "little cherry" restaurant that offers a stupendous view of the mountains, mainly the north face of the Pizzo delle Saette. The ancient stone houses of Isola Santa are well worth visiting after the hike and of course the restaurant.

How to reach the trailhead

Take the road *Strada del Cipollaio* from Querceta towards Castelnuovo Garfagnana. Enter the 1 km long *Galleria del Cipollaio* tunnel at 21.5 km; here you cross to the Garfagnana side. As you drop down the other side of the mountain, you pass a house on the left (Casa Henraux) and after a couple of kilometers turn left at a junction onto a road coming from Massa (*La Strada di Pian della Fioba*). Pass through the first group of houses of Arni, then, 2 km after the junction, at the first switchback (here there is a blue road sign to Massa and a brown sign to Passo del Vestito) leave the main road and go straight on. Park in the village parking area on the right, 100 meters after the switchback (elevation 916 m).

Shuttle: The hike finishes at Capanne di Careggine, a small village, just off the road to Castelnuovo Garfagnana, about 8 km east of Arni. Leave a car there, or have someone pick you up. To reach Capanne di Careggine, stay on the Strada del Cipollaio after you have gone through the Cipollaio tunnel, and instead of turning left at the road to Arni (and Massa), continue on the Strada del Cipollaio through a shorter tunnel and continue down along the Turrite Secca. Be sure to watch on your left for wonderful views of Penna di Sumbra. Turn left about 3 km past the short tunnel at the junction with the road going to Capanne di Careggine. Continue on this road until you reach the restaurant *La Ceragetta*, where you may park your shuttle car.

The hike

From the parking lot in Arni, cross the stream on a narrow pedestrian bridge past a fountain where you may fill your water bottle. Stay on the trail up and around the fountain to a paved road. Continue up the paved road past a few stone houses where, on the right, the trail climbs up a

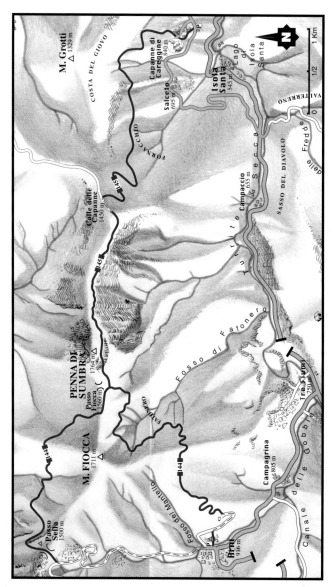

few concrete steps and takes off among cultivated fields. The trail continues climbing through fields and flowers, and soon across gorse bushes until it reaches the first ridge, ½ h. It continues climbing up for some hundreds of meters along the ridge with views of the town of Arni, down to the left, and the valley of Turrite Secca on the right. The trail goes to the right with a long traverse of the south slopes of Monte Fiocca on steps carved in the marble. It continues almost level for several hundred meters along the south side of Monte Fiocca, reaches the southeast ridge of Monte Fiocca, goes down for a few meters (some exposure) and then very soon it goes up again and reaches the first trees of a beech grove. Be careful here, the trail appears to go down along a wide path but in fact it goes straight ahead on rock (follow the red marks). It crosses the beech grove, called il *Fatonero*, then becomes a grassy treeless path eventually arriving at Passo Fiocca, a large perfect saddle of marble (2 ½ h from Arni). A blazed trail (#145) now ascends the west ridge of Penna di Sumbra and leads up to the grassy slope about 100 m below the summit. From here, a metal cable has been installed to assist your safe ascent up the steep, grassy slope to the summit (some exposure), ¾ h from Passo Fiocca. You are rewarded with broad views of the main peaks of the Apuane Alps, Lake Vagli with the submerged village of *Fabbrica* or *Fabbriche di Careggine* (see the Dec. 1994 issue of National Geographic Magazine), the Apennines and Garfagnana.

From the top trail #145 descends along the east ridge of the mountain. The terrain is sometimes grassy, sometimes rocky, and the ridge drops off sharply on the right into a vertical rock face up to 500 m high. The trail soon leaves the exposed ridge and descends through a grove of beech trees and bushes. As the trail leaves the wood, there is a picnic table under a tree (*Colle delle Capanne*, 1452 m, 1¼ h from the summit). Do not be tempted to follow the trail that descends left. It does not go to Capanne di Careggine, but to Maestà del Tribbio, which is not our destination. Stay to the right on #145, which is very narrow in the grass. After a long descent on grassy slopes, passing close to some old, ruined stone houses, follow the trail which seems to disappear into a cleft in the rock cliff, a hide-out for partisans during World War II. The trail continues almost horizontally. Follow the red marks, or blazes. Retreat if you lose them and try again. Finally the trail enters a grove of chestnut trees, continuing down a long way to Capanne di Careggine. After reaching the road, and about ten meters after passing the church along the road, the trail is to the right. Continue down to the restaurant La Ceragetta, 1½ h from the picnic table at 1452 m.

It is well worth visiting the stone houses of Isola Santa ("Holy Island") which served as a resting place where pilgrims stayed while crossing the valley. From the restaurant, drive back to the main road and turn left toward Castelnuovo Garfagnana. Continue a few hundred meters past the junction. Park along the road. (If the local restaurant *Da Giacco'* is open, as a courtesy avoid parking in their lot). From the restaurant walk back 100 m to a footpath on your left. Follow the trail downhill and explore picturesque Isola Santa with its ancient stone houses, its church with a beautiful bell tower and the lake.

A less strenuous alternative hike: Monte Fiocca loop (Difficulty: M)

This alternative takes you back to Arni, your starting point, and therefore no shuttle is involved.

From Passo Fiocca, take trail #144 to the left around the north side of Monte Fiocca reaching Passo Sella (1500 m), a beautiful, large grassy saddle, in about 1½ h. Immediately below the pass on the south side, a marmifera connects Arni with the marble quarries, which are on the west, seaward slopes of Monte Sella. Before you take the marmifera down to Arni (it takes about 1 h), walk up and go through a very short tunnel to a viewpoint overlooking the sea and the steep, narrow valleys below you.

Where to end the hike

At *La Ceragetta* (see above) for a drink, a meal and terrific mountain views. Their menu includes good local, traditional food, such as *tordelli al sugo*, which is tortelli pasta filled with meat or ricotta cheese and dressed with a meat sauce, or *risotto ai funghi*, rice with mushrooms. The restaurant is at the end of your hike. If you choose the less strenuous hike, drive from Arni to Capanne di Careggine, or try *Trattoria La Romana*, located a few hundred meters past the junction on the main road to Castelnuovo Garfagnana. Here you should ask for *focaccia con lardo di Colonnata* (in off-season, available weekends only) and a glass of local wine. *Lardo* is just what it sounds like: bacon with almost no lean meat. Focaccia is flat bread. Colonnata is a town on the Versilia side, very close to Carrara, famous for its numerous marble quarries and its lardo. The sandwich is toasted and delicious, and a cultural experience!

Hike 5 - Monte Sagro

Difficulty	*Moderate*
Length	*8 km*
Elevation gain	*550 m*
Walking time	*3 ½ h*
Highest elevation	*1749 m (Monte Sagro)*
Trailhead	*Foce di Pianza (1279 m)*
Trails	*#172 from Foce di Pianza to Foce della Faggiola (1464 m);*
	from Foce della Faggiola a path (blue marks) leads to the summit (1749 m);

Illustration 11 - Monte Sagro (1749 m), west slope, from Foce di Pianza (1279 m)

from the summit along the northwest ridge to trail
#173;
#173 from the north ridge of Monte Sagro to Foce
di Pianza.

Points of interest   *Monte Sagro, view from the top*
Marble quarries of Monte Sagro
Exploration of Carrara, famous for its white marble
Scenic drive to Foce di Pianza

Monte Sagro is very close to the sea, like Monte Altissimo, and is the first high mountain you see coming from the north along the motorway from Genova to Livorno. From the sea it looks very high and the white slopes all around are reminiscent of the snow and glaciers of the Alps. The slopes are in fact covered with marble debris, the so called *ravaneto*, which has been released from the quarries above them. This hike has some of the best panoramic views in the Park. You will have a spectacular view of neighboring peaks, the marble quarries, and get a close view of the coastline, Bocca di Magra (mouth of the Magra River), the Gulf of La Spezia with the tiny islands of Tino and Palmaria, and Portovenere. Portovenere is a picturesque marine town in Liguria on the Bay of the Poets so-called because of its connection with Byron and Shelley; Shelley drowned off this coast.

How to reach the trailhead

From Carrara (86 m) take the State road #446d toward Fosdinovo (500 m). Fosdinovo is a walled medieval town around the old castle of Malaspina, where Dante spent some time while writing part of his Divine Comedy. On the way you will pass the town of Gragnana (219 m) and then Castelpoggio (547 m), it has a good view of the coast. If the shops are open, stop for a local snack: a *panino con mondiola*, a sandwich of mortadella and local bread made in a wood oven. Mondiola can also be found in Garfagnana, but here, instead of mortadella, they use a special kind of salami. Continue on the same road and 9.5 km from Carrara, take the road on your right to Campo Cecina. The road has good views all the way up, and at 9.5 km from the junction, there is large parking area (1230 m) where you can stop to enjoy the view below you of Carrara and the valleys which are almost completely white because of the many marble quarries. From here the road splits in two: the road on the left goes towards

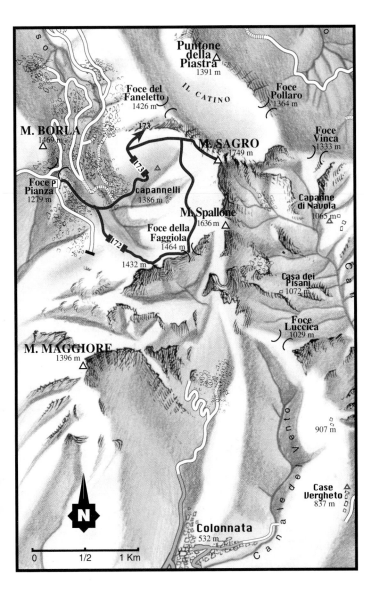

Puntone
della
Piastra
1391 m

IL CATINO

Foce
Pollaro
1364 m

Foce del
Faneletto
1426 m

173

M. BORLA
1469 m

M. SAGRO
1749 m

Foce
Vinca
1333 m

173

Foce
Pianza
1279 m

P

capannelli
1386 m

M. Spallone
1636 m

Capanne
di Navola
1065 m

Foce della
Faggiola
1464 m

172

1432 m

Casa dei
Pisani
1072 m

Foce
Luccica
1029 m

M. MAGGIORE
1396 m

Canale del Vento

907 m

Case
Vergheto
837 m

N

Colonnata
532 m

0   1/2   1 Km

Campo Cecina and Acquasparta in about 1 km (from Acquasparta, a rocky trail leads to the Rifugio Carrara,1320 m, and takes about 10 minutes); take the road to the right and in a little more than 1 km reach Foce di Pianza. Park here in a wide area covered with marble debris, with a view of Monte Sagro on one side and Carrara and the sea on the other

The hike

Trail #172 follows the top of the low, flat ridge from Foce di Pianza to Monte Sagro. Once you have reached the ridge, continue along it to the right following the red marks toward Foce della Faggiola. The trail climbs slowly, crossing a small grove of beech trees, until it reaches the west ridge above Colonnata. Follow the ridge on your left to reach the Foce della Faggiola (1464 m), 1 h. The name *faggiola* comes from the local term for the fruit of the Common or European Beech (*faggio*, in Italian) and has nothing to do with *fagiolo*, which is the Italian name for bean. Leave trail #172, which crosses the pass and descends toward Foce Luccica along the south slopes of the mountain (see hikes 15 and 16); instead, turn left to follow the blue marks that lead you to the top of Monte Sagro. From Foce della Faggiola you cross meadows and then follow a narrow path along the west side of Monte Sagro and up the northwest ridge, and along it up to the summit (1 h from Foce della Faggiola). The view from the summit is one of the most extensive in the Apuane Park: the coast, Bocca di Magra (Magra river mouth), La Spezia Gulf, the islands and, from south to east, Monte Grondilice, Garnerone Crest, Foce di Giovo (Giovo Pass), Pizzo d' Uccello and, beyond them, Monte Tambura, Pisanino and Cavallo.

The return trip is short, it takes less than 1½ h. Follow the northwest ridge first and then continue along the west ridge (very easy scrambling, but watch for loose rocks) until you reach trail #173. Turn left on this trail and follow it up to Foce di Pianza.

Where to end the hike

If Rifugio Carrara (0585 841972) is open, you will find good, inexpensive meals there. Otherwise, Campo Cecina (Acquasparta, to be precise) has a good, but a little more expensive, restaurant: *Il Belvedere* (0585 841973). They serve tasty first courses including homemade *tordelli di carne*, or *ravioli di ricotta*, or their speciality *taglierini con i fagioli* and for a main course *coniglio* or *cervo alla cacciatora* (stewed rabbit or deer).

Hike 6 - Pizzo d'Uccello

Difficulty	*Moderate*
Lenght	*8 km*
Elevation gain	*700 m*
Walking time	*4 ½ h*
Highest elevation	*1781 m (Pizzo d'Uccello)*
Trailhead	*Rifugio Donegani (1122 m)*
Trails	*#37 from Rifugio Donegani to Foce di Giovo (1500 m);*
	#181 from Foce di Giovo to Giovetto (1497 m); from Giovetto follow the path almost all the way along the south ridge up to the summit (1781 m); return by the same route.
Points of interest	*Serenaia Valley*
	Foce di Giovo
	Scrambling on Pizzo d'Uccello
	Pizzo d'Uccello
	Marble quarries

Illustration 12 - Pizzo d' Uccello (1781 m), south slope

Coming from the north, along the motorway from Parma towards La Spezia, in the vicinity of the exit to "Pontremoli" in clear weather you will see a majestic group of big mountains, with four high peaks with very steep slopes. They are, from left to right: Monte Pisanino, the highest in the Apuane, Pizzo d' Uccello, Monte Grondilice and Monte Sagro. It is really a very impressive view, not to be missed. Pizzo d' Uccello is the most northerly of the high mountains, and one of the rockiest and boldest peaks of the Apuane Alps; the North Wall provides up to 700 m of serious rock-climbing. The hike goes to the top of the mountain along a simple but exposed route (*via normale*). If anyone in your party fears heights, the last exposed stretch to the summit should be avoided.

How to reach the trailhead

On the road from Castelnuovo Garfagnana to Aulla, about 1 km past the center of Piazza al Serchio toward Aulla, take the road on your left to Gramolazzo and Minucciano. Pass through the town of Nicciano and drive along the north bank of Lake Gramolazzo, and then through the town of Gramolazzo, 8 km from the junction. Continue on the same road for about 3 km from Gramolazzo. Just before a tunnel, turn left on the road to Serenaia and Rifugio Donegani. Serenaia is a large, relatively flat area surrounded by high mountains, about 6 km from the junction. Continue for about ½ km to reach Rifugio Donegani (1122 m). Park here. Across the valley you will see Monte Pisanino (1946 m) the highest peak in the Apuane Alps.

The hike

The hike starts from Rifugio Donegani. Cross the road just in front of the Rifugio and follow the red marks going almost straight up to connect with a marmifera. Go left along the road up to the marble quarries. At the first quarry, trail #37 leaves the road on the right (follow the red marks on the left side of a gate). It ascends in several switchbacks through a grove of beech trees up to Foce di Giovo, a large grassy saddle, 1 h from the Rifugio. From the saddle there are views of the Serenaia Valley to the east and Vinca on the other side of the saddle. From Foce di Giovo, follow the rock shoulder connecting Foce di Giovo to the southeast ridge of Pizzo d' Uccello. At Foce del Giovetto (1497 m) trail #181, coming on your right from Foce Siggioli and going to Foce di Giovo converges with

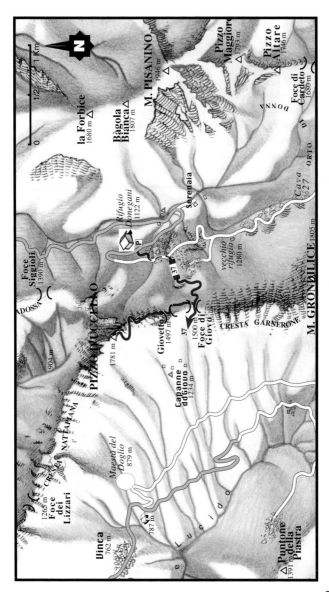

N

1 Km
1/2
0

la Forbice
1680 m △

Bàgola
Bianca △
1807 m

M. PISANINO
1946 m △

Pizzo
Maggiore
1793 m △

Pizzo
Altare
1746 m △

Foce di
Cardeto
1680 m

DONNA

D'

ORTO

Cava
27

M. GRONDILICE 1805 m

Serenaia

Rifugio
Donegani
1122 m

P

37

vecchio
rifugio
1280 m

CRESTA GARNERONE

Foce
Siggioli
1390 m

ADOSSA

904 m

PIZZO D'UCCELLO

1781 m △

Giovetto
1497 m

37
1500 m
Foce di
Giovo

CRESTA NATTAPIANA

CRESTA

1265 m
Foce
dei
Lizzari

Maestà del
Dogio
879 m

Capanne
dd Giovo
1234 m

Puntone
della
Piastra
1391 m △

Ulnca
762 m

787 m

e Lucido

trail #191, which descends to the left and goes towards Foce dei Lizzari. Continue up and down along the ridge until you reach the base of the southeast ridge of Pizzo d' Uccello. Scramble up to the summit following the blue marks, but watch for loose rocks in the narrow, steep couloirs. Keep your party together, with only a few people at a time in the couloir. The rest should remain in a protected area until the party above has moved out of the couloir. The ascent is exciting, enjoyable and not difficult, although you may have to use your hands occasionally to help you climb (1½ h from Foce di Giovo). From the summit there are splendid views of the valleys below and the surrounding mountain peaks: Monte Sagro, Contrario, Cavallo, Pisanino and the Apennines in the east.

Return to Rifugio Donegani (2 h from the summit) by the same route.

Some alternatives to the climb of Pizzo d' Uccello

There are pleasant beech woods around Serenaia. You may pick mushrooms, but be sure you know your mushrooms: the killer *amanita phalloides* is around!

You may prefer to hike to the rocky Foce Siggioli (1390 m) following trail #187 through a beech wood, see map of "Hike 13 - Pizzo d' Uccello loop". From Foce Siggioli you can view the huge, almost vertical wall of Pizzo d' Uccello. This hike takes 2 h for the round trip. To reach the trailhead, follow the paved road going up from the rifugio. After the first switchback, about 50 m on the right, there are red marks for trail #187. Difficulty: E. Foce di Giovo and Foce Siggioli are connected by trail #181. The walk takes a little more than 1 h. Be alert to some danger from loose stones on the steep, narrow path. From Foce Siggioli, a *Via Ferrata* allows hikers to reach the bottom of the north wall of Pizzo d' Uccello. See the paragraph "Via Ferrata and Sentiero Attrezzato (cable route)" in the chapter "Before Starting Your Hike". You will need a climbing harness, helmet and nylon slings with carabiners for self belay on the cable to use the Via Ferrata (a couple of hours round trip from Foce Siggioli). The Via Ferrata is part of the "Hike 30 - Solco di Equi and Via Ferrata to Foce Siggioli", which is described in the chapter on "Climbs in the Apuane Alps".

You may hike to Foce di Cardeto (1680 m). Take either trail #178 from Serenaia (1050), or trail #180, which starts a little below the Rifugio Donegani on the right side going down the road, see map of the "Hike

14 - Monte Pisanino". Near the middle of the hike, these two trails rejoin. This is a very enjoyable walk, first through beech woods then on more rocky terrain up to the pass. It takes a couple of hours from the Rifugio, and an hour at least to get back. On the way back you may use the other trail for variety. Difficulty: E

Where to end your hike

Rifugio Donegani is a wonderful place for a delicious and inexpensive meal. It is not always open, so be sure to call ahead to make a reservation (0583 610085). In our case, we arrived back from the hike much earlier than planned, 3:30 pm, but they were flexible; the meal received rave reviews from all the hungry diners.

Hike 7 - Monte Tambura, from Arnetota

Difficulty	*Strenuous*
Lenght	*8 km*
Elevation gain	*1000 m*
Walking time	*5 h*
Highest elevation	*1890 m (Monte Tambura)*
Trailhead	*Arnetola (900 m)*
Trails	*#35 (via Vandelli) from Arnetola to Passo Tambura (1620 m);*
	#148 from Passo Tambura to the summit of Monte Tambura (1890 m);
	back along the same route.

Illustration 13 - Monte Tambura (1890 m), south-west slope (Garfagnana side)

Points of interest   *Marble quarries (Arnetola and along the trail)*
Via Vandelli
Monte Tambura
Exploration of Vagli di Sotto
Lake of Vagli (National Geographic Magazine,
Dec. 1994 issue, Geographica feature)

Monte Tambura is one of the highest mountains of the Apuane Alps. It was referred to as *Tambernicchi* by Dante Alighieri in the Divine Comedy (Dante, Inferno Canto XXXII, 28). This trail follows the route of the old, circa 1750, road between Arnetola and Resceto over the Passo Tambura. It is known as *Via Vandelli*, and is named after its builder, the Engineer and Abbot Domenico Vandelli. It was commissioned by Francesco III d' Este, Duke of Modena, as a connection from Modena to the area. The road fell into disuse for a variety of reasons (amongst them stories of robbery and murder), and is now, fortunately for us, used as a recreational trail. Other stretches of the road still exist between Arnetola and Modena.

How to reach the trailhead

Take the road from Poggio (a village on the main road from Castelnuovo Garfagnana to Piazza al Serchio and Aulla) toward Vagli di Sopra along the Edron Valley. After 6.5 km, you reach the dam that created the artificial lake of Vagli. At the bottom of the lake is *Fabbriche di Careggine*, or simply *Fabbrica*, a 13th Century village that was famous for its iron works. About every ten years the lake is drained for maintenance on the dam and the 32 houses and the church can be visited. The last time the reservoir was drained was in 1994. The road runs along the north-west side of the lake. On the left, the picturesque village of Vagli di Sotto is perched on the hill overlooking the lake. The lake water has eroded the hillside and threatens the stability of the village; the authorities are encouraging the villagers to move to a new village on the north-west side of the lake, but some are reluctant to move so the village is still occupied. At the village of Vagli di Sopra (*Castrum Vallis de Supra*), 11.5 km, turn left, go through the town and enter the valley of Arnetola. At the junction with an unpaved road, go right to follow the road switch-backing up to a flat area, called Arnetola. You will see blocks of marble all around you and, on the hillsides, working marble quarries.

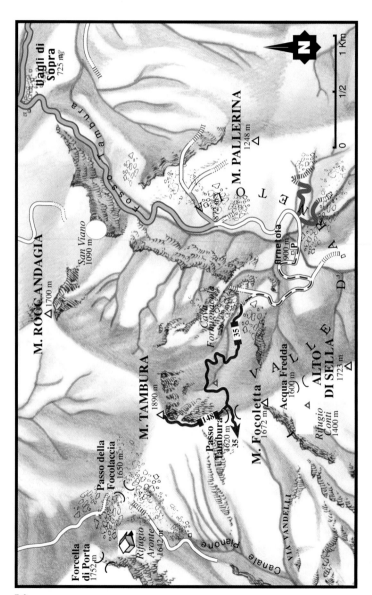

Park your car here (900 m, 2.5 km from Vagli di Sopra) before the road starts going up steeply.

The hike

From Arnetola, (900 m) continue on foot up the road, which now becomes a marmifera (trail #31). As you pass some stone houses, the road forks. Keep to the right. After about 50 meters trail #31 turns left along a steep marmifera and goes towards Passo Sella, see "Hike 25 - Monte Fiocca"), we stay on the right branch (trail #35), still a dirt road, and follow some switchbacks leading to a marble quarry (*Cava Formignacola*). From here the trail leaves the road on the left and passes through a grove of beech trees, crosses a scree field that spills over from the top of Monte Tambura, and climbs up in more switchbacks to Passo Tambura (2 h). On the way, you will pass through a lovely, bucolic meadow with a fresh water spring. From Passo Tambura, leave the "via Vandelli" (trail #35), which descends the western slopes of the mountain. Turn right onto trail #148, which climbs up marble scree, intersects the south ridge of the mountain, then follows the ridge line almost all the way up to the summit (1 h from the pass). The summit rewards you with views of almost all the Apuane peaks, the islands, the Magra River, the Gulf of La Spezia and the coastline.

To go back to Arnetola follow the same route (about 2 h).

Where to end the hike

For a pizza and local wine you may stop at the *Bar Pizzeria Coltelli Dino*, in Vagli di Sopra, via Vandelli 2 (0583 664058). For a complete meal, drive to Vagli di Sotto and go to the *Trattoria del Pescatore* (0583 664052), just before the bridge into the old town, for local home-made pasta and rabbit, chicken or roast lamb.

Hike 8 - Monte Forato loop

Difficulty	*Moderate*
Lenght	*10 km*
Elevation gain	*800 m*
Walking time	*5 h*
Highest elevation	*1281 m (Costa Pulita)*
Trailhead	*Fornovolasco (480 m)*

Illustration 14 - Monte Forato (1223 m), west slope

Trails	*#6 from Fornovolasco to Foce di Petrosciana (961 m);*
	from Foce di Petrosciana to Monte Forato (1223 m) and from here to Foce di Valli (1266 m) a trail along the ridge (red marks, but no number);
	#130 from Foce di Valli (1266 m) to Fornovolasco.
Points of interest	*Monte Forato*
	The walk along the ridge and along Costa Pulita
	A walk around Fornovolasco
	A visit to the Grotta del Vento (Wind Cave, take the short tour, fee)
	Scenic drive
	Eremo di Calomini (a Sanctuary in a niche in the rock)

Monte Forato, in the southern Apuane, is one of the most distinctive mountains in the Apuane Alps. The mountain has two peaks connected by a natural arch about 30 meters across. The word *forato* means "pierced". It is said that a small aeroplane has actually flown the arch. The more adventurous of your group will walk over the top of the arch, while everyone can go underneath (a trail actually passes through the arch). Prior to 1996, you could see the small village of Cardoso, 265 m in Versilia, through the arch, but the village was almost entirely submerged and washed away in the floods in June of that year. The town of Fornovolasco was seriously damaged by the same flood, as was the *Albergo Rifugio La Buca*. During a recent visit, in May 1997, the rifugio and the restaurant were fully in operation, while the town is still being rebuilt. Fornovolasco is celebrated for the *Grotta del Vento* (Wind Cave), which is open to visitors. There are different tours, the short version lasting one hour, and the longer one all of three hours. The valley along the creek "Turrite di Gallicano" from Gallicano to Fornovolasco is very narrow and very interesting. Driving up towards Fornovolasco at about 3 km from Gallicano on the right high in the rock is the white *Eremo di Calomini*, a sanctuary inside a niche in the high bluff overhanging the valley. The road continues climbing, enters a narrow canyon where on the left can be seen the high dam of a small artificial lake and reaches the village of Fornovolasco (480 m), 10 km from Gallicano.

How to reach the trailhead

On the main road from Lucca to Castelnuovo Garfagnana, in the town of Gallicano take the road going to Fornovolasco (road sign) and the Grotta del Vento (brown sign) and drive 9 km to the main parking area in Fornovolasco. Park your car here. In May 1997 the last stretch of the road was still blocked. If the road is still blocked, follow the detour through the town of Vergemoli. The road from Vergemoli to Fornovolasco has been recently paved.

The hike

From the parking lot, go toward Albergo Rifugio La Buca. Why not pause for a cappuccino? Cross the small bridge over the creek and you are at the trailhead of trails #130, #12 and #6. Do not take trail #130, which goes straight up across the town, but follow trails #6 and #12, which initially coincide. Go left under a vault (an arched passage between two houses) and enter the narrow valley that goes to Foce di Pietrosciana. In less than ½ km the trail crosses the road from Fornovolasco to the Grotta del Vento and continues across the road along the same valley. The trail then enters a grove of chestnut trees. Shortly thereafter the trail splits, #12 to the right and #6 to the left. Leave trail #12 which passes close to the *Tana Che Urla* (the Shouting Cave), 572 m long and the first cave to be explored in the Apuane Alps, in 1704. Continue on the left taking trail #6 which goes down slightly until it reaches the river bed. The trail now goes up following and frequently crossing the river bed. Follow the red marks; the last flood damaged the trail and now it is not easy to follow. The trail eventually reaches a dirt road. Follow it to the right (no more signs) and shortly turn left at the first junction. Follow the dirt road up and soon you'll find the red marks and the river bed again. Continue going up until you find on your left the way up to the old trail. The trail switchbacks until it reaches Foce di Pietrosciana, 961 m elevation, 1½ h from Fornovolasco. On the other side is the Versilia region and the sea. From here on the right, starts trail #131, which initially descends slowly still on the Garfagnana side, and then climbs up to Foce di Valli. Do not follow trail #131, but climb the easy rocks on your right. The itinerary (red marks) is very enjoyable, along the rocky, brushy mountain ridge. Some stretches have metal cables, but they are nonetheless very easy. The trail soon reaches the beginning of a *Via*

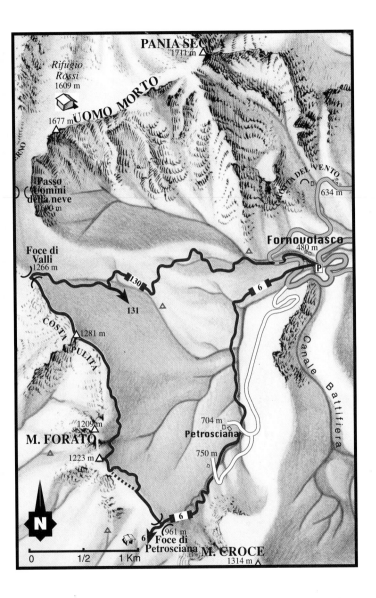

PANIA SECCA
1711 m ▲

Rifugio
Rossi
1609 m

UOMO MORTO

1677 m ▲

Passo
Uomini
della neve
00 m

COSTA DEL VENTO

634 m

Fornovolasco
480 m

P

Foce di
Valli
1266 m

130

131

▲1281 m

COSTA PULITA

6

Canale Battiffera

▲1209 m

M. FORATO

1223 m ▲

704 m

Petrosciana

750 m

6

N

0   1/2   1 Km

6
961 m
Foce di
Petrosciana

M. CROCE
1314 m ▲

Ferrata, where a metal cable and a ladder help hikers climb the rocks ahead, if they have thought to bring a climbing harness, helmet, slings and a carabiner. If you are not so well supplied, do not follow the via ferrata; instead, take the trail, which continues on your right (red marks), passing to the right of rocks with no difficulty at all. The two trails rejoin before you reach the summit of the first peak of Monte Forato. Soon you are at the Arch, 1 h from Foce di Petrosciana. There are spectacular views from the arch. If the weather is sunny and calm, climb the peak (elevation 1209 m) on the right of the arch, called *Cima*

Illustration 15 - Pania della Croce (1859 m), south slope, from Foce di Valli (1266 m)

Nord (North Peak) and enjoy your picnic lunch there.

From the Arch, the trail continues along the ridge, up and down the so-called *Costa Pulita* (Clean Ridge) between 1200 m and 1281 m, and reaches Foce di Valli (1266 m elevation, 1 h from the Arch). It is a very large grassy saddle (with a few trees) between Pania della Croce and Costa Pulita. From here you have wonderful views of Pania della Croce, Uomo Morto and Pania Secca. Trail #130, which goes to Fornovolasco, starts here, as well as trail #131, which connects Foce di Valli and Foce di Petrosciana by a lower path. The two trails initially coincide and both go down on your right. They immediately descend through rough, steep, grassy meadows, and continue going down almost to the border between meadow and wood, until they split. Trail #131 continues almost straight down towards Foce di Petrosciana, while our trail #130 goes to the left and soon crosses a small canyon. Trail #130 goes down the other slope of the valley past terraced fields and a couple of houses. Soon it enters a beech wood, which blends into a grove of chestnut trees, and eventually reaches a dirt road. Turn to the right along the road and soon you reach on your left the trail going down through the wood. Continue down in the wood until you reach the road from Fornovolasco to the Grotta del Vento (the Wind Cave). Turn right along the road and shortly, across the road, continue going down on trail #130 (watch for the red marks). Soon you reach the center of Fornovolasco completing the loop (2 h from Foce di Valli).

Where to end the hike

At the *Albergo Rifugio La Buca* in Fornovolasco (0583 722013) they serve American-sized portions of local Italian food. Ask your host, Vito Mori, in advance for *Farinata*, a special soup common in Lucca and Garfagnana. Farinata is made of beans, maize flower, lardo and cabbage (a special type called in Italian *cavolo nero*, i.e. black cabbage). Other specialities are *tordelli alla carne* (tortelli pasta filled with meat), *tagliatelle ai funghi* (homemade pasta with mushrooms) and local trout.

Hike 9 - Monte Grondilice loop

Difficulty	*Strenuous*
Lenght	*12 km*
Elevation gain	*1000 m*
Walking time	*6 h*
Highest elevation	*1805 m (Monte Grondilice)*
Trailhead	*Vinca (808 m)*
Trails	*#38 from Vinca towards Capanna Garnerone (1260 m);*
	#37 from Capanna Garnerone to Foce di Monte Rasori (1318 m);
	#186 from Foce di Monte Rasori to Foce di Grondilice (1773 m) and Cava 27 (1500 m);
	#179 from Cava 27 to Foce di Giovo (1500 m);
	#175 from Foce di Giovo to Vinca.

Illustration 16 - Monte Grondilice (1805 m), south-east slope

Points of interest   Tour of the picturesque town of Vinca
Foce di Monte Rasori
Monte Grondilice
Foce di Giovo

This hike is entirely inside the north part of the Apuane Alps. The environment changes dramatically from the woods on the Vinca side to the wild and rocky slopes of Monte Grondilice, from the rocky, narrow Passo di Grondilice, to the grassy, bucolic saddle of Foce di Giovo. This pass is also named *Finestra* (window) *di Grondilice.*

How to reach the trailhead

Take road #63 from Aulla toward Passo del Cerreto. At 12 km, go right at the junction to Castelnuovo Garfagnana, road #445. Then at km 3.5, take another right to enter and cross Gragnola and drive toward Equi Terme. In 4.2 km, pass through the town of Monzone the take the road to Vinca. Once in Vinca, drive toward the center of town (take the road on your left going upward, no outlet). Park in the square, where you will find a convenient fountain of fresh water to fill your water bottles. When in town, if you find an open *Bar* or an *Alimentari* shop, do not fail to taste the local *focaccia*, a kind of flat homemade bread.

The hike

From the parking lot, enter the village. Follow the red marks on the stone walls of the houses up to the top of the town. After you pass the last house, trail #38 enters a chestnut grove, crosses a creek bed, and reaches a dirt road. Here on your right you will find a *Maestà* (about 900 m, ½ h from the parking lot). Take the gravel road into the woods, passing the Boy Scouts campground on your right (there is a wooden house and a fountain). Continue up along the winding road. After you leave the woods, you will see a couple of houses on your left. All around you will see mountains as if you were in an amphitheater. From left to right they are: Pizzo d' Uccello, Cresta Garnerone, Monte Grondilice, and finally Monte Sagro on your right, with its steep and lofty east ridge. A few hundred meters beyond the houses on your left, take a trail (no number, but red marks) which leaves the road and goes up toward *Capanna Garnerone*, 1 h from Vinca. Shortly you will join trail #37 coming from

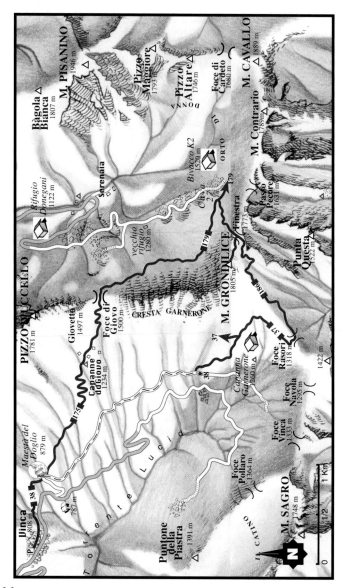

M. PISANINO

Bàgola Bianca 1807 m

Pizzo Maggiore 1793 m

Pizzo Altare 1746 m

Foce di Cardeto 1680 m

M. CAVALLO 1889 m

M. Contrario 1789 m

Passo Pecore 1631 m

Bivacco K2 1520 m

DI ORTO DONNA

Rifugio Donegani 1122 m

Serenaia

179

Cima 27

Finestra 1773 m

179

Punta Questa 1522 m

vecchio rifugio 1280 m

179

M. GRONDILICE 1805 m

186

PIZZO DI UCCELLO 1781 m

Giovetta 1497 m

Foce di Giovo 1500 m

CRESTA GARNERONE

37

186

Capanne dd Gioo 1234 m

Capanna Garnerone 1260 m

Foce Rasori 1318 m

1422 m

Maestà del Doglio 879 m

175

36

Foce Navola 1295 m

Foce Vinca 1333 m

Uinca P 808 m

38

38

787 m

Torrente Lucid

Foce Pollaro 1364 m

M. SAGRO 1748 m

Puntone della Piastra 1391 m

IL CATINO

N

0   1/2   1 Km

Foce di Giovo on your left, and going to Capanna Garnerone. Go right on this trail to reach Capanna Garnerone (about 1300 m, 1½ h from Vinca), in a coniferous wood. Capanna Garnerone is a metal hut, unmanned, which can accommodate up to 18 people. It has a completely furnished kitchen and a gas-stove. No food is available, so bring your own, should you wish to stay here. You will find drinkable water and a toilet outside. The rifugio is owned by the Carrara section of CAI, from which you may obtain the key (see the chapter "The local CAI Sections" for address and telephone number). When it is available, and if you have time, this is a nice, spartan and inexpensive base camp for some days hiking around and/or climbing the Cresta Garnerone, Torrione Figari or Punta Questa, which are all very close to the rifugio. Refer to the chapter "Climbs in the Apuane Alps".

Continue past the rifugio to the *Fonte* (fountain) *Vacchereccia*. From there, the trail soon splits, trail #173 leaves to the right toward Foce di Navola, and we continue on trail #37 which goes on the left toward Foce di Monte Rasori. In 15 minutes, you will reach the Foce di Monte Rasori (1318 m), a large, panoramic saddle with views of the sea, Monte Sagro and Monte Grondilice. In between, on your left you can see the two peaks, Torrione Figari and Punta Questa, along the south ridge that extends down from Monte Grondilice. From Foce di Monte Rasori, go left along the grassy ridge; avoid the level trail that runs horizontally to your right and goes to Punta Questa. Instead, climb upward to the foot of some steep rocks ahead of you. Follow the red marks and ascend the steep, rocky trail (watch for falling rocks). The environment is now dramatically different: wild, no vegetation, severe and rocky. Soon the trail becomes very steep, traversing steep scree slopes to finally reach Finestra di Grondilice (1773 m, 1¼ h from Foce di Monte Rasori). From here in about ½ h for the round trip, you can follow a narrow blazed trail on the left, that leads to the summit of Monte Grondilice (easy scrambling; a little exposure; watch for falling rocks). From the summit, you have wonderful views of the surrounding mountains and the sea.

Return to Finestra di Grondilice, and from there, descend via the trail on the other side of the pass to *Cava 27* (cava means quarry). You are now in the valley of *Orto di Donna* and *Serenaia*, the valley of Rifugio Donegani. The peaks, from left to right, are Monte Pisanino (1946 m, the highest peak in the Apuane Alps), Zucchi di Cardeto (1746 and 1793 m), Monte Cavallo (1895 m) and Monte Contrario (1789 m). Just before the quarry on your left, take trail #179. The trail descends through a beech grove down to Foce di Giovo (1500 m), a large grassy saddle that connects the valley of Orto di Donna and Serenaia with the valley of Vinca (1½ h from Finestra di Grondilice). Cross the pass on your left and pick up trail #175 along the west slopes toward Vinca. The trail traverses steep meadows, passing the remains of old houses, Capanne di Giovo, passes close to a nearby water fountain and eventually through a chestnut wood (look for mushrooms) to reach Vinca (1 h from the Giovo pass).

Where to end the hike

Whether you came from Aulla or another direction, you must not miss the opportunity to taste the *Panigacci* and *Testaroli al pesto* at the *Ristorante La Gavarina d' Oro*, on the Via Castello, Podenzana, Aulla (tel. 0187 410021, closed on Wednesday). To find the restaurant, once you are in Aulla, follow the road signs to Podenzana. It is on the other side of the Magra River, which flows through Aulla. Cross the bridge and continue on the road going upward. You will pass under the motorway Parma-La Spezia, and continue for about 5 km. At the junction with the road to the Castle (blue road sign to Casalina, Castello and Caviana), turn right on the road to the Ristorante La Gavarina d' Oro (you see the brown sign at the junction). You can also have delicious local food at the restaurant of the *Hotel la Posta* (0585 97937) of Elena and Livo Pietrini in Equi Terme. Equi Terme is a spa town not far from Vinca. It has an old center and two prehistoric caves, well worth visiting.

Hike 10 - Monte Tambura loop, from Resceto

Illustration 17 - Via Vandelli towards Passo della Tambura (1620 m)

Difficulty	*Very strenuous*
Length	*15 km*
Elevation gain	*1500 m*
Walking time	*8 h*
Highest elevation	*1890 m (Monte Tambura)*
Trailhead	*Resceto (485 m)*
Trails	*#35 from Resceto, and then #166, #166 bis and #36 to Passo Focolaccia (1650 m);*
	#148 from Passo Focolaccia to the summit of Monte Tambura (1890 m);
	#148 from the summit of Monte Tambura to Passo Tambura (1620 m);
	#35 (via Vandelli) from Passo Tambura to Resceto.
Points of interest	*Lizza and Marble quarries (Focolaccia and along the trail)*
	Via Vandelli (this is one of the most interesting parts of the old road)
	Monte Tambura, one of the highest of the Apuane Alps
	The drive from Massa to Resceto along the valley of the river Frigido
	Exploration of Resceto

Monte Tambura is one of the highest mountains of the Apuane Alps. It was mentioned as *Tambernicchi* by Dante Alighieri in the Divine Comedy (Dante, Inferno, Canto XXXII, 28). This trail starts as the *Via Vandelli*, connecting Resceto to Passo Tambura, and beyond to Arnetola in Garfagnana. It is part of a road built around 1750 by the Abbot and Engineer Domenico Vandelli. The trail was commissioned as a road by Francesco III d' Este, Duke of Modena, who meant to connect Massa to Modena. Years later, the road fell into disuse, as it became notorious because of stories of robbery and murder. The long trail from Resceto to Passo Tambura, rises more than 1100 m in countless switch-backs through dramatic scenery. It seems incredible that almost 250 years ago horse-drawn carts went up and down this narrow, steep, treacherous, exposed stony path. The first 3-4 km of the trail from Resceto, recently restored to its original cobbled pavement, appears wide and smooth, but it is always steep. The Via Vandelli starts from a small house, the *Casa del Fondo*, which means House at the Bottom (elevation 627 m), above the main parking lot in Resceto at the end of the road ascending from the town. The environment immediately becomes dramatic: a treeless, steep, grassy slope, a narrow bridge over a deep gorge surrounded by high rocky mountains, and broad views as you rapidly gain elevation.

How to reach the trailhead

Take the road from Massa to Resceto along the valley of the Frigido River. From the center of Massa follow the signs to Forno and Resceto. Pass through the village of Canevara and at 6.5 km from Massa at the junction take the road on the right (signs to Gronda and Resceto). Pass through the villages of Guadine and Gronda (2 km from the junction). In Gronda take the road on your left and enter a picturesque canyon. After a few switchbacks, in one of which there is a memorial dedicated to Abbot Vandelli, you will reach the town of Resceto (5 Km from the junction), elevation 485 m. Park in the parking lot at the top of the town.

The hike

From Resceto follow the main road going upward to the mountains (no outlet). The road ends after few hundreds meters at the Casa del Fondo (627 m) and the start of the Via Vandelli. Trail #35 ascends steadily until it crosses a mountain ridge and enters a narrow valley; on the slope to the right you can see all the Via Vandelli switchbacks going up towards Passo Tambura, which is still out of sight. Continue for a few meters, leaving the Via Vandelli on the right, and take trail #166 straight ahead. The trail now follows an old lizza, steep and relentless, which leads eventually to Passo Focolaccia. Follow the *via di lizza* (a steep rocky path used for sliding down blocks of marble, see "Local Terms" in the chapter "Before Starting Your Hike") for a few hundred meters and then take the steep, narrow and grassy left fork, trail #166 bis, going uphill. While the lizza follows the bottom of the long steep canyon, this trail ascends to the ridge in few short switchbacks. From the ridge you have good views of the wild environment, of the narrow valleys and of Resceto. The trail follows the ridge for a while, then continues on the left side along another steep and stony lizza (*lizza Silvia*), which leads to marble quarries far above. Here you can still see some wood piro standing along the lizza. As mentioned in the "Local Terms", *piro* is a piece of wood, planted in the ground, around which ropes were wrapped to hold and give direction to the blocks of marble in their way down the lizza. Sometimes, instead of wood,

Forcella
di Porta
1752 m

Passo della
Focolaccia
1650 m

Rifugio
Aronte
1642 m

148

M. TAMBURA
△ 1890 m

36

36

166

166

Canale Pianone

Passo della
Tambura
1620 m

35

M. Focoletta
△ 1672 m

Acqua Fredda
1600 m

VIA VANDELLI

35

627 m

Casa del
Fondo

Rifugio
Conti
1400 m

ALTO
DI SELLA
1723 m
△

Canale Piastriccioni

P

Resceto
485 m

Focola
del Vento
1358 m

M. SELLA
1739 m △

N

0   1/2   1 Km

piro is made of marble: a marble piro is visible along the lizza from Cave Cervaiole to the town of Azzano. The climbing is long and hard, the lizza full of loose marble stones, but the scenery is very pleasant, the vegetation wild and grassy with a few isolated bushes. Trail #166 bis ends at a marble quarry where it joins trail #36, which comes from the town of Forno via *Case della Vettolina* (Vettolina Houses, elevation 1059 m) (see "Hike 17 - Monte Cavallo loop").

Continue on up trail #36 to the right, following the steep lizza. Climb the steps carved in the rock past the remains of an old warehouse near a rocky saddle, 2 ½ h from Resceto. From the saddle there is a wonderful view of the coast on your left, and in front, on the opposite slope, you will see the rocky *Coda del Cavallo* (the Tail of Monte Cavallo), with an overhanging wall and a marble quarry at the bottom. Drop down from the saddle back to the old warehouse, climb up to the ridge and soon you reach a dirt road, a marmifera, used for the marble quarries all around you. Follow the road going upward, pass beside a new house and a big tank, and continue up to Passo Focolaccia (1650 m), 1 h from the saddle. Before you reach the pass look to your left between the ridge and the road to see the *Rifugio Aronte*. It is the oldest (1902) and the highest (1642 m) hut in the Apuane Alps. The rifugio is very small, only one room for about 10 people, unmanned, with a stove and maybe wood and blankets. The pass has been completely devastated by the road and the surrounding marble quarries. Before you reach the pass go right to reach the northwest ridge of Monte Tambura. Continue along this ridge, with its panoramic views, for about 1 km before passing a false summit, to reach the summit of Monte Tambura with its spectacular views of the mountains, the coastline, the islands and the sea. You are about 1 hour from Passo della Focolaccia.

From the summit, follow the south ridge of the mountain to Passo Tambura. The trail descends almost all the way along the ridge, sometimes along marble scree to eventually reach the pass, about 30 minutes from the summit. From Passo Tambura (1620 m) follow right along the Via Vandelli, trail #35, on the west slopes of the mountain towards Resceto. The Via Vandelli drops down in long switchbacks and soon reaches a notch in the ridge (1442 m) on your left, ¾ h from Passo Tambura. For an interesting and very short side trip, follow the trail through the notch, which leads you in few minutes to the manned *Rifugio Nello Conti*, almost at the top end of the steep and wild *Canale dei Piastriccioni*. A visit to the rifugio is worth the short deviation and, if open, a drink will restore your energy and enthusiasm. After your break, return to the Via Vandelli to continue down by innumerable switchbacks. This part of the trail has recently been restored and looks almost like a road with its stony, smooth pavement, buttressed from below by dry-stone walls. Once at the bottom cross the narrow bridge and ascend to rejoin trail #166 (closing the loop). Continue down along via Vandelli and then along the road, until you reach the town of Resceto, 2¼ h from Rifugio Conti.

Where to end the hike

At the end of the village of Resceto on the way to Massa on the right try the Bar Trattoria of the local *Circolo ARCI* (*circolo* means club). *Tordelli*, *lasagne*, rabbit and polenta or a variety of salt cod and polenta are among the delicious specialities.

Hike 11 - Monte Sella

Difficulty	*Strenuous*
Length	*12 km*
Elevation gain	*1250 m*
Walking time	*7 h*
Highest elevation	*1739 m (Monte Sella)*
Trailhead	*Resceto (485 m)*
Trails	*#165 from Resceto (485 m), along Canale dei Piastriccioni;*
	#160 from Canale dei Piastriccioni to Cava Bagnoli and summit of Monte Sella (1739 m); back along the same route.
Points of interest	*Ponte del Pirosetto (Pirosetto bridge)*
	Marble quarries (Cave Bagnoli and of Monte Sella)
	Monte Sella
	The drive from Massa to Resceto along the valley of the river Frigido
	Exploration of Resceto

Monte Sella is located in the central part of the Apuane Alps. The mountains here are among the highest in the entire chain. The western slopes are very steep and rocky with little vegetation in the higher part, it is mainly *paleo* (grass) with tiny, sparse beeches in the lower part. The slopes from the top fall for a thousand meters down towards dark and narrow canyons. This description cannot do justice to the dramatic scenery in this area.

How to reach the trailhead

Take the road from Massa to Resceto along the valley of the Frigido River. From the center of Massa follow the signs to Forno and Resceto. Pass through the village of Canevara and at 6.5 kilometers from Massa at the junction take the road on the right (signs to Gronda and Resceto). Pass through the villages of Guadine and Gronda (2 km from the junction). In Gronda take the road on your left and enter a picturesque canyon. After a few switchbacks, in one of which there is a memorial dedicated to Abbot Vandelli, is the town of Resceto (5 Km from the junction, elevation 485 m). Park in the parking lot at the top of the town.

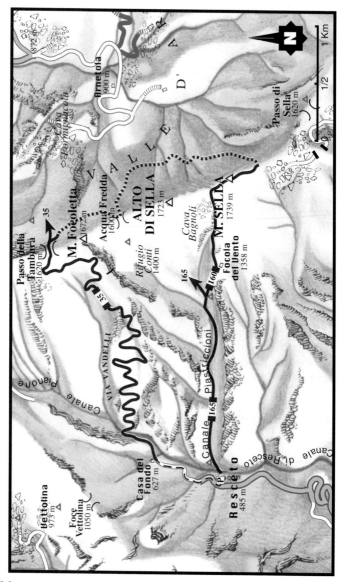

The hike

From the parking lot go back to the center of the town. You will find a bar in the main square. From here go downhill and cross the bed of Canale di Resceto. The trail 165 follows a dirt road, steep and stony (marble debris) along the *Canale dei Piastriccioni* (Piastriccioni canyon), one of the tributaries of the Frigido river. At the first small stone building, you will find a fountain of fresh water where you may fill your water bottles. The trail leaves the road, going up a few steps on the right, and continues higher in the same direction, still along the Canale dei Piastriccioni. At an old bridge, called *Ponte del Pirosetto*, no longer usable - it is part of an old lizza, go down a few meters and cross the stream coming from the right, it comes from the upper part of the Canale dei Piastriccioni. The trail goes up along an old lizza. After a few hundred meters you pass close to an old, ruined building, on the right. Continue for a few meters along the lizza and then turn right on rock and steps carved in the rock. Soon you reach a lateral valley. The trail continues first along the left bank of the stream, crosses the stream after a while and then climbs along the right bank of the same stream, up to a big stone, under which you will find a spring of fresh water, 2 h from Resceto. At this point the trail splits into two parts, the one on the left is trail #164, which leads to Rifugio Conti at the *Finestra* (window) *Vandelli*, the other to the right, still trail #165, continues along the same valley.

Follow trail #165 and after a few hundred meters reach the junction with another trail. Turn right on this trail, #160, it goes up toward *Focola del Vento*, *Cava Bagnoli* and then Monte Sella. The trail is very steep and stony. Party members should stay very close together to avoid the danger of rock fall. The trail is long, always steep, narrow and rocky. Finally it reaches the ridge and continues along it up to the Focola del Vento, where there is a high electricity pylon, 1 h from the spring. The view is impressive and the sea is finally visible. Also visible, down to the left is a lizza with a monorail in the middle. At the Focola del Vento follow trail #160 going up along the lizza and passing through the Bagnoli marble quarry, until you reach the summit of Monte Sella, 1 h from the Focola del Vento. The views from the summit are really rewarding.

From the summit return along the same route.

Alternative route: Monte Sella loop, through "Via Ferrata Vecchiacchi"

Provided you have no fear of heights and are adequately equipped, instead of going back along the same route, you may complete a very interesting loop around Monte Sella, by the *Via Ferrata Vecchiacchi*, and then back to Resceto along the Via Vandelli. Your equipment should be: climbing harness, a sling and a carabiner for self-belay on the cable, and helmet. The itinerary includes the Via Ferrata Vecchiacchi, from the summit to Passo della Tambura (1620 m), and trail #35 from the pass to Resceto, along the astonishing Via Vandelli. With this variant the hike becomes 16 km long, the elevation gain 1500 m, the time 9 h, and difficulty is VS.

From the summit follow the south ridge, where shortly you will find the start of the Via Ferrata Vecchiacchi, on your left along the east slopes of the mountain on the Garfagnana side. When you reach a shoulder of the mountain a metal cable allows you to descend safely along the very steep grassy slope of the mountain. The Via Ferrata Vecchiacchi crosses the full expanse of the east side of the mountain and drops about two hundred meters. Then go uphill again (do not take trail #146 going to Arnetola) until you reach the crest at *Focetta dell'Acqua Fredda* (Cold Water Pass), almost 1600 m elevation. On this pass two other trails converge from the west (sea) side of the mountain: #165, the same trail you left at Canale dei Piastriccioni, and #164, recently restored with a metal cable, coming from Rifugio Nello Conti. After a short detour on the east side, to avoid the rocky peak of Monte Focoletta, the trail reaches Passo Tambura, 1620 m, 2 h from Monte Sella. From here follow trail #35, the Via Vandelli, going down on your left along the west slopes of the mountain.

The description of the route down along via Vandelli, is the same as for "Hike 10 - Monte Tambura, from Resceto"and is repeated here: ... From Passo Tambura (1620 m) follow right along the Via Vandelli, trail #35, on the west slopes of the mountain towards Resceto. The Via Vandelli drops down in long switchbacks and soon reaches a notch in the ridge (1442 m) on your left, ¾ h from Passo Tambura. For an interesting and very short side trip, follow the trail through the notch, which leads you in few minutes to the manned *Rifugio Nello Conti*, almost at the top end of the steep and wild *Canale dei Piastriccioni*. A visit to the rifugio is worth the short deviation and, if open, a drink will restore your energy and enthusiasm. After your break, return to the Via Vandelli to continue down by innumerable switchbacks. This part of the trail has recently been restored and looks almost like a road with its stony, smooth pavement, buttressed from below by dry-stone walls. Once at the bottom cross the narrow bridge and ascend to rejoin trail #166 (closing the loop). Continue down along via Vandelli and then along the road, until you reach the town of Resceto, 2 ¼ h from Rifugio Conti.

Where to end the hike

The Bar Trattoria of the local *Circolo ARCI* (circolo means club) is at the end of the village on the way to Massa. *Tordelli, lasagne,* rabbit and polenta, or a variety of salt cod and polenta are among the delicious specialities.

A Hike along the East Ligurian Coast

Illustration 18 - Vernazza (Cinque Terre)

Hike 12 - Cinque Terre (literally: five lands)

Difficulty	*Moderate*
Lenght	*12 km*
Elevation gain	*650 m*
Walking time	*5 h*
Highest elavation	*about 300 m, on the path from Monterosso to Vernazza*
Trailhead	*Monterosso*
Trail	*#2 from Monterosso*
Points of interest	*The five villages: Monterosso, Vernazza, Corniglia, Manarola and Riomaggiore*
	Terraced fields
	Olive, orange and lemon groves
	Mediterranean bush
	A wide variety of coastal views

This is one of the most beautiful coastal paths in Italy. The environment is unique: steep hills, terraces and olive groves or vegetable gardens, agave and cactus on slopes running down to the sea and, above all, the total absence of cars. In the past, it was only possible to reach the villages by boat or on foot. The train arrived in 1874, while roads arrived only a few decades ago. The road however is inland and, thanks to the very steep slopes on the sea side, it is almost invisible. All the villages are very picturesque and have interesting old churches. The best time to walk here is between September and May. In summer it is too hot, but at least you can go swimming.

How to reach the trailhead

Arrive in Monterosso by train. Make sure the train stops there. Usually local trains from La Spezia or from Sestri Levante stop in all the five towns. Leave the station and turn left on the main road along the coast. Pass through a car-pedestrian tunnel to the center of town. Immediately after the tunnel, there is a long railway bridge which passes over the center of the village cutting it in two: to the west there is a bay with a sandy beach and a walkway going up over the rock to the entrance to "Porto Roca Hotel". On the other side of the bridge is the main part of the village. From Monterosso there are two different trailheads:

1. To find the first, pass under the bridge and turn right through the public garden. At the south end of the garden go straight on, passing on the left the "Palazzo Comunale" (City Hall) with blue marks on the left (the name of this path is "Sentiero Azzurro", which means Blue Trail) to the start of blue trail #2. The blue trail starts climbing some steps on the right among the last houses of the village and continues on the level above the Porto Roca Hotel, on the right.

2. There are better views from the walkway above the coast, which is the other trailhead. After the tunnel go right on the road, parallel to the beach and on the walkway going up towards the Porto Roca Hotel. Here the red marks indicate the start of trail #2.

The hike

Just before the gate of the hotel, the trail turns right along a short and panoramic itinerary, carved in the rock, overhanging the sea. The trail starts going up around the Porto Roca Hotel, and just past the hotel it joins the blue trail. At the junction the trail continues on the right, following up and down a winding old footpath, which was, until recently, the only connection between the towns and the outside world, with the exception of the sea and the railroad. The trail runs along the edges of terraced fields, sometimes beside dry stone walls, sometimes climbing countless stone steps, going around the many ridges which run down to the sea, crossing small streams by ancient stone vaulted bridges, overlooking steep green slopes and deep, wild bays and coves. The path connects the small, picturesque, medieval towns of Vernazza (about 1½ h from Monterosso), Corniglia (2 h from Vernazza, the most strenuous stretch with a lot of ups and downs), Manarola (1 h from Corniglia, along an almost completely flat stretch), and eventually Riomaggiore (½ h from Manarola, along a wonderful walkway, high above the coast). Each of the towns has shops, restaurants, bars, hotels and a train station. It is thus possible to end your walk at any one of them and return by train. The stretch between Manarola and Riomaggiore is very short and has been named *Sentiero dell' Amore* (Lovers' Lane) because of its romantic beauty.

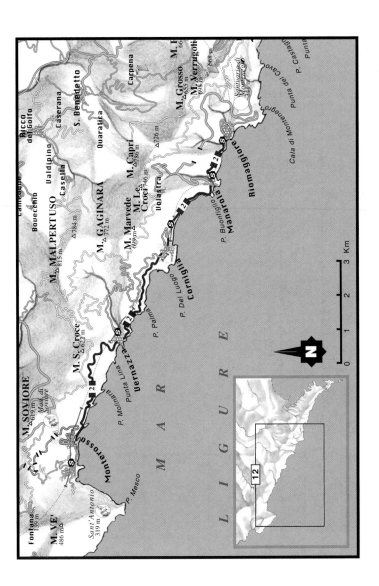

105

Where to end the hike

Whether you end your hike in Riomaggiore or any of the other towns, you can find a good seafood restaurant. Listed in the Chapter "Where to stay, What to eat, Where to eat, Rifugio" are some of the Ligurian specialities. Look out for:

- *trenette al pesto*, a special kind of pasta with pesto sauce;
- *trofie al pesto*, small dumplings with pesto sauce;
- *mesciua*, a soup with chick-peas, beans and wheat grains;
- *pansotti*, a kind of ravioli stuffed with cheese and chard and served with a creamy walnut sauce;
- *gianchet*, very small fish, sometimes baby sardines, coated with egg and bread crumbs and deep-fried;
- *focaccia al formaggio*, flat bread with cheese inside;
- *zuppa di tartufi*, local shell fish soup, very difficult to find, expensive, but worth the price;
- *vino delle Cinque Terre*, local wine;
- *sciacchetrà*, a local strong sweet dessert wine.

Other Hikes in the Apuane Alps

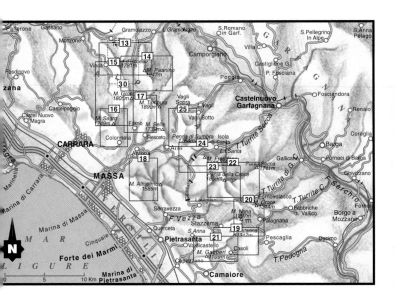

Map 16 - "other Hikes in the Apuane Alps" Reference Map

Hike 13 - Pizzo d'Uccello loop

Difficulty	*Moderate*
Length	*11 km*
Elevation gain	*700 m*
Walking time	*5 ½ h*
Highest elevation	*1781 m (Pizzo d' Uccello)*
Trailhead	*Rifugio Donegani (1122 m)*
Trails	*#187 from the trailhead to Foce Siggioli (1390 m); #181 from Foce Siggioli to Giovetto (1497 m); from Foce Giovetto along the south ridge to the summit of Pizzo d' Uccello (1781 m) and back to Giovetto;*

Illustration 19 - Rifugio Donegani (1122 m)

	#181 from Giovetto to Foce di Giovo (1500 m);

#181 from Giovetto to Foce di Giovo (1500 m);
#37 from Foce di Giovo to Rifugio Donegani.

Points of interest   *One of the best views of the north wall of Pizzo d'Uc-*
cello
The view from Pizzo d' Uccello
Foce di Giovo, a wide grassy saddle
Marble quarries
Serenaia high plain

Pizzo d' Uccello is one of the rockiest and boldest peaks of the Apuane Alps. From Foce Siggioli you have one of the best views of the north wall of the mountain (more than 700 m high). The stretch to the summit of Pizzo d' Uccello is exposed and should be avoided by less experienced hikers. The rest of the hike is very interesting and enjoyable.

How to reach the trailhead (same as for Hike 6 and Hike 14)

On the road from Castelnuovo Garfagnana to Aulla, about 1 km past the center of Piazza al Serchio toward Aulla, take the road on your left to Gramolazzo and Minucciano. Pass through the town of Nicciano and drive along the north bank of Lake Gramolazzo, and then through the town of Gramolazzo, 8 km from the junction. Continue on the same road for about 3 km from Gramolazzo. Just before a tunnel, turn left on the road to Serenaia and Rifugio Donegani. Serenaia is a large, relatively flat area surrounded by high mountains, about 6 km from the junction. Continue for about ½ km to reach Rifugio Donegani (1122 m). Park here. Across the valley you will see Monte Pisanino (1946 m) the highest peak in the Apuane Alps.

The hike

From Rifugio Donegani follow the road going up. Soon after the first switchback you reach the trailhead of trail #187 on the right. Take trail #187 which leaves the road, climbs the grassy slope on the right and crosses a wood of beech trees along the east slope of the mountain. In a little more than 1 h it reaches Foce Siggioli (1390 m). The view from the foce is astonishing. The huge wall of Pizzo d' Uccello rises on your left, more than 700 m high. From the summit the long ridge, running to the west-north-west and called Nattapiana, stretches for more than two

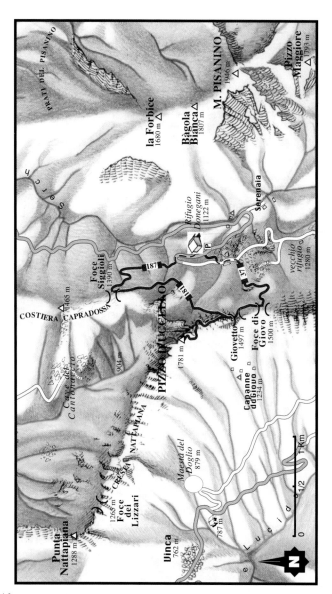

PRATI DEL PISANINO

M. PISANINO
1946 m

Pizzo
Maggiore
1793 m

la Forbice
1680 m

Bàgola
Bianca
1807 m

Serchio

Rifugio
Donegani
1122 m

Serenaia

P

vecchio
rifugio
1280 m

Foce
Siggioli
1390 m

187

181

37

COSTIERA CAPRADOSSA
1465 m

904 m

PIZZO DI UCCELLO

1781 m

Giovetto
1497 m

Foce di
Giovo
1500 m

Cave dei
Cantonacci

Capanne
dd Giovo
1234 m

CRESTA NATTAPIANA

Maestà del
Doglio
879 m

1 Km

Foce
dei
Lizzari
1265 m

787 m

1/2

Punta
Nattapiana
1288 m

Ulinca
762 m

e Lucia

0

N

110

km, enclosing the narrow valley of the Solco di Equi. Here starts the "Via Ferrata" which goes to the bottom of the wall along a steep and very exposed ridge (see "Hike 30 - Solco di Equi and Via Ferrata to Foce Siggioli", in the chapter "Climbs in the Apuane Alps"). From Foce Siggioli take trail #181, which goes back up on your left across the upper part of the east slope of the mountain. The trail is steep and narrow (some exposure, watch for loose stones) and leads to the Giovetto pass (1497 m) in less than 1 h. Here is the point where the party may split: the less experienced hikers may either wait for the others here or go ahead a little further on trail #181 up to Foce di Giovo and, while waiting, enjoy the beautiful grassy saddle and the views. For this group the hike becomes Easy. The group proceeding to the summit from Giovetto should turn right along the south ridge of Pizzo d'Uccello (blue marks). Scramble up to the summit, but watch for loose rocks in the narrow, steep couloirs. Keep your party together, with only a few people at a time in the couloir. The rest should remain in a protected area until the party above has moved out of the couloir. The ascent is exciting, enjoyable and not difficult, although you may have to use your hands occasionally to help you climb (1½ h from Giovetto). From the summit there are views of the valleys below and the surrounding mountain peaks, Monte Sagro, Contrario, Cavallo, Pisanino and the Apennines in the east.

From the summit go back following the same route as far as Giovetto and from here continue on trail #181 up to Foce di Giovo (1500 m), 1 h from the summit. Here the two groups may reunite. From Foce di Giovo there are views of the Serenaia Valley to the east and Vinca on the other side of the saddle. From the Foce di Giovo go east following trail #37 towards the rifugio Donegani, see "Hike 6 - Pizzo d' Uccello". The trail descends with several switchbacks through a grove of beech trees and reaches a marble quarry and a dirt road (marmifera). Follow the red marks indicating trail #37 (easy to miss), otherwise follow the road down and eventually you will reach Rifugio Donegani, 1 h from Foce di Giovo.

Where to end the hike

Enjoy a delicious and inexpensive meal at the Rifugio Donegani (0583 610085).

Hike 14 - Monte Pisanino

Difficulty	*Strenuous*
Length	*12 km*
Elevation gain	*1000 m*
Walking time	*6 ½ h*
Highest elevation	*1946 m (Monte Pisanino)*
Trailhead	*Rifugio Donegani (1122 m)*
Trails	*#180 from Rifugio Donegani to Foce di Cardeto (1680 m);*
	from Foce di Cardeto to the summit, a trail with blue marks and no number;
	back along the same route.
Points of interest	*Monte Pisanino*
	Serenaia valley
	Foce di Cardeto

Monte Pisanino, the highest of the Apuane Alps at 1946 m, is a truncated pyramid with very steep and grassy slopes all round, it is located in a lateral branch of the main divide of the mountains.

How to reach the trailhead (same as for Hike 6 and Hike 13)

On the road from Castelnuovo Garfagnana to Aulla, about 1 km past the center of Piazza al Serchio toward Aulla, take the road on your left to Gramolazzo and Minucciano. Pass through the town of Nicciano and drive along the north bank of Lake Gramolazzo, and then through the town of Gramolazzo, 8 km from the junction. Continue on the same road for about 3 km from Gramolazzo. Just before a tunnel, turn left on the road to Serenaia and Rifugio Donegani. Serenaia is a large, relatively flat area surrounded by high mountains, about 6 km from the junction. Continue for about ½ km to reach Rifugio Donegani (1122 m). Park here. Across the valley you will see Monte Pisanino (1946 m) the highest peak in the Apuane Alps.

The hike

From the rifugio a few minutes down the road, on the right hand side, is the trailhead of trail #180. Continue along trail #180 through a beech

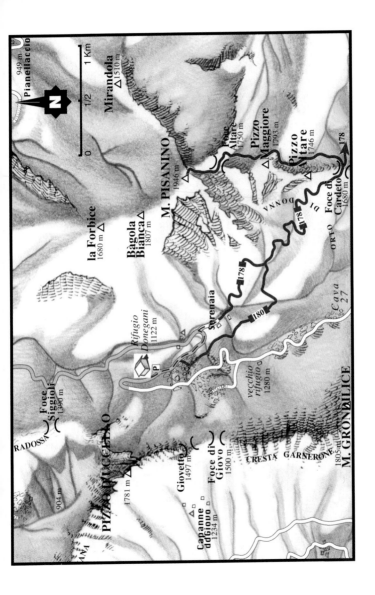

wood, to the intersection with trail #178 which comes from Serenaia. Turn right along this trail (#178) up to Foce di Cardeto (1680 m), which is a gap in the rock between Monte Cavallo and Pizzo Altare, 2 h from Rifugio Donegani. This stretch is very enjoyable, first in the wood and then on a rocky and open path up to the pass. A few meters down from the pass on the other side, on the left, take the visible trail with blue marks but no number up to Foce Altare (Altar Pass, 1750 m) along a narrow path (some exposure) on the east slopes of Pizzo Altare and Pizzo Maggiore, 1 h from Foce di Cardeto. From Foce Altare climb through the *Canale delle Rose* (Couloir of the Roses), very steep and grassy (watch for loose stones), and reach the short flat crest. From here it is a short scramble (some exposure) to the summit of Monte Pisanino (1946 m), the highest of the Apuane Alps, 1 h from Foce Altare. There are great views over Lake Gramolazzo and the whole amphitheater of mountains around Serenaia and Rifugio Donegani.

From the summit, return along the same route, in about 2 ½ h.

Where to end the hike

Enjoy a delicious and inexpensive meal at the Rifugio Donegani (0583 610085).

Hike 15 - Monte Sagro loop, from Vinca

Difficulty   *Very Strenuous*
Length   *16 km*
Elevation gain   *1300 m*
Walking time   *8 h*
Highest elevation *1749 m (Monte Sagro)*

Illustration 20 - From the summit of Monte Sagro (1749 m), towards south-west. On the bottom left the Casa dei Pisani *(Pisans' House) in Canal Regolo.*

Trailhead	the main square of the town of Vinca (808 m)
Trails	#38 from Vinca to Foce di Vinca (1333 m) and from there to Foce Luccica (1029 m);
	#172 from Foce Luccica to Foce della Faggiola (1464 m);
	from Foce della Faggiola a path (blue marks) reaches the west ridge first and then, along the northwest ridge, the summit of Monte Sagro (1749 m);
	from the summit back along the northwest ridge first and then along the west ridge to the junction with trail #173;
	#173 from this junction to Foce del Faneletto (1426 m) and on to Foce del Pollaro (1364 m) and then to the junction with trail #38 (below Foce di Vinca);
	#38 from the junction to Vinca.
Points of interest	The town of Vinca
	Crossing 5 different valleys
	The view from Monte Sagro
	Marble quarries

Monte Sagro has one of the best views in the Park. In addition to the spectacular views from the top, you cross five contrasting valleys, some wooded and green, others steep and wild, others white due to the numerous marble quarries on their slopes.

How to reach the trailhead (same as for "Hike 9 - Monte Grondilice loop")

Take road #63 from Aulla toward Passo del Cerreto. At 12 km, go right at the junction to Castelnuovo Garfagnana, road #445. Then at km 3.5, take another right to enter and cross Gragnola and drive toward Equi Terme. In 4.2 km, pass through the town of Monzone and then take the road to Vinca. Once in Vinca, drive toward the center of town (take the road on your left going upward, no outlet). Park in the square, where you will find a convenient fountain of fresh water to fill your water bottles. When in town, if you find a *Bar* or an *Alimentari* shop open, do not fail to taste the local *focaccia*, a kind of flat homemade bread.

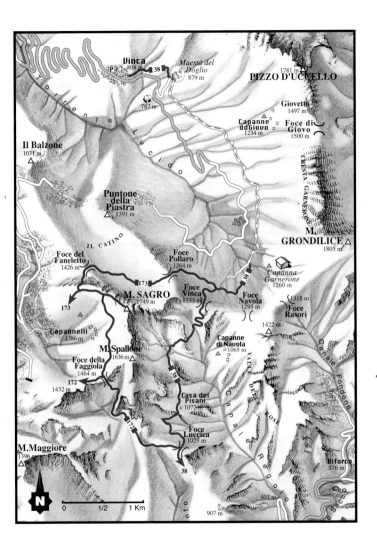

Vinca
808 m 🅿 38

Maestà del
Doglio
879 m

PIZZO D'UCCELLO
1781 m

787 m

Giovetto
1497 m

Capanne
di Giovo
1234 m

Foce di
Giovo
1500 m

Il Balzone
1071 m △

Puntone
della
Piastra
△ 1391 m

IL CATINO

CRESTA GARNERONE

M.
GRONDILICE △
1805 m

Foce del
Faneletto
1426 m

Foce
Pollaro
1364 m

Capanna
Garnerone
1260 m

173

Foce
Vinca
1333 m

38

M. SAGRO
1749 m
△

Foce
Navola
1295 m

1318 m
Foce
Rasori

173

Capannelli
1386 m

1422 m △

Foce della
Faggiola
1464 m

M. Spallone
1636 m △

Capanne
di Navola
1065 m △

38

172
1432 m

Casa dei
Pisani
1072 m

VALLE DELLE ROSE

172

Canale Fondone

M. Maggiore
1396 m
△

Foce
Luccica
1029 m

38

Canale Regolo

Biforco
376 m △

403 m △

907 m △

Torrente Secco

N

0   1/2   1 Km

The hike

From the square, enter the town. Follow the red marks on the stone walls of the houses up to the top of the town. After you pass the last house, take trail #38 which enters a chestnut grove, crosses a creek bed and reaches a dirt road. Here on the right is a *Maestà* (about 900 m, ½ h from the square). Take the gravel road up into the woods, pass the Boy Scouts campground on your right (there is a wooden house and a fountain) and continue up on the winding road. After you leave the woods you will see a couple of houses on the left and then be in an amphitheater of mountains (from left to right): Pizzo d'Uccello, Cresta Garnerone, Monte Grondilice, up to Monte Sagro on your right, with its steep and exposed east ridge. Continue almost to the top of the valley, until trail #38 leaves the road. Turn on trail #38 and reach Foce di Vinca (1333 m),1 h from the Maestà. From here the trail enters the steep and wild valley of Canal Regolo, passes beside two big ruined buildings (the last is called the *Casa dei Pisani*, Pisans' House, 1077 m elevation) and reaches Foce Luccica (1029 m), 1½ h from Foce di Vinca. From Foce Luccica take trail #172 a little down on the right and climb along the south slopes of Monte Spallone up to Foce della Faggiola (1464 m), 1½ h from Foce Luccica. There are broad views from the trail which is steep and slightly exposed. In some stretches, especially in the high grass (*paleo*) and after having reached a dirt road, it is very easy to lose the trail (follow the red marks with extreme care). The name *faggiola* comes from the local name of the fruit of the Common or European Beech (in Italian *Faggio*) and has nothing to do with *fagiolo*, which is the Italian name for bean. At the pass leave trail #172, which goes to Foce di Pianza and turn right following the blue signs leading to the top of Monte Sagro (1749 m), along the west side of the mountain first and then along the north-west ridge,1 h from Foce della Faggiola. From here the views are amongst the most beautiful and extensive in the Apuane Alps: the sea, the coast, Bocca di Magra (Magra river mouth), La Spezia Gulf, the islands and, from south to east, Monte Grondilice, Garnerone Crest, Foce di Giovo (Giovo Pass), Pizzo d'Uccello, and beyond them Monte Tambura, Pisanino and Cavallo.

From the summit return down the northwest ridge first and then continue along the west ridge (very easy scrambling, watch for loose stones) until you reach trail #173. At the junction turn right on #173 up to Foce Faneletto (1426 m, metal cable) and continue along the bottom of the north wall of Monte Sagro. Continue through Foce del Pollaro (1364 m) and along a very steep stretch (metal cable) to the junction with trail #38, just below Foce di Vinca, 1½ h from the summit. Turn left on trail #38 and go back to Vinca, 1 h from the junction.

This hike to Monte Sagro could be combined with the other to Monte Grondilice and may become a very enjoyable 2-day hike, see "Multi-day hikes in the Apuane Alps".

Where to end your hike

As suggested in the "Hike 9 - Monte Grondilice" you can enjoy a meal of *Panigacci* and *Testaroli al Pesto* at the *Ristorante La Gavarina d' Oro*. For details see "Where to stay, What to eat, Where to eat, Rifugio". But you can also have delicious local food at the restaurant of the *Hotel la Posta* (0585 97937) of Elena and Livo Pietrini in Equi Terme. Equi Terme is a spa town not far from Vinca. It has an old center and two prehistoric caves, well worth visiting.

Hike 16 - Monte Sagro loop, from Colonnata

Difficulty	*Very Strenuous*
Length	*15 km*
Elevation gain	*1400 m*
Walking time	*8 h*
Highest elevation	*1749 m (Monte Sagro)*
Trailhead	*Colonnata (532 m)*
Trails	*#38 from Colonnata to Case Vergheto (837 m) first and then to Foce Luccica (1029 m);*
	#172 from Foce Luccica to Foce della Faggiola (1464 m);
	from Foce della Faggiola a path (blue marks) reaches the west ridge first and then, along the northwest ridge, the summit of Monte Sagro(1749 m);
	from the summit back along the northwest ridge first and then along the west ridge to the junction with trail #173;
	#173 from the junction to Foce del Faneletto (1426 m), to Foce del Pollaro (1364 m) and then to Foce di Vinca (1333 m);
	#38 from Foce di Vinca to Foce Luccica and back to the trailhead.
Points of interest	*Five different valleys*
	The view from Monte Sagro
	The Vergheto houses
	The drive to the town of Colonnata
	Exploration of Colonnata
	Marble quarries

This has almost the same itinerary as hike 15, but starting from a different place. This time the hike starts from Colonnata (532 m), famous for *lardo* and for its numerous marble quarries. There are spectacular views from the top of Monte Sagro. By starting from Case Vergheto (837 m) the hike could become shorter and less strenuous whilst remaining varied and interesting.

How to reach the trailhead

From the north-east side of Carrara follow the road signs to Colonnata. The winding road passes close to several marble quarries (gift shops along the road) and climbs in 7 km to Colonnata, at 532 m elevation. The drive is very interesting: you will see marble quarries and marmifera all around and the valleys are almost completely white with marble debris. At the entrance to Colonnata there is a parking lot. Park here.

The hike

From the parking area continue walking along the main road and just before the main square, at the first intersection, turn right. Here starts trail #38. Trail #38 leaves the last houses of Colonnata, climbs slightly up towards *Canale del Vento* (Wind Valley), crosses a bridge over a stream and enters a wood of chestnut trees before reaching, after a few switchbacks, the houses of Vergheto (837 m) and a refreshing fountain. From here the trail soon reaches Foce Luccica (1029 m), 1½ h from Colonnata. A few meters before reaching the pass, take trail #172 on your left. It climbs the south slopes of Monte Spallone and reaches Foce Faggiola (1464 m) in 1½ h from Foce Luccica. The trail is steep, very panoramic and occasionally exposed. In some stretches, especially those with high grass (*paleo*) and also after having reached a dirt road, it is very easy to lose the trail (follow the red marks with extreme care). At the pass leave trail #172, which goes to Foce di Pianza, and turn right following the blue signs. The trail leads to the top of Monte Sagro (1749 m), along the west side of the mountain first and then along the northwest ridge, 1 h from Foce della Faggiola. From the top you will see one of the most beautiful panoramas of the Apuane Alps: the coastline quite close by with *Bocca di Magra* (Magra river mouth), La Spezia Gulf, the islands, and inland all around are severe and majestic mountains.

From the summit return back along the north-west ridge and continue along the west ridge (very easy scrambling but watch for loose rocks) until you find trail #173. At the junction turn right on #173 up to Foce Faneletto (1426 m, metal cable), continue along the bottom of the north wall of Monte Sagro, then through Foce del Pollaro (1364 m) and along a steep stretch (metal cable, watch for loose rocks), reaching the junction with trail #38, coming from Vinca. Take trail #38 to Foce di Vinca (1333 m), 1½ h from the summit. From here continue on trail #38, cross the

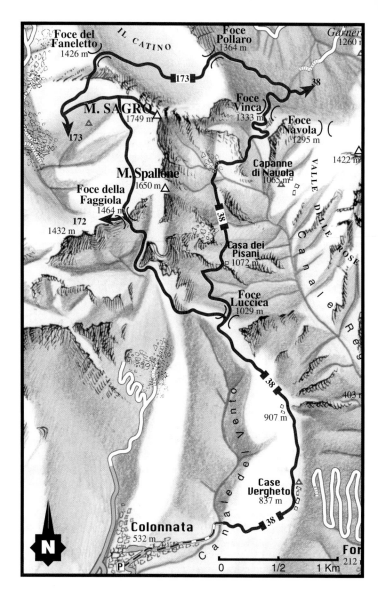

Foce del
Faneletto
1426 m

IL CATINO

Foce
Pollaro
1364 m

Garner

1260 m

173

38

M. SAGRO
1749 m

Foce
Vinca
1333 m

Foce
Navola
1295 m

173

Capanne
di Nauola
1065 m

VALLE DELLE ROSE

1422 m

M. Spallone
1650 m

Foce della
Faggiola
1464 m

38

Casa dei
Pisani
1072 m

Canale Reg

172
1432 m

Foce
Luccica
1029 m

38

403 m

Canale del Vento

907 m

Case
Vergheto
837 m

38

Colonnata
532 m

N

P

0   1/2   1 Km

Canale del Vento

For

212

122

pass and go south-west towards Foce Luccica. Continue along trail #38 after Foce Luccica and again reach Case Vergheto (about 1½ h from Foce di Vinca). From Case Vergheto continue on trail #38 to Colonnata, in less than 1 h.

A shorter and less strenuous hike

The hike could become shorter and less strenuous if you started from Case Vergheto directly. To reach Case Vergheto from Massa drive to Forno, cross the town and follow the road upward along the valley. A little more than ½ km from Forno turn left on the new road going to

Illustration 21- I Capannelli del Sagro (1386 m), on the west slope of Monte Sagro

Case Vergheto. From Case Vergheto the hike is still strenuous, but only 12 km long with 1000 m elevation gain. The walking time is now 6 h, and difficulty is only S.

Where to end the hike

Colonnata is very well known for its famous *lardo*. You should on no account fail to taste it at one of the two restaurants, both very good: *Venanzio* (closed on Thursday and Sunday night), Piazza Palestro 3, 0585 73617, or *Locanda Apuana*, Via Comunale 1, 0585 768017.

Hike 17 - Monte Cavallo loop

Difficulty	*Very Strenuous*
Length	*14 km*
Elevation gain	*1400 m*
Walking time	*7 ½ h*
Highest elevation	*1752 m (Forcella di Porta)*
Trailhead	*Casa Biforco (376 m), Forno*
Trails	*#167 from Casa Biforco to Casa Carpano (1047 m), Forcella di Porta (1752 m) and Passo della Focolaccia (1650 m);*
	#36 from Passo della Focolaccia to Casa Biforco.
Points of interest	*Valle degli Alberghi (Valley of hotels)*
	Casa Carpano (Carpano House)
	Marble quarries
	Via di lizza

Illustration 22 - Monte Cavallo (1895 m), west slope (Versilia side), from the road from Massa to Forno

This hike takes you through one of the wildest parts of the Apuane Alps. It starts climbing an old *via di lizza* toward the *Valle degli Alberghi* and continues along the steep slopes and south ridge of Monte Contrario. It crosses the upper part of the valley of Canal Cerignano (Cerignano Valley) just below the crest of Monte Cavallo (Mount Horse), reaches Passo della Focolaccia and descends almost the whole length of the divide between Canale Cerignano and Canale Pianone with wonderful views over the two lateral valleys.

How to reach the trailhead

From Massa drive to Forno, go through the town and follow the road upward along the valley. A little more than ½ kilometer out of Forno you will pass a new road going to Case Vergheto on your left. Do not take it, but keep right towards Casa Biforco (376 m), where the road again splits in two. The road was damaged during the last flood of June 1996, but it is still possible to reach this fork. The valley, up to here named Canale Secco (Dry Valley), also splits in two, Canale Fondone (Fondone Valley) on the left and Canale Cerignano (Cerignano Valley) on the right. Park the car just before the fork, near an old ruined loading station, but please do not obstruct the passage of other cars or trucks. From the car reach the split and find the start of trails #167 and #36. Trail #167 follows the valley on the left (Canale Fondone), while trail #36 the valley on the right (Canale Cerignano), which will be our way back to the car.

The hike

Trail #167 starts from the fork and follows the valley on the left and passes close to Casa Biforco. Soon it leaves Canale Fondone and enters the Valle degli Alberghi (Alberghi is the name of the valley, which means " Hotels", because there were dormitories for the marble workers here), climbing up to the right along an old and steep via di lizza. Finally it reaches a ruined house, below the Casa Alberghi. Follow the trail on the right, now narrow and less visible, and reach Casa Carpano (Carpano House, 1047 m) a little more than 2 h from Casa Biforco. From Casa Carpano the trail, not always easy to follow, continues, it is very steep and there are some exposed sections along the south ridge of Monte Contrario. The trail obliquely traverses the south slope of Monte Cavallo and reaches Forcella di Porta (1752 m) and very soon thereafter it

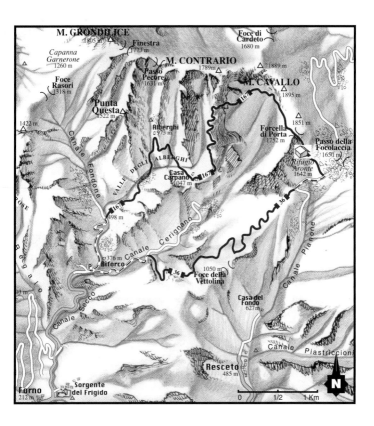

M. GRONDILICE
1805 m

Capanna
Garnerone
1260 m

Finestra
1773 m

Foce di
Cardeto
1680 m

M. CONTRARIO
1789m

1889 m

Passo
Pecore
1631 m

M. CAVALLO
1895 m

Foce
Rasori
1318 m

Punta
Questa
1522 m

Forcella
di Porta
1752 m

1851 m

Passo della
Focolaccia
1650 m

1422 m

Alberghi
973 m

Canale Fondone

VALLE DEGLI ALBERGHI

Rifugio
Aronte
1642 m

Casa
Carpano
1047 m

167

167

498 m

36

Canale Pianone

376 m
Biforco

Canale Cerignano

P

04 m

Canale Secco

1050 m
Foce della
Vettolina

36

Casa del
Fondo
627 m

Canale Piastriccioni

Resceto
485 m

Forno
212 m

Sorgente
del Frigido

N

0   1/2   1 Km

127

reaches Passo della Focolaccia (1650 m), 2 h from Casa Carpano. The pass has been completely devastated by the road and the surrounding marble quarries. Very close to the pass is the Rifugio Aronte, the oldest (built in 1902) and the highest (1642 m) hut in the Apuane Alps. The rifugio is very small, only one room for about 10 people, unmanned, with a stove and maybe wood and blankets. The itinerary, from Passo della Focolaccia to the junction with trail #166 bis, is the same as that of "Hike 10 - Monte Tambura loop, from Resceto".

From Passo della Focolaccia follow the marmifera going down along the western slopes (coastal side) of the mountain, past a new house (for marble workers) and a big water tank, and continue for a couple of km. Suddenly from the road, on your right, trail #36 goes down along a ridge (be careful, the red marks on the ridge must not be missed, otherwise you may find yourself following along the marmifera red marks of other old trails, no longer used). Trail #36 reaches a ruined warehouse below a saddle. From the saddle there are wonderful views of the coast on your left, and in front, on the opposite slope, is the rocky *Coda del Cavallo* (the Tail of Monte Cavallo), with an overhanging wall and a marble quarry at the bottom. From the saddle the trail goes down by steps carved in the rock, following a steep lizza (*lizza Silvia*) and reaches at a marble quarry the junction with trail #166 bis going towards Resceto (see "Hike 10"). Trail #36 crosses the quarry, goes down along a grassy slope, reaches the remains of the houses of Vettolina (1059 m), and, immediately after the intersection with trail #170, comes very close to Foce della Vettolina (1050 m), 1 h from the last saddle. Continue on trail #36 down toward Forno. The trail soon starts to descend reaching the marmifera along the Canale Pianone. Follow the marmifera down until you find the confluence with Canale Fondone and immediately thereafter reach your car, 1½ h from Foce della Vettolina.

Where to end the hike

Unfortunately there are no restaurants in Forno nor in the villages between here and Massa. Therefore drive to Resceto, and, just at the entrance to the town on the left, you will find the *Bar Trattoria Circolo ARCI* (circolo means club). *Tordelli*, *lasagne,* rabbit and polenta or a variety of salt cod and polenta are among the delicious specialities.

Hike 18 - Passo degli Uncini - Monte Carchio

Difficulty	*Moderate*
Length	*10 km*
Elevation gain	*700 m*
Walking time	*5 h*
Highest elevation	*1380 m (Passo degli Uncini)*
Trailhead	*Foce Pasquilio (827 m)*
Trails	*#33 from Pasquilio to Passo degli Uncini (Hooks Pass, 1380 m) and back to the west ridge of Monte Focoraccia;*
	from the ridge to the summit of Monte Focoraccia (1149 m) and along the south-west crest up to the top of Monte Carchio (1087 m);
	from Monte Carchio along a marmifera up to the west ridge, and along the west ridge in a coniferous wood down to Foce Pasquilio (red marks in the wood).
Points of interest	*Marble quarry on top of Monte Carchio*
	Views from Monte Focoraccia and Monte Carchio
	Scenic drive to Foce Pasquilio

This is one of the most scenic hikes in the south-west area of the Apuane Alps. The stretch between Monte Focoraccia and Passo degli Uncini is a little exposed. Pasquilio is a location very close to the town of Massa, with a few houses scattered on the southern slopes and a chapel in a beautiful position overlooking the sea. The location is well known because it was part of the *Linea Gotica* (Gothic Line) during the last war. It was here that a Japanese corps of American troops breached the Gothic Line. This military line was created by the Germans to stop the allied troops on their way north through Italy. There is a memorial to these events on marble at the pass.

How to reach the trailhead

There are two routes to choose from:

1. take the road from Massa to Castelnuovo Garfagnana (*Strada di Pian della Fioba*, see the chapter "The Apuane Alps"); pass through the town of San Carlo Po (famous for mineral waters) and after the town

of Pariana (283 m elevation) there is a junction on the right. Following the instructions on a road sign continue for 50 meters beyond the junction, make a U turn and finally take the road to Pasquilio which is now on your left. Does it sound strange to you? Yes, it is strange but since the roads here are very narrow this is the only way to take the turn to Pasquilio. Or,

2. take the state road Aurelia, #1, between Pietrasanta and Massa and then take the road to Montignoso and follow the signs to Pasquilio.

In both cases, when the road reaches its highest point you are at Foce (Pass) Pasquilio which is also called *Foce del Campaccio* (827 m). Park the car here and enjoy the view.

The hike

From the north-east corner of Foce Pasquilio take trail #33. Do not follow the red signs going upward inside the wood of conifers (it is the return route from Monte Carchio). After going up for a few meters trail #33 continues horizontally in the wood, then goes down for a short stretch and then up again slowly climbing the western grassy slope of the mountain. The trail passes close to a spring (on the right) and reaches a narrow cut in the rock of the west ridge of Monte Focoraccia, 1 h from Pasquilio. From here the trail continues slightly down with steps in the rock (some exposure) and then just beyond a "false pass" reaches Passo Focoraccia (1059 m) along the north-east ridge of the mountain. The trail goes steeply down for about 50 meters and then up again going slowly up alternately along the east and then the west slope (some exposure). Finally it reaches the bottom of a very steep and stony couloir (watch for loose rocks in the narrow couloir). The trail climbs up the couloir with a series of short switchbacks and reaches the south-west ridge of Monte Altissimo. Passo degli Uncini (Hooks Pass, 1380 m) is a few hundreds meters farther along the ridge on the right (east), 1½ h from the cut on the ridge of Monte Focoraccia.

On the way back, follow the same route until you arrive at the narrow cut in the rocks along the west ridge of Monte Focoraccia, which you can easily recognize, since it is at the end of the short stretch of the trail with steps in the rock and some exposure. Once you are at this pass, 1 h from Passo degli Uncini, instead of following trail #33, go up on your left along the ridge to reach the top of Monte Focoraccia and follow the south-west crest up to the top of Monte Carchio (1087 m). There are

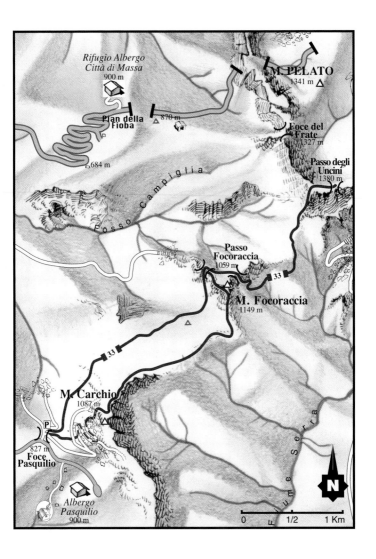

Rifugio Albergo
Città di Massa
900 m

Pian della
Fioba

870 m

684 m

M. PELATO
1341 m

Foce del
Frate
1327 m

Passo degli
Uncini
1380 m

Fosso Campiglia

Passo
Focoraccia
1059 m

33

M. Focoraccia
1149 m

33

M. Carchio
1087 m

P

827 m
Foce
Pasquilio

Albergo
Pasquilio
900 m

Fiume Serra

N

0   1/2   1 Km

some old red marks along the way. This is a very scenic route with wonderful views. Eventually you reach an old marble quarry and a marmifera which continues in the direction of the sea. When the marmifera splits take the right (lower) marmifera. After some switchbacks take a path (red marks) near the picnic area through a wood of conifers until you reach Foce Pasquilio, about 1 ½ h from Monte Focoraccia.

Where to end your hike

La Gotica (0585 819230) is very close to the pass Pasquilio and offers very good food. Try the *Focaccia* or *Panzanelle* with fresh *Pecorino* cheese, home made pasta with mushrooms and to finish *Bollenti di necci* (made of chestnut flour and ricotta cheese). At the present time the Albergo Pasquilio is closed.

Hike 19 - Monte Matanna loop

Difficulty	*Moderate*
Length	*10 km*
Elevation gain	*850 m*
Walking time	*5 h*
Highest elevation	*1317 m (Monte Matanna)*
Ttrailhead	*Trescolli (523 m)*
Trails	*#106 from Trescolli to Foce di San Rocchino (San Rocchino Pass, 801 m);*
	#3 from San Rocchino to Foce di Grattaculo (Pass of Grattaculo, 860 m) and then to Foce del Pallone (Balloon Pass, 1080 m);
	from Foce del Pallone along the east-south-east ridge to the summit of Monte Matanna (1317 m) and back to the same pass, red marks;
	#105 from Foce del Pallone to Foce del Crocione (Big-Cross Pass, 978 m);
	#2 from Foce del Crocione down towards Casoli along the southwest slopes up to the paved road; along the paved road from the intersection up to Trescolli.
Points of interest	*Terraced fields along the hillside above the coast*
	View from the top of Monte Matanna
	Scenic drive to Casoli
	Exploration of Casoli and Camaiore
	Visit to Grotta all' Onda (Wave Cave, optional)

This hike is in the southern part of the Apuane Alps. It starts by crossing cultivated terraced fields along the hillside, continues on very old paths and reaches the summit along a panoramic ridge. While the mountain is not very high, the climbing is hard but enjoyable, and the view from the top is still very extensive: green valleys towards the coast, the sea, the islands and the rocky peaks of the southern Apuane. The visit to the *Grotta all' Onda* (Wave Cave) requires a small deviation from the direct route between Foce del Crocione and Trescolli.

How to reach the trailhead

Trescolli, also known as Tre Scogli or Tre Scolli, is at the end of the road from Casoli. Take the road from Viareggio to Camaiore, and from Camaiore take the road to Casoli. After Casoli, continue along the same road until the end. Here you are at Trescolli. On your left is a parking lot for the customers of the restaurant *Domenici*. If you are going to have a meal at the restaurant, ask the restaurant if you may park there, otherwise park along the road (limited space). From the car walk up along the road for about ½ km to the trailhead #106.

The hike

The trail goes up steadily until it reaches Foce di San Rocchino, elevation 801 m, ½ h. On the right is a very small chapel dedicated to San Rocco. From San Rocchino turn right on trail #3 going north-east to Foce di Grattaculo (Pass of Grattaculo, a vulgar name for a rear part of the anatomy, 860 m). From Grattaculo stay on trail #3 which traverses almost all of the south-east slope of Monte Matanna (there is a fountain along the way) and reaches Foce del Pallone (Balloon Pass, 1080 m), 1¼ h from San Rocchino. There is a *marginetta* here, close to the pass, on the trail that goes to Albergo Alto Matanna. From Foce del Pallone turn left on the ridge running east-south-east to reach the summit of Monte Matanna (1317 m), ¾ h from the last pass. There are wide views of the coast, sea, islands and the mountains around: Monte Altissimo, Monte Corchia, Procinto, Monte Nona, Pania della Croce, Uomo Morto, Pania Secca, and the Apennines.

From the summit go back along the same ridge to Foce del Pallone, and from there continue east on trail #105 along an old, wide path. Soon trail #105 leaves the wide path on the left to reach Foce del Crocione, 978 m, 1 h from the summit. Turn right on trail #2 going down to the south along the narrow valley. The trail descends in several switchbacks, reaches a fountain, crosses a bridge over a narrow stream, passes a small marginetta, on the right, and ends at the paved road from Casoli to Trescolli, 1¼ h from Foce del Crocione. Turn right on the road and reach Trescolli in about 15 minutes.

Visit to Grotta all'Onda (Wave Cave)

The visit is optional, and the detour makes the hike 1 h longer. From trail #2, at 682 m elevation, a footpath starts (red marks, no number)

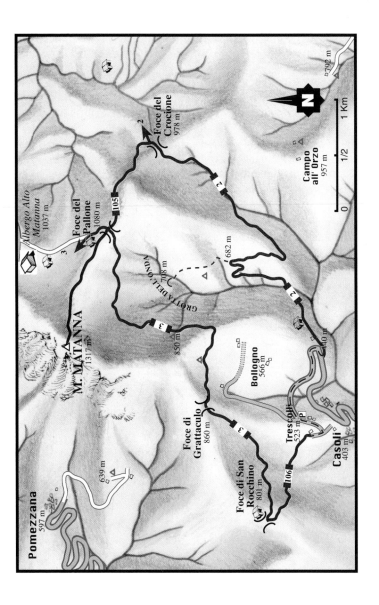

Pomezzana
597 m

639 m

M. MATANNA
1317 m

Foce di Grattaculo
860 m

Foce di San
Rocchino
801 m

Albergo Alto
Matanna
1037 m

Foce del
Pallone
1080 m

105

3

Foce del
Crocione
978 m

2

2

682 m

GROTTA DELL'ONDA
708 m

850 m

3

Bollogno
566 m

640 m

Trescoli
523 m

Casoli
403 m

106

3

Campo
all' Orzo
957 m

792 m

N

0   1/2   1 Km

leading to Grotta all' Onda, where prehistoric remains were found (they are now in the *Museo Civico Archeologico Versiliese,* in Pietrasanta). At the beginning of the twentieth century a balloon was installed close to the cave to carry tourists from Grotta all' Onda to Foce del Pallone (hence its name), along a fixed cable. Unfortunately the balloon was destroyed by lightning after a year's use and was never restored. From the cave there are two routes back:

1. continue along the trail, which is not very visible, up to the intersection with trail #106, and then down along this trail to Trescolli, 2 ½ h from the summit; or

2. take the recommended route which involves going back to trail #2.

Where to end your hike

The restaurant *Domenici*, at Trescolli (0584 988019), can offer you not only a parking place but also a very good meal with local food and wine.

Hike 20 - Monte Croce loop

Difficulty	*Moderate*
Length	*9 km*
Elevation gain	*600 m*
Walking time	*4 h*
Highest elevation	*1314 m (Monte Croce)*
Trailhead	*Palagnana (757 m)*

Illustration 23 - Maestà *(or* marginetta*), at Passo delle Porchette (982 m)*

Trails	#8 from Palagnana to Foce delle Porchette (Piglet Pass, 982 m);
	#108 from Foce delle Porchette to the south ridge of Monte Croce;
	along the south ridge of Monte Croce (blue marks) to the top (1314 m);
	from the summit along the east ridge to trail #108;
	#108 towards east to the il Termine pass (1119 m);
	#135 from il Termine to Palagnana.
Points of interest	The view from the top of Monte Croce
	Typical rural life in Garfagnana
	Visit to Palagnana
	S. Anna Church
	Scenic drive to Palagnana along the valley of Turrite Cava

From the summit of Monte Croce you will enjoy one of the best views of Pania della Croce, Uomo Morto and Pania Secca. The hike is in the southern part of the Apuane on the Garfagnana side of the chain. The town of Palagnana, together with the small clusters of houses on the slopes and the terraced fields around, will give you some insight into rural life in this area.

How to reach the trailhead

From the road between Lucca and Castelnuovo Garfagnana, at 6 km from Borgo a Mozzano, take the road, along a very interesting and picturesque valley, going to Fabbriche di Vallico and then to Palagnana (about 15 km from the junction with the main road). Park the car at the parking lot just before the first houses of the town. The first building on the right, above the parking lot, is the *Locanda dalla Gè*, where you can stop before starting your hike to have a coffee or cappuccino, and after the hike for a tasty local meal. Continue along the main road and shortly among the houses (30 meters up) on the left is the trailhead for trails #8 and #3.

The hike

From the main road turn left on trail #8 (here trails #8 and #3 coinci-

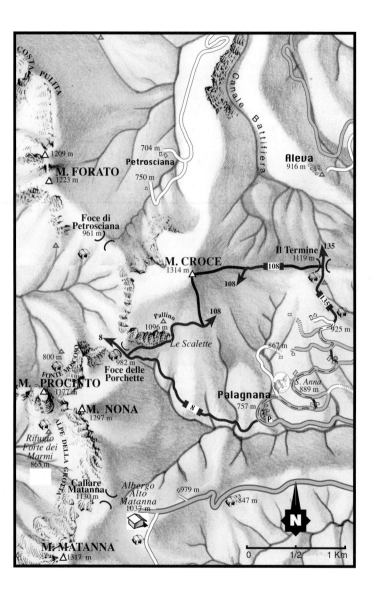

COSTA PULITA

△ 1209 m

M. FORATO
△ 1223 m

704 m
Petrosciana

750 m

Canale Battiffera

Aleva
916 m

Foce di Petrosciana
961 m

△

M. CROCE
1314 m △

108

108

Il Termine 135
1119 m

108

135

925 m

Pallino
1096 m

Le Scalette

867 m

8

800 m

982 m
Foce delle Porchette

FONTE MOCCOSO

S. Anna
889 m

Palagnana
757 m

P

M. PROCINTO
△ 1177 m

△**M. NONA**
1297 m

ALPE DELLA GROTTA

8

Rifugio Forte dei Marmi
865 m

Callare Matanna
1130 m

Albergo Alto Matanna
1037 m

979 m

847 m

N

M. MATANNA
△ 1317 m

0   1/2   1 Km

de) along the narrow path between the first houses of the town, and continue until you reach a stream. Here trail #3 crosses the stream and goes towards Albergo Alto Matanna, while trail #8, which should be followed, remains on the same side of the stream and starts climbing up in short switchbacks. The path is one of the oldest in the area, it was used to connect Palagnana with Cardoso on the other (Versilia) side of the mountains. It goes up very gently and reaches *Foce delle Porchette* (982 m) in a little under 1 h from the town. Here there is a small *Maestà* and views of the sea, the deep valley on the Versilia side and Pania della Croce. Just before reaching the pass take trail #108 on the right and continue along the grassy slope, climbing easy rocks along a narrow couloir (dry in Summer; there is a short exposed stretch), called *le Scalette* (the short staircase) to reach a spring in a small flat area at the foot of the south face of Monte Croce; the spring is called *Pallino* (the small ball, elevation 1096 m). From here go right and shortly you will reach the south ridge of Monte Croce. Leave the trail and climb along the ridge (blue marks) up to the summit,1 h from Foce delle Porchette. From the summit there are great views of Pania della Croce, Uomo Morto and Pania Secca, in front of you and the Apennines on one side and the sea on the other.

From the top go down along the east ridge to rejoin trail #108 and turn left on it. In Spring the south-east slope of the mountain is almost completely covered by narcissus and asphodel flowers. Turn left on trail #108 towards the east and along the north slopes of the wooded ridge up to il Termine pass (1119 m). Here there is an old milestone engraved with the initials: DM for *Ducato di Modena* in one side and GDT for *Granducato di Toscana* in the other, and a Maesta' on your right. From the pass turn right on trail #135, which in short switchbacks in the wood reaches a road. Follow the road and look for the next red marks. Anyway do not worry, eventually the road takes you to Palagnana and to your car, 2 h from the summit. On the way down is the lovely S. Anna Church (889 m) with its tall bell tower. Have a break there and enjoy the view of the bucolic valley.

Where to end your hike

Go to the *Locanda dalla Gè* in Palagnana (0584 776050). Ask for *Conchiglie alla montanara*, a shell shaped pasta dressed with herbs (from the mountain) sautéd in olive oil, or try the *Testaroli alla*

Palagnina, which are almost the same as the Testaroli (see the chapter "Where to stay, What to eat, Where to eat, Rifugio"), but in this case to the bread dough has been added maize flour. For a main course try *baccala' al forno*, *pancetta di vitello al forno* or *cinghiale al forno*, which are salted cod, veal flank or boar respectively, baked in a wood fired oven. *Buon appetito!*

Illustration 24 - Pania della Croce (1859 m), Uomo Morto (1677 m) and Pania Secca (1711 m), from the summit of Monte Croce (1314 m)

Hike 21 - Monte Gabberi loop

Difficulty	*Easy*
Length	*8 km*
Elevation gain	*500 m*
Walking time	*3 ½ h*
Highest elevation	*1108 m (Monte Gabberi)*
Trailhead	*Farnocchia (646 m)*
Trails	*#3 from Farnocchia toward Foce San Rocchino (801 m), up to the intersection with trail #107; #107 from the intersection to Monte Gabberi (1108 m) and back to the intersection with the trail to Farnocchia; the trail toward Farnocchia (red/white marks, no number) close to the north-west ridge between Monte Gabberi and Monte Lieto and then along the north-west slope up to the intersection with trail #4; #4 from the intersection with the above trail to Farnocchia.*
Points of interest	*View from the summit of Monte Gabberi Visiting Farnocchia Scenic drive to Farnocchia*

Monte Gabberi is one of the closest mountains to the coast. From the summit there is a wide panorama of the coast and sea, lake Massaciuccoli and the mountains around. This is a short and beautiful hike, which starts from the pretty village of Farnocchia and crosses chestnut stands at the lower level and beech woods towards the top.

How to reach the trailhead

To get to Farnocchia: from the road going from Querceta to Castelnuovo Garfagnana, at about 1 km after Ruosina, take the road on your right to Ponte Stazzemese and Stazzema. Once in Ponte Stazzemese (158 m) take the road on your right going up towards Stazzema. A few hundred meters after the village of Culerchia (247 m) turn right on the road to Pomezzana and Farnocchia. At the next junction, 1.5 km, take

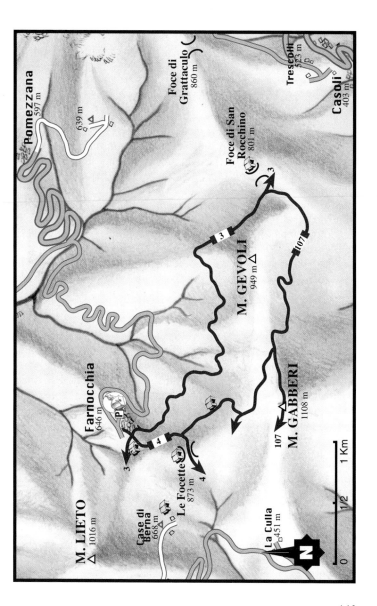

Pomezzana 597 m

639 m

Foce di Grattaculo 860 m

Foce di San Rocchino 801 m

Trescolli 523 m

Casoli 403 m

3

3

M. GEVOLI 949 m

107

Farnocchia 646 m

P

M. LIETO 1016 m

3

4

4

Le Focette 873 m

Case di Berna 668 m

M. GABBERI 1108 m

107

107

La Culla 451 m

N

0   1/2   1 Km

143

the road on the right to Farnocchia, about 4 km further. Just before the paved road ends in town, turn left and park in the large square, with the old church of San Michele (dating from at the latest 1018) and its square stone bell tower.

The hike

From the square follow the route through tiny streets to the nearby *piazza del Carmine*, with another old church, *S. Maria del Carmine*, an "Alimentari" shop and, on the right in an adjoining small square, the *Bar Trattoria da Franca*, a very good place to stop before and after the hike. Take the narrow street up on the left of the Alimentari shop and after a few meters, at the junction, turn left on trail #3 towards San Rocchino; the right hand trail goes to the town of Santa Anna, sadly well known for the massacre of more than 600 people (women, children and seniors), in 1944. The trail leaves Farnocchia and goes south-east towards Foce San Rocchino, first slowly down and soon uphill. The trail crosses almost the whole of the north slope of Monte Gabberi and in about 2.5 km reaches a pass, 1¼ h from Farnocchia. At the pass leave trail #3, which goes left to nearby Foce San Rocchino (801 m). Take instead trail #107 on the right towards Monte Gabberi. Climb the east ridge (views of Procinto, Monte Nona and Monte Matanna, looking back) and continue along the crest. There is a junction with a trail, blue sign and marks, going to Farnocchia. Continue straight along the bushy crest to another junction with a trail with red and white signs to S. Anna, la Culla and Farnocchia (this trail will be your way back to Farnocchia); keep going along the crest. Another junction with a trail with blue marks to Farnocchia is passed, but continue up along easy rocks and shortly you will reach the summit of Monte Gabberi, 2 ½ h from Farnocchia. There are lovely views of the sea and coast, Lake Massaciuccoli with on its eastern shore the small town of Torre del Lago, where is found the Villa of Giacomo Puccini (1858-1924), author of *La Boheme, Tosca, Madame Butterfly* and many other operas.

From the summit go back along the same trail #107 as far as the junction with red and white signs to S. Anna, La Culla, Farnocchia (15 minutes from the summit) that was passed during the ascent. Turn left on this unnumbered trail and follow the red marks downhill. In 15 minutes you will reach a junction: on the left are signs to S. Anna and La Culla, on the right on the trunk of a tree a sign to Farnocchia. Both these trails lead to Farnocchia; the trail on the left through *Le Focette* pass, but the trail on the right is shorter. Follow then the trail on the right, go down in short switchbacks to a junction with a level trail, blue marks. Go left, pass close to a nice old *marginetta* very soon reaching the junction with trail #4. Turn right on trail #4 and go down towards Farnocchia. The trail soon reaches a small marginetta, at the intersection with trail #3, and in a few meters reaches Farnocchia, 1 h from the summit.

Where to end your hike

Just at the end of the hike you will find the *Bar Trattoria da Franca* (0584 777022, closed on Wednesday) with homemade food like *tordelli*, *polenta* with *cinghiale* (boar), *farro* soup and vegetables (*minestra di farro e verdure*), taglierini and beans (*taglierini e fagioli*), and in the fall the meal can be rounded off with roasted chestnuts, here called *mondine*. On Wednesday the trattoria is closed, so on the way back to your hotel, stop at Mulina di Stazzema at the *Trattoria Luciana* (0584 777008), where you can have home made pasta or farro soup and, in season, polenta with mushrooms.

Hike 22 - Pizzo delle Saette and Pania della Croce loop

Difficulty	*Strenuous*
Length	*12 km*
Elevation gain	*950 m*
Walking time	*6 ½ h*
Highest elevation	*1859 m (Pania della Croce)*
Trailhead	*Piglionico (1120 m)*
Trails	*#7 from Piglionico to Rifugio Rossi (1609 m);*
	#126 from Rifugio Rossi, through Foce Puntone (Puntone Pass, 1611 m) and along the Vallone dell' Inferno (Hell Couloir), to a pass on the north ridge of Pania della Croce;
	along the north ridge to the top of Pania della Croce (1859 m) and back to the pass;
	#126 from the pass to the north ridge at about 1750 m elevation between Pania della Croce and Pizzo delle Saette;

Illustration 25 - L'Uomo Morto (1677 m) and Pania Secca (1711 m) from "Passo degli Uomini della Neve"

along the north ridge (blue marks) up to the top of Pizzo delle Saette (1720 m);
along the trail (no number, red marks) going down along the east slope of Pizzo delle Saette up to the junction with trail #139;
#139 from the intersection to the junction with trail #127;
#127 from the intersection to Piglionico.

Points of interest   *Pania della Croce*
Pizzo delle Saette
Rifugio Rossi, the highest manned rifugio in the Apuane
Borra di Canala, one of the wildest canyons in the Apuane

Pania della Croce is the Queen of the Apuane Alps and this is the easiest and shortest way to the top. The hike is very interesting and enjoyable. The stretch from Pania della Croce to Pizzo delle Saette is, in some parts, exposed. Also exposed is the stretch down from Pizzo delle Saette to the top of Borra di Canala. There are two alternative routes given below, they avoid the exposed stretches whilst still providing an interesting and enjoyable walk.

How to reach the trailhead

Take the road from Lucca to Castelnuovo Garfagnana to the town of Gallicano, 186 m elevation, 35 km from Lucca and 12 km from Castelnuovo Garfagnana. From the north-east side of Gallicano take the road to Molazzana (474 m, 4.5 km from Gallicano), continue and at 6.5 km from Gallicano take the road on your left to Alpe S. Antonio and Piglionico. After 4 km take the road on the left going to Piglionico. The paved road ends and a gravel road starts; in a little over four kilometers Piglionico is reached (1120 m). Park there, near the chapel. Continue walking along the road and at its end find the trailhead.

The hike

Trail #7 enters a wood of beech trees and in several switchbacks goes up until it reaches high meadows with views of the rifugio and of

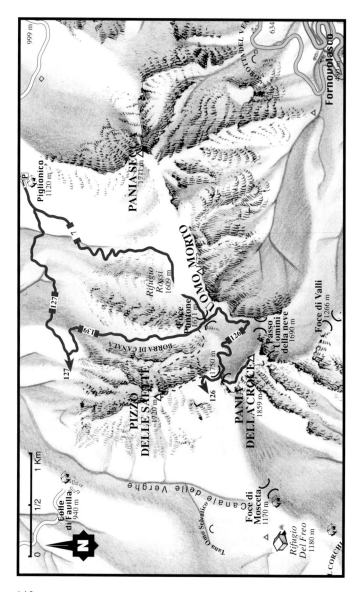

PANIA SECCA 1711 m

Piglionico 1120 m

Rifugio Rossi 1609 m

UOMO MORTO 1677 m

Foce Pontone 1611 m

BORRA DI CANALA

PIZZO DELLE SAETTE 1720 m

PANIA DELLA CROCE 1859 m

Passo Uomini della neve 1690 m

Foce di Valli 1266 m

Foce di Mosceta 1170 m

Canale delle Verghe

Tana Omo Selvatico

Rifugio Del Freo 1180 m

L. CORCHI

Colle di Favilla 940 m

Fornovolasco

999 m

634

GROTTA DEL VENTO

1750 m

127

139

127

L7

126

126

N

0   1/2   1 Km

Pania Secca on the left. Continue along the grassy slope to Rifugio Rossi (1609 m), 1½ h from Piglionico. Please, stay on the trail along this stretch, to avoid damaging the ground (because it is easily eroded) and falling into one of the caves. Because of these risks some stretches of this trail are fenced. Not far from the rifugio, at 1453 m elevation, is the entrance to the so-called *Abisso Enrico Revel,* an almost perfectly vertical pit, more than 300 m deep, which, not long ago, was considered the deepest single vertical pit in the world. If the rifugio is open do not fail to have a coffee or cappuccino there. From Rifugio Rossi continue along the same trail, cross Foce del Puntone (Puntone pass, 1611 m) and enter the wild and rocky *Vallone dell' Inferno* (Hell couloir). Here we leave trail #7 and turn right on trail #126, which climbs the stony valley in short switchbacks (watch out for falling stones). Snow is sometimes found in this valley even in summer, especially on the left under the east ridge of Pania della Croce, in one deep natural cavity, where the snow is protected from the sun by the high rocks all around and where drifts have been pressed down by snow dropping from the slopes above. In the past people from the valley used to come here and collect snow, through a pass along the east ridge of Pania della Croce. Hence this pass was named *Passo degli Uomini della neve* (Men-of-the-snow pass). The trail finally reaches a pass on the north ridge of Pania della Croce, 1 h from the Rifugio. At the ridge leave the trail and go left (south) along the crest. It takes a few minutes to reach the summit (1859 m). The views encompass the entire Apuane Alps, the sea and the islands, Garfagnana and the Apennines.

From the summit go back along the crest to the pass and take trail #126, which descends gently along the north-west slope of the mountain and again reaches the ridge at a little lower than 1750 m elevation, between Pania della Croce and Pizzo delle Saette. At this point leave trail #126, which goes towards Rifugio Del Freo, and follow the north ridge (blue marks) up to the top of Pizzo delle Saette (1720 m), 1½ h from the summit of Pania. The route stays very close to the crest going up and down (some exposure). After about two thirds of the route, along the crest, a trail (red marks) goes down the east slope of the mountain (it will be part of the itinerary back to Piglionico). Continue down along the ridge until you reach the base of the terminal peak of Pizzo delle Saette. Go slightly to the left and climb the steep, narrow and rocky couloir in short switchbacks until you reach the summit. Watch for loose stones while climbing and descending the steep couloir. From the top of Pizzo delle Saette pause to enjoy the view of the deep valley of Turrite Secca surrounded by mountains: Penna di Sumbra, Fiocca, Sella, Macina, Freddone, Altissimo and Corchia (going from east to west).

From the top go back along the same route, until you reach the red marks of a trail going down along the east slope of the mountain. Go down this trail, which is at first very steep (some exposure) and then almost flat along the bottom of the wall between Pania della Croce and Pizzo delle Saette, in an astonishing chaos of debris and rocks. Continue until you reach, just below Foce del Puntone, a junction with a trail (#139) coming from Rifugio Rossi, ¾ h from Pizzo delle Saette. Follow this trail down the large, steep, rocky couloir, called *Borra di Canala*, one of the wildest in the Apuane Alps. Go down the trail up to the junction with trail #127, ¾ h. At the junction turn right on trail #127, which goes round the north slope of the mountain hardly losing height. Towards

Illustration 26 - L'Uomo Morto (1677 m) and Rifugio Rossi (1609 m), from the ridge between Pania della Croce and Pizzo delle Saette

the end the trail climbs up about 50 m and eventually reaches the junction with trail #7, 1 h from the last junction. The loop has now been completed. Turn left and soon you will be in Piglionico.

A shorter hike, without exposure

To avoid the stretches with some exposure (i.e. between Pania della Croce and Pizzo delle Saette, and from Pizzo delle Saette to the top of Borra di Canala), you can go from the Rifugio Rossi to the Foce del Puntone and from here directly to the top of Borra di Canala at the intersection with the trail coming from Pizzo delle Saette. The hike is still very beautiful and interesting, and becomes Moderate, 9 km long, with 550 m elevation gain, and takes 3 ½ h.

You may still climb Pania della Croce, going up to the summit and back to Foce del Puntone, along the steep Vallone dell' Inferno, this adds a further 1½ h. This is the simplest and shortest hike to the summit of Pania della Croce. The hike becomes Strenuous, 11 km long, with 900 m elevation gain, takes about 5 h and is very enjoyable.

Where to end the hike

From Piglionico drive back to Gallicano and stop at the Hotel Restaurant *Eliseo* (0583 74031). The vegetable soup (made with herbs from the local mountains) is delicious as is the *farro* soup, and for a main course ask for a char-broiled local trout.

Hike 23 - Monte Corchia loop

Difficulty	*Moderate*
Length	*10 km*
Elevation gain	*700 m*
Walking time	*5 h*
Highest elevation	*1677 m (Monte Corchia)*
Trailhead	*Passo di Croce (Cross Pass, 1160 m)*
Trails	*Along the west ridge and the Pirosetto couloir to the summit of Monte Corchia (1677 m); from the summit, along the east ridge, to the Rifugio Del Freo (1180 m); #129 from Rifugio Del Freo to Fociomboli (1260 m); along the dirt road from Fociomboli to Passo di Croce.*
Points of interest	*Monte Corchia*
	Rifugio Del Freo
	Mosceta
	Marble quarries
	The scenic drive to Passo di Croce

This hike has the highest starting point of all the hikes described in this book. The hike is varied and panoramic, it involves climbs up grassy slopes, rocky ridges and a steep couloir (a very short stretch with a little exposure) and takes you to one of the most visited parts of the Apuane Alps, Mosceta and Rifugio Del Freo. The view from the summit of Monte Corchia is wide and spectacular.

How to reach the trailhead

On the road from Querceta to Castelnuovo Garfagnana, 18 Km from Querceta, at about 600 m elevation, there is a junction with the paved road going to Passo di Croce. Follow this road until you reach the pass (1160 m elevation, about 5 km from the junction). The road becomes dirt and before the fork in the road, stop and park your car. The start of the hike is just at the fork.

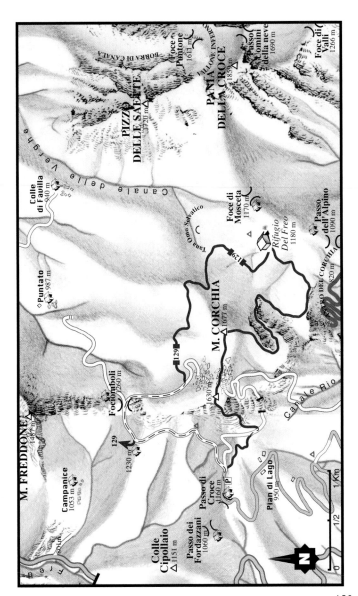

Foce di Canala

Croce Pontone
1611 m

Foce di Valli
1266 m

Passo Zomini della neve
1690 m

VALLONE INFERNO

PIZZO DELLE SAETTE
1720 m

PANIA DELLA CROCE
1859 m

Colle di Favilla
940 m

Canale delle Verghe

Foce di Mosceta
1170 m

Passo dell'Alpino
1090 m

Tana Omo Salvatico

120

Rifugio Del Freo
1180 m

CANALE DEL CORCHIA
820 m

Puntato
987 m

M. CORCHIA
1677 m

129

1260 m
Fociomboli

129

1230 m

1630 m

Canale Rio

M. FREDDONE
1487 m

Campanice
1053 m

Colle Cipollaio
1151 m

Passo dei Fordazzani
1060 m

Passo di Croce
1160 m

P

Pian di Lago
950 m

Fred

N

0   1/2   1/Km

153

The hike

From the fork go up to the ridge on your right and go up along it following the red marks. The trail follows the ridge, almost all the way up, and joins the road 20 minutes later, after 100 m elevation gain. Follow the road up for about 50 meters and on the left of the road are the marks of the trail. Climb up the grassy slope to regain the ridge and go up towards the *Torrioni del Corchia* (Corchia Towers). The trail goes around one of the towers and enters the narrow couloir between the last two towers (*Canale del Pirosetto*). The trail climbs a big stone in the middle of the couloir (a little exposure), follows a narrow and grassy path and reaches a small crest (watch for falling stones while climbing the narrow steep couloir). The trail continues along the north-east ridge (a very short stretch with a little exposure) and soon reaches the west peak (1630 m) of Monte Corchia. It follows the crest eastward past a marble quarry and takes you to the main summit of the mountain (1677 m), 2 h from Passo di Croce. The view all the way up and from the summit is wide and spectacular. Among the closer peaks are, from west to east: Monte Altissimo, Macina, Sella, Fiocca, Penna di Sumbra, Pizzo delle Saette and Pania della Croce.

From the summit continue east along the ridge (red marks) until you reach a saddle facing *Canale delle Volte*. From the other side of the saddle a trail goes, through meadows, to the *Rifugio Del Freo* (1180 m), 1 h. It is time for a drink at the rifugio, if open. From Rifugio del Freo take trail #129 which climbs the east and north slopes of Monte Corchia (follow the red marks carefully) up to a dirt road. Turn right on the road and reach Fociomboli, a pass at 1260 m elevation, 1 h from the rifugio. From Fociomboli follow the dirt road which returns to the trailhead at Passo di Croce in about ½ h.

Where to end the hike

On the way back, you have a choice between a snack at the *Trattoria da Tassilone* in Terrinca, 0584 778140, for a pizza and wine, or a complete and delicious meal at the *Hotel Raffaello* (0584 778063) in Levigliani; their speciality is *spalla di capretto* (roast shoulder of kid) (make a reservation in advance), see the chapter "Where to stay, What to eat, Where to eat, Rifugio".

Hike 24 - Monte Freddone loop

Difficulty	*Moderate*
Length	*10 km*
Elevation gain	*750 m*
Walking time	*5 h*
Highest elevation	*1487 m (Monte Freddone)*
Trailhead	*Tre Fiumi (750 m)*
Trails	*#128 from Tre Fiumi to the north-east ridge of Monte Freddone;*
	along the north-east ridge to the top of Monte Freddone (1487 m);

Illustration 27 - Monte Freddone (1487 m), south-east slope

*from the summit down to Fociomboli (1270 m)
crossing the east-south slopes of the mountain (red
marks);
#129 from Fociomboli to the road "Strada del
Cipollaio";
down along the paved road to Tre Fiumi.*

Points of interest   *View from the summit of Monte Freddone
Marble quarries
The village of Campanice and its small church
Scenic drive to Tre Fiumi*

An easy scramble along the north-east ridge of Monte Freddone (some exposure). The hike takes you to the small and beautiful village of Campanice with its ruined stone houses. The small church and the bell tower are, however, both still intact. If you wish to avoid the scrambling and exposure, you can easily bypass the summit and still have a very enjoyable hike.

How to reach the trailhead

Take the road from Querceta to Castelnuovo Garfagnana (*Strada del Cipollaio*), go through the tunnel, *Galleria del Cipollaio* and 1.5 km after the tunnel and about 500 meters before the junction with the road from Massa (km 24.5 from Querceta) you will find, on the left, a very small parking area. This area is called *Tre Fiumi* (Three Rivers, about 750 m elevation). Park your car here. The trailhead #128 is just across the road on the slope, opposite your parking place.

The hike

Trail #128 connects Tre Fiumi with Mosceta through the abandoned stone houses of *Puntato*. The trail starts from the road and climbs the wooded (Chestnuts) north slope of Monte Freddone. It reaches a *Maestà* at 1150 m elevation and continues traversing, almost flat, the north slope of the mountain. Finally it reaches the north-east ridge of Monte Freddone, 1 h from Tre Fiumi. From here can be seen the valley of *Canale delle Fredde*, the ruined houses and church of Puntato, and farther away the church and houses of *Col di Favilla*. Leave the trail and follow the ridge going up to the right. There are no marks but the route is easily

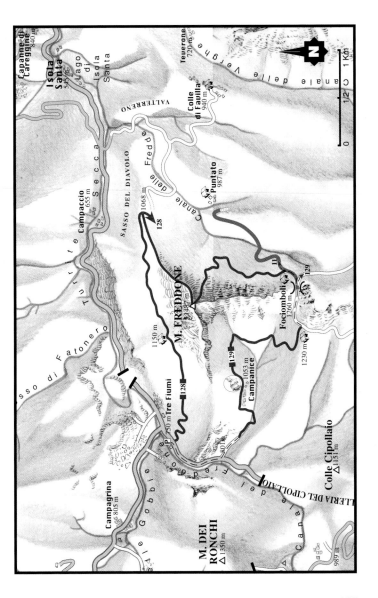

Capanne di Careggine 840 m
Isola Santa 550 m
Lago di Isola Santa
Isola Santa
Teuerone 720 m
Canale delle Verghe
Colle di Fauilla 940 m
VALTERRENO
Puntato 987 m
Canale delle Fredde
SASSO DEL DIAVOLO
Campaccio 655 m
Turrite Secca
1068 m
128
128
M. FREDDONE 1447 m
Fociomboli 1260 m
129
1150 m
1230 m
Campanice 1053 m
129
808 m
Fatonero
Tre Fiumi 750 m
128
P
Sasso di Fatonero
Campagrina 805 m
Canale delle Gobbie
Canale del Freddone
GALLERIA DEL CIPOLLAIO
Colle Cipollaio 1157 m
Canale del Cipollaio
M. DEI RONCHI △ 1350 m
989 m

N

0   1/2   1 Km

157

recognised. There is an easy rock climb which involves some hand holds. Then follows a quite flat stretch, and then a small drop before the trail starts to climb again on the left, in the wood, leaving the ridge. Once out of the wood, continue climbing the steep slope, on the left of the north-east ridge of the mountain and, without a defined route, among fissured rocks and grassy spots. In Spring suddenly and unexpectedly you may find in the fissures of the rocks splendid purple-pink peony (*Poeonia officinalis*) flowers in bloom. The slope becomes steeper and steeper (watch for loose rocks), and finally you reach the edge of the ridge. Go left along the ridge, climb the easy rocks above (use your hands) and shortly you reach a false summit and, immediately after, the summit of Monte Freddone (1487 m), 1½ h from the trail. From the summit there are wide views of the deep valley of Turrite Secca and all the mountains around: Macina, Sella, Fiocca, Penna di Sumbra and Pizzo delle Saette, Pania della Croce, Corchia, Altissimo.

From the summit go back a few meters and follow the red marks going down the very steep and grassy south-east slope. The trail continues down a couloir (watch for loose rocks) and then crosses, with several ups and downs, the wooded (beech trees) east slope of the mountain and eventually reaches a Maestà and a dirt road. Turn right on the road and follow it for a few meters up to Fociomboli (1260 m), a pass between Monte Freddone and Monte Corchia, 1¼ h from the summit. From Fociomboli go right (west), cross the pass and go along the dirt road for about 100 meters. At a Maestà (off the road, 1230 m elevation), go right leaving the road and take trail #129. The trail immediately enters a wood of beech trees and goes down, very steeply at the beginning and later gently, to the picturesque old village of *Campanice*, with abandoned stone houses and a small church and a bell tower still intact, 1053 m elevation. The trail passes through the ruined houses of the village, between two box hedges, and goes down to a stream. Cross the stream and go down to the right until you reach first a dirt road (*marmifera*) and after a further 100 meters the road "La Strada del Cipollaio". Turn right along the road, in 500 m you reach the parking place, 1¼ h from Fociomboli.

How to avoid scrambling and the stretches with exposure

Once at the north-east ridge of Monte Freddone, continue along trail #128 going towards the abandoned village of Puntato. Cross the Canale delle Fredde and at the junction turn right on trail #11which leads you to Fociomboli through a wooded and picturesque landscape, 1½ h from the ridge. At Fociomboli you can rejoin the scramblers. The entire hike becomes Moderate, 8 km long, with 600 m elevation gain and takes 3 ¾ h.

Where to end the hike

From the parking place drive down for less than a km towards Castelnuovo Garfagnana and find on your right the *Trattoria La Romana* (0584 789023) for a *focaccia al lardo di Colonnata* (in off-season, available weekends only). For a complete meal, drive down towards Castelnuovo Garfagnana and after about 500 meters take the road to Massa on your left. At the entrance to the town of Arni at the first houses on the left is the *Albergo Aronte* (0584 77917) where they serve tasty local food and good wine.

Hike 25 - Monte Fiocca

Difficulty	*Strenuous*
Length	*11 km*
Elevation gain	*850 m*
Walking time	*5 ½ h*
Highest elevation	*1711 m (Monte Fiocca)*
Trailhead	*Arnetola (900 m)*
Trails	*#31 from Arnetola to Passo Sella (Sella Pass, 1500 m);*
	#144 from Passo Sella to Passo Fiocca (1560 m); from Passo Fiocca to the summit (1711 m) by the east ridge.
Points of interest	*Passo Sella and Passo Fiocca*
	View from the summit of Monte Fiocca
	Marble quarries of Arnetola
	Lake of Vagli
	Vagli di Sotto and Vagli di Sopra
	The scenic drive along the Edron valley

The trail from Arnetola to Passo Sella is one of the most beautiful in the Apuane Alps, for most of the way it is through a wood of beech trees. From the summit of Monte Fiocca there are wonderful views of the mountains and of the Turrite Secca valley.

How to reach the trailhead

From the road from Castelnuovo Garfagnana to Aulla, at the town of Poggio (7.5 km from Castelnuovo) take the road towards Vagli di Sopra along the Edron valley. At the town of Vagli di Sopra,11.5 km, turn left, cross the town and enter the valley of Arnetola. At the junction take the right-hand road going upward. After a few switchbacks there is a flat area, *Arnetola*, with marble blocks all around and active marble quarries on the surrounding hills, elevation 900 m, about 2 km from Vagli di Sopra. Park your car here, before the unpaved road starts going up steeply.

The hike

From Arnetola (900 m) walk up along the road, which now becomes

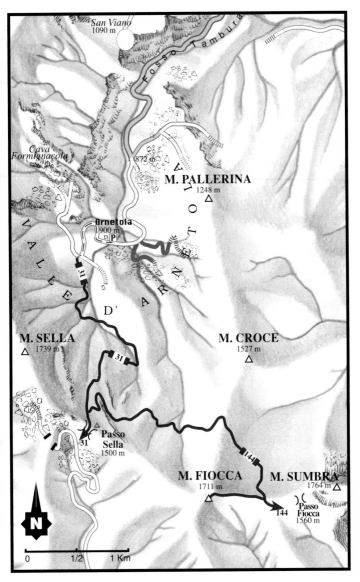

San Viano
1090 m

Fosso Tambura

Cava
Formignacola

872 m

M. PALLERINA
1248 m

Arnetola
900 m P

VALLE

D'

ARNETOLA

31

M. SELLA
1739 m

31

M. CROCE
1527 m

Passo
Sella
1500 m

31

144

M. FIOCCA
1711 m

M. SUMBRA
1764 m

144

Passo
Fiocca
1560 m

N

0   1/2   1 Km

a *marmifera* (trail #31). As you pass a few stone houses the road forks; take the road to the right and after about 50 meters turn left on trail #31 along a steep old marmifera, while the dirt road (trail #35) goes towards Passo Tambura, see "Hike 7 - Monte Tambura, from Arnetola". Trail #31 climbs up on the old marmifera, paved with oxidized blocks of marble, and in a few switchbacks reaches a dirt road. The trail continues left on the road and shortly becomes one of the most beautiful paths in the Apuane Alps, passing through a dense wood of beech trees. Finally the trail leaves the wood and just before reaching the pass, joins trail #144. Stop a moment at Passo Sella (Sella Pass, 1500 m), a perfect grassy saddle and enjoy the views of the mountains. Back at the intersection, continue on trail #144. The trail crosses the north slopes of Monte Fiocca and in 1¼ h the trail takes you to the east ridge of Monte Fiocca. Here leave trail #144 (which soon reaches Passo Fiocca and from there goes to Arni) and continue on the right along the east ridge up to the summit (1711 m), 1½ h from Passo Sella.

Return by the same route.

A slightly different way up

Instead of taking trail #144, you can reach Passo Sella first and from there follow the west ridge of Monte Fiocca up to the summit. The route is shorter but there is a very short passage on rock with some exposure. To return take trail #144 and follow the route given above.

Where to end the hike

At the *Bar Pizzeria Coltelli Dino* (0583 664058), in Vagli di Sopra via Vandelli 2, you may have a pizza and local wine. If the Pizzeria is not open or you prefer a complete meal, drive to Vagli di Sotto and go to the *Trattoria del Pescatore* (0583 664052), just before the bridge to the old town. You can enjoy homemade pasta and roasted local rabbit, chicken or lamb.

Multi-day hikes in the Apuane Alps

In the Apuane Alps it is of course possible to do multi-day hikes. You can backpack, carrying a tent and supplies, in which case you have a large choice of hikes. You may also take advantage of the local rifugio, and then the choice is more limited but still very wide and the food and company are very enjoyable. In either case it is possible to combine two or more of the hikes already described. In particular the itinerary given below is suggested - it is labelled hike #26 - as an example. In an analogous fashion, many other hikes could be planned. There are also suggested itineraries crossing part of the chain. In particular there is an itinerary called *Garfagnana Trekking*, the relevant publication is detailed in the "References" section. The best periods for the multi-day hikes are from April-May to June, and from September to November or even December. In April some of the highest peaks may be still covered by snow. In winter you may need ice-axe and crampons. May and June are the best months for the flowers (see "The Flowers of the Apuane Alps"). Try to avoid summer, because it is usually too hot and dry. But in this season, you can have the great pleasure of swimming after your hike.

Hike 26 - Monte Sagro and Monte Grondilice

1st day Itinerary

from the town of Vinca (808 m), Rifugio Capanna Garnerone (1260 m), Foce di Vinca (1333 m), Foce Luccica (1029 m), Foce della Faggiola (1464 m), Monte Sagro (1749 m), Foce di Pianza (1279 m), Monte Borla (1469 m), to Rifugio Carrara (1320 m). Dinner and night, at the rifugio.

Difficulty	*Very Strenuous*
Length	*15 km*
Elevation gain	*1300 m*
Walking time	*7 ½ h*
Highest elevation	*1749 m (Monte Sagro)*

2nd day itinerary

from Rifugio Carrara (1320 m), Monte Borla (1469 m), Foce di Pianza (1279 m), Foce del Fanetetto (1426 m), Foce di Vinca (1333 m), Foce di Monte Rasori (1318 m), Foce Grondilice (1773 m), Monte Grondilice (1809 m), Foce Grondilice, Cava 27 (about 1500 m), Foce di Giovo (1500 m), up to Vinca (808 m).

Difficulty	*Strenuous*
Length	*14 km*
Elevation gain	*1000 m*
Walking time	*7 h*
Highest elevation	*1809 m (Monte Grondilice)*

How to reach the trailhead

The trailhead is the same as for hikes 9 and 15. Take the road #63 from Aulla toward Passo del Cerreto. At 12 km, go right at the junction to Castelnuovo Garfagnana, road #445. Then at km 3.5, take another right to enter and pass through Gragnola and drive toward Equi Terme. After 4.2 km, go through the town of Monzone then take the road to Vinca. Once in Vinca, drive toward the center of town (take the road on your left going upward, no outlet). Park at the square, where you will find a convenient fountain of fresh water to fill your water bottles. When in town, if you find a *Bar* or an *Alimentari* shop open, do not fail to taste the local *focaccia*, a kind of flat homemade bread.

The Hike

Go to "Hike 15 - Monte Sagro loop, from Vinca" and to "Hike 9 - Monte Grondilice loop" for the description of almost all the itinerary for both days. Here is given just the route to Rifugio Carrara from the summit of Monte Sagro, and to Foce di Monte Rasori from Foce di Vinca. These are the only two stretches not described in the above hikes.

First day

1. From the town of Vinca to the junction of trail #173 with the west ridge: see Hike 15.

2. From the west ridge to Rifugio Carrara (1320 m). Having left the summit of Monte Sagro and gone down the northwest ridge first and then the west ridge (very easy scrambling, watch for loose stones) one joins #173. At the junction, instead of turning right as suggested in the Hike 15, turn left on trail #173 towards Foce di Pianza (Hike 5 - Monte Sagro). Trail #173 reaches Foce di Pianza along the ridge connecting Monte Spallone and Monte Borla, 1½ h from the summit. It crosses the dirt road and continues a little below the south ridge of Monte Borla. It climbs slowly going all around the east slopes and finally crosses the north ridge of the mountain. The trail crosses the meadows of Campo Cecina and goes down to the north-west to Rifugio Carrara (1320 m), ¾ h from Foce di Pianza. Rifugio Carrara can be reached along the road from Foce di Pianza to Carrara. Walk along the road for about 1 km and turn right at the first junction, along the road going to Acquasparta. In about another km, immediately after a fountain of fresh water, turn right on the trail going to Rifugio Carrara. In a little over ½ h you will reach the rifugio.

Second day

3. Back to the Foce di Pianza and from there to the west ridge junction on the same trail as yesterday (1½ h from the rifugio).

4. From west ridge junction to Foce di Vinca - see Hike 15, 2 ½ h from the rifugio.

5.   From Foce di Vinca to Foce di Monte Rasori: from Foce di Vinca, instead of taking trail #38 as suggested in the Hike 15, continue along trail #173, which goes to Foce di Navola (1295 m). From Foce di Navola leave trail #173 and instead follow trail #37 and reach Foce di Monte Rasori (1318 m), ½ h from Foce di Vinca.

6.   From Foce di Monte Rasori to Vinca - see Hike 9.

Where to end the hike

At the Rifugio Carrara they serve very good meals. So, no problem for the first night. For the second night, as suggested for hikes 15 and 9, enjoy a meal of *Panigacci* and *Testaroli al Pesto* at the *Ristorante La Gavarina d' Oro* (0187 410021) in Podenzana, close to Aulla. But you can also have delicious local food at the restaurant of the *Hotel la Posta* (0585 97937) of Elena and Livo Pietrini in Equi Terme. Equi Terme is a spa town not far from Vinca, it has an old center and two prehistoric caves, well worth visiting.

Other Hikes along the East Ligurian Coast

Illustration 28- San Fruttuoso

Hike 27 - Camogli - San Fruttuoso - Portofino - Santa Margherita Ligure

Difficulty	*Strenuous*
Length	*15 km*
Elevation gain	*600 m*
Walking time	*5 ½ h*
Highest elevation	*about 300 m (Costa del Termine)*
Trailhead	*Camogli (Genova)*
Trails	*"Two small red balls" trail from Camogli (50 m) to San Rocco (220 m), to San Fruttuoso (sea level), and from there to Portofino (sea level); from Portofino to Santa Margherita, either by bus or by walking along the 5 km of paved road between the two villages.*
Points of interest	*Camogli (it perhaps inspired the architects who dreamt of building skyscrapers) Monte Portofino San Fruttuoso and its Abbazia (abbey, recently restored) Portofino and Santa Margherita, two of the most picturesque villages on the Ligurian coast*

Delightful coastal hike around Monte Portofino (610 m). The hike has splendid views of the high cliffs above the sea and most of the way one is immersed in Mediterranean maquis. There is time to visit the ancient Abbey of San Fruttuoso and the picturesque towns of Camogli, Portofino and Santa Margherita Ligure.

How to reach the trailhead

Camogli is a small fishing town between Genova and La Spezia, about 25 km from Genova. You can reach Camogli by train either from Genova or from La Spezia, along the main train route Roma-Torino. You can also drive to Camogli: take the exit "Recco" from the "Genova-Livorno" autostrada (A12) (motorway) and follow the road signs to Camogli, 1.5 km from Recco. You can reach Recco by car also along the State road #1, *Via Aurelia*, the ancient Roman road connecting Rome and Provence. The road between Genova and La Spezia is very close to the coast and was considered as one of the most beautiful in Italy by Charles Dickens, who visited the area in 1844-45: "There is nothing in Italy, more beautiful to me, than the coast-road between Genoa and Spezzia". Park anywhere you can find space, preferably close to the railway station. Camogli, called *Camoglia* by Dickens, is very pretty with its fishing port and very colorful houses going from the seaside up over the steep slopes of the mountain. Every year in May, on the second Sunday of the month, for the *Sagra del Pesce* festival (the Blessing of the Fish) freshly caught fish is cooked in pans more than 4 meters wide, it is offered free to the public.

The hike

From the railway station turn left along the main road and at the first junction continue on the right slowly downhill. At the corner, beside the "Civico Museo Marinaro" (Town Maritime Museum), you will find two signs posted: the first, Camogli-San Fruttuoso-Portofino Mare, 5 h, trail "two small red balls"; the second, Camogli-Pietre Strette-San Fruttuoso, 2 ½ h, trail "empty red circle". Both walking times are too optimistic, according to our standards; each of the hikes is likely to take at least half an hour longer than indicated. Take the "two small red balls" trail here, and indeed continue to follow it for the rest of the walk. At the first large curve where, on a concrete pylon, there are the symbols of both the trails, leave the road and go left on a narrow road going up beside the stream. In a few meters, turn right, cross a bridge over the stream and turn left on an old footpath. The trail goes steadily up between two stone walls and finally arrives at the large stone steps up to San Rocco, ½ h from Camogli.

As you enter San Rocco it is traditional to stop at "Panificio Maccarini" (bakery), well known for the *Galletta del Marinaio* (sailors' hard flat bread). The bakery is also a bar and here it is possible to taste not only the galletta, but also many other local specialities: *focaccia al formaggio* (flat homemade bread with cheese on top), *torta di zucca* (flat pumpkin pie), *torta di bietola* (flat bok-choy pie), *polpettone di patate e funghi* (potatoes and mushroom pie), *polpettone di patate e fagiolini* (potatoes and long bean pie). From the large terrace in front of the church there are extensive views of Camogli and the whole coast as far as Genova and the Paradiso Gulf.

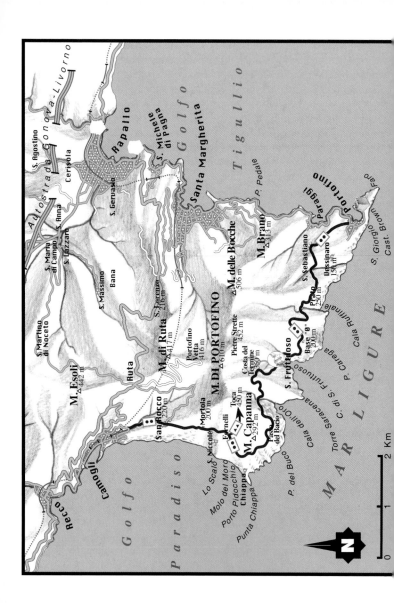

Leaving the church continue right on the walkway high above the coast. At the next junction the "two small red balls" trail turns to the left, passes through the group of houses called Mortola and soon reaches another junction (sign posted "Fornelli"). From this junction the "two small empty red triangles" trail goes on the left towards Toca (see later "How to avoid the exposed stretches"), while our trail continues straight on towards San Fruttuoso. The trail runs, quite flat at the beginning, high above the coast through Mediterranean bush and crosses some ridges. Passing around the ridges there are spectacular views of secluded coves, high cliffs and steep bush-covered slopes. The vegetation is typically Mediterranean, with *corbezzolo* (Strawberry trees, Arbutus unedo), *erica* (Heather, Erica herbacea), *mirto* (Myrtle, Myrtus communis), *lentisco* (Mastic Tree, Pistacia lentiscus) and, at higher elevations, pine trees. Some stretches around the ridges are slightly exposed but along these you will find metal cables which make the going easier and safer. Long ascents alternate with steep descents; the trail passes "Passo del Bacio" (Pass of Kisses), "Costa del Termine" and eventually goes down to San Fruttuoso, 3 h from San Rocco. Have a look at the abbey (pre-tenth century) which has recently been restored and have a drink at the local Bar Restaurant *Da Giovanni*. Boat services run between San Fruttuoso and Camogli and between San Fruttuoso and Santa Margherita Ligure. In summer the service is daily, while in the other seasons it is limited to Sundays and holidays. Two companies run the service: the first, "Servizio Marittimo del Tigullio" (0185 284670), connects San Fruttuoso with Santa Margherita Ligure, the second, "Golfo Paradiso" (0185 772091) connects San Fruttuoso with Camogli. They are private services, please call in advance to be sure that the service is running.

From San Fruttuoso the "two small red balls" trail resumes at the other side of the bay and with several zigzags climbs steadily to the so-called *Base 0* (225 m elevation) and from there it continues on the level at the top of the cliffs passing through the houses at Prato (245 m) and then at San Sebastiano (165 m). It eventually reaches Portofino Mare, at sea level, 2 h from San Fruttuoso. The stretch between San Fruttuoso and Portofino is probably the most enjoyable and interesting of the entire hike, with spectacular views of the sea and cliffs, passing through dense and luxuriant Mediterranean vegetation. Portofino is one of the most romantic and picturesque towns along the Ligurian coast. With its beautiful bay, Castello (Castle) of San Giorgio, the church of San Giorgio (containing relics of Saint George) and coloured houses, restaurants and bars around the harbor it is really worth a visit.

From Portofino take the bus to Santa Margherita, unless you want to walk the 5 km of road which connects the two towns. The road is paved and has good views. If you walk this stretch it adds an hour to the duration of the walk. Santa Margherita is also very beautiful and fortunately less crowded and expensive than Portofino.

Camogli reminds me of the joke about "the power of 7". Do you know it? Here it is:

> "Per la strada che va a Camogli,
> incontrai un uomo con sette mogli.
> Ogni moglie aveva sette tasche,
> in ogni tasca c'erano sette gatte;
> ogni gatta aveva sette gattini.
> Tra gattini, gatte, tasche e mogli,
> quanti andavano a Camogli?"

You do not know Italian? Well, here it is in English (but here Camogli has become St. Ives):

> "As I was going to St. Ives,
> I met a man with seven wives;
> Every wife had seven sacks,
> Every sack had seven cats,
> Every cat had seven kits.
> Kits, cats, sacks, and wives,
> How many were going to St. Ives?"

How to avoid the exposed stretches

If you wish to avoid the exposed stretches take the same route from Camogli up to the "Fornelli" junction. From here, turn left on the trail with the symbol "two small red empty triangles" to "Toca", at 450 m elevation, 1 h from the junction. From here, take the trail with the symbol "a triangle of three small red triangles in the vertices" by an interesting and panoramic itinerary to "Pietre Strette" (tight stones), 452 m elevation, ¾ h from Toca. From Pietre Strette the trail with the symbol "red empty circle" goes down with several zigzags to San Fruttuoso in another 45 minutes. From San Fruttuoso follow the directions given above. If you wish, you may reach San Fruttuoso directly from Portofino and return along the same route. In this case, the hike becomes Easy, the length 8 km, the elevation gain 500 m, the walking time 4 h and the highest elevation 250 m.

Where to end your hike

You have already had focaccia al formaggio in San Rocco, so why not feast on a good pizza in one of the several Pizzerie in Santa Magherita Ligure? However for a complete local meal go to *Da Baisin*, in Santa Margherita, via Algeria 5, tel. 0185 286763. They serve local specialities including *pansotti*, a ravioli stuffed with cheese and chard and served with a creamy walnut sauce, and *zuppa di pesce* (fish soup).

Hike 28 - Riomaggiore - Portovenere

Difficulty	*Moderate*
Length	*10 km*
Elevation gain	*700 m*
Walking time	*5 h*
Highest elevation	*511 m (Telegrafo)*
Trailhead	*Riomaggiore*
Trails	*#3 from Riomaggiore to Telegrafo (511 m);*
	#1 from Telegrafo to Portovenere, along the ridge;
	from Portovenere to La Spezia by bus.
Points of interest	*Riomaggiore*
	Santuario di Montenero (also known as Montenegro)
	Portovenere
	Bay of the Poets (Byron and Shelley)
	Views of the coast

Illustration 29 - On trail #3 from Riomaggiore to "Santuario di Montenegro"

Together with the Cinque Terre this is one of the finest coastal hikes in Italy. Some stretches of this hike are even more beautiful than the Cinque Terre, with better views of the coast and of the Gulf of La Spezia. From the "Santuario di Montenero" there are spectacular views of Riomaggiore, of the other villages along the coast up to Monterosso and of the promontory of Punta Mesco to the north. To the south are views of the coast up to Portovenere, the island of Palmaria and the smaller island of Tino. Another part of the walk commanding panoramic views is that between Campiglia and

Portovenere. This path is at the top of the cliffs and has breathtaking views of Portovenere, the Bay of the Poets, the islands of Palmaria and Tino and even of the smaller island of Tinetto.

How to reach the trailhead

The loop can start from La Spezia or, if you wish, from Riomaggiore. In the first case, from La Spezia take the train to Riomaggiore on the railway La Spezia-Genova, get off at the first stop from La Spezia. Be sure the train stops there; usually local trains (*treno locale*) stop in Riomaggiore. In the second case you should go to Riomaggiore by car and come back by train to collect it at the end of the hike. The choice yours. Once in Riomaggiore, you have to choose between two different trails to reach the first destination called Telegrafo (511 m elevation): trail #3 or #3a. Trail #3 is recommended, it is wider and less steep than the other. It has been regularly used for many years since it was the only connection between Riomaggiore and the village of Biassa on the other side of the hills towards La Spezia.

From the railway station, turn right and walk through the rail-pedestrian tunnel to the town center. After the tunnel on the right steps take you under the railway and to a small arbour with interesting views of the town; on the left is the center of the town, with shops, bars and restaurants along both sides of the road. Going up along the road, among the first houses on the right you will find the start of trail #3a marked in red. Carry on along the road up to the junction with the main road coming from La Spezia. If you arrive by car, you are already there. Here there is the main parking lot of the town.

The hike

Across the main road trail #3 goes up along the bank of the creek. It takes about ¾ h to reach the *Santuario di Nostra Signora di Montenero*, a church of the 14th century, 341 m elevation. This is a vantage point overlooking Riomaggiore and all the other villages scattered along the coast as far as Monterosso and the promontory of Punta Mesco. On the other side, to the south, you can see the coast as far as Portovenere, the island of Palmaria and the tiny island of Tino. Trails #3 and #3a join together here and they continue up behind the church. When they split again turn right on trail #3 and in ¾ h you will reach Telegrafo (511 m).

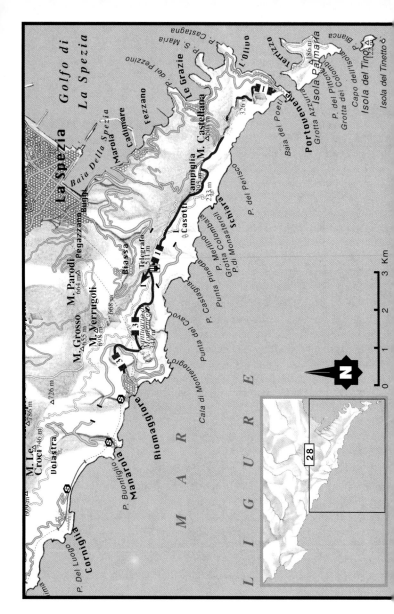

Here a road comes up from Biassa on the other side of the hill and the trail joins trail #1 (from Portovenere to Levanto). More importantly here is the *Bar Trattoria Da Natale* (tel. 0187 920792) where you should stop for a drink and try the *mesciua*, a soup made of beans, chickpeas and wheat grains.

Leaving the restaurant turn right on trail #1 along the ridge through a coniferous wood. Follow the red marks and in about 1 h you come to the pretty village of Campiglia which has good views of the coast and the sea. Pass through the village and follow trail #1 around the small church on the right. Soon there is a paved road which you follow for a short distance until, at the first curve, you leave it on the right. From here the trail goes high above the sea and there are broad views to the island of Palmaria and the tiny island of Tino along the coast to the south. In less than 1 km the trail reaches the paved road. Do not take this road, the trail continues straight along the edge (the marks here are not very clear; if you find yourself going down along a paved road, you are on the wrong track; go back, the paved road would take you very far from Portovenere). The trail continues in the bushes, close to the edge of the cliff, and soon reaches a paved road again. Here the signs and marks are clear. Turn right on the road, which winds slowly uphill, and follow the red/white marks. In about 300 m, at the junction with a dirt road on the left, the trail continues along by a shortcut through the wood and reaches the road again after a few meters. Continue along the road following the red/white marks and after about ½ km, at the first hairpin bend, leave the road, which turns to the right, and go straight forward along a dirt road, which soon becomes a narrow footpath. The trail runs quite flat along the south-east slopes of the hill and finally starts going down steeply, with views of the gulf of La Spezia, the castle, the bay and the island of Palmaria. The trail is now very steep and goes straight towards the Castle. Eventually a long series of steps beside the wall of the town takes you down to the picturesque village of Portovenere, 1½ h from Campiglia.

The entrance to the medieval village is on the right through a big gate in the wall. It is a real pleasure to walk along the narrow and colorful streets. At the south end of the village on top of a promontory is the gothic church of San Pietro (13th Century) with its black and white striped walls. On the other side of the promontory is the so-called Bay of the Poets (the poets were Byron and Shelley). From Portovenere take the bus to the railway station of La Spezia. You can buy bus tickets at the *Pro Loco*, the local tourist Office, just to the right of the gate through which you entered. The ride to the station takes from ½ to 1 h, depending on traffic.

Where to end the hike

Try one of the several good restaurants in Portovenere, but be careful they may be more expensive than the restaurants in the Apuane. But if quality is more important than cost there is only one place to go: *La Taverna del Corsaro*, in Portovenere, calata Doria 102, tel. 0187 900622, which is both a good restaurant and a pleasant place to eat. Look out for the Ligurian specialities (see "What to eat" in the chapter "Where to stay, What to eat, Where to eat, Rifugio").

Illustration 30 - The church of San Pietro in Portovenere

Hike 29 - Monterosso - Levanto

Difficulty	*Easy*
Length	*8 km*
Elevation gain	*400 m*
Walking time	*3 h*
Highest elevation	*350 m (Punta Mesco)*
Trailhead	*Monterosso*
Trails	*#10 from Monterosso to Punta Mesco (350 m); #1 from Punta Mesco to Levanto; from Levanto back to your starting railway station, by train.*
Points of interest	*The towns of Monterosso and Levanto The views from Punta Mesco and along the trail*

Punta Mesco is a beautiful promontory covered in Mediterranean bush and stands of Umbrella Pine trees. This short and easy hike gives you wide views of the coast from Monterosso to Portovenere to the south and from Levanto to Portofino to the north.

How to reach the trailhead

Go to Monterosso by train. On leaving the station turn right along the main road and continue until the road starts to go uphill. Here on the right are signs #1 and #10. On the left you can see the Clubhouse of the local Sailing Club, with a huge statue, "il Gigante" (the Giant), sculptured in the rock supporting part of the roof.

The hike

Trail #10 starts going up towards Levanto and shortly leaves the last houses of the town. It climbs several steps, follows a narrow path beside a paved road, runs along the road for a short stretch and finally leaves the road on the right following a steep footpath. It continues traversing the east slopes of the Promontory and reaches the ridge. Here turn left to Punta Mesco, with the ruins of a small church (*Sant' Antonio*) and an abandoned construction, *Semaforo* (light-house), 350 m elevation, about 1 h from the railway station of Monterosso. There are extensive views, from the top of the promontory, of Monterosso and the whole Cinque Terre riviera up to the islands of Palmaria and Tino. From Punta Mesco go back along the ridge and continue on trail #10 up for about 10 meters to the junction with trail #1. Trail #1 comes from Levanto on the left and goes from here first along the ridge and then along the main divide up to Portovenere. From the junction, turn left on trail #1, going towards Levanto along the west slopes of the Promontory. The trail initially goes down slowly and continues going down by steep steps until it reaches a paved road. Just at the left hand corner between the footpath and the road there is the restaurant *la Giada del Mesco* in a splendid location with spectacular views of the sea. They can also accommodate a few people. Turn left on the road and, after a short stretch along the paved road, take the trail on the left. The trail descends gently with views of the coast and Levanto. Finally by a long series of steps the trail reaches the Castle (*Castello di Levanto*) and from here by further steps, steep and narrow, reaches the road along the coast. Turn right towards the center of town and from there to the railway station, which is about ½ km from the beach, in the north-east part of the town, 2 h from Punta Mesco. From Levanto take the train back to the railway station you started from. The ride is very short and interesting.

Where to end your hike

La Giada del Mesco (see above, 0187 808705) has wonderful views and good local food, but it will seem expensive if you have grown accustomed to the prices in the Apuane. If you need accommodation try *Pensione Ristorante Meri*, 0187 823059, in Costa di Framura, north of Levanto, beyond Bonassola. In addition to the room you can find good *trofie al pesto*, fresh grilled fish, and other local food and wine. If you do not have a car in Levanto you can reach Framura by train (the second station from Levanto in the direction Sestri Levante, after Bonassola station). From the railway station at Framura a long series of steps takes you first to Anzo (part of Framura), then to Setta (another section of Framura) and finally to Costa di Framura. Keep going after the church and in less than 100 m along the paved road, on the left, you will find the Pensione Meri. From the station there are about 200 m elevation gain and it takes ¾ h.

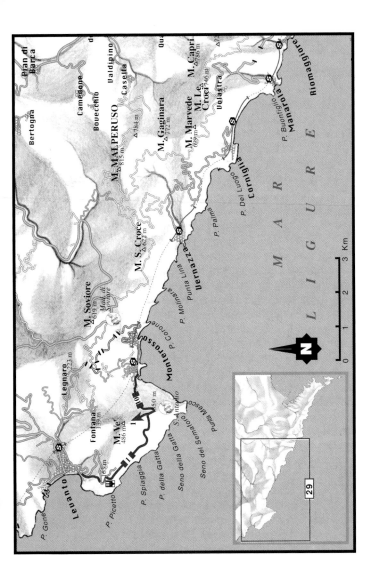

Climbs in the Apuane Alps

Angelo Nerli

For an introduction to climbing in the Apuane Alps, I wanted to choose routes with the right combination of attractive settings and sound rock. Also, I wanted to focus on trips of moderate length and difficulty. The routes here have a difficulty of II to IV in the European grading system and 5.5 - 5.7 in the Yosemite system used in the USA. However, finding the right climbs is not easy in the Apuane Alps.

The mountains are moderate in altitude with the highest, Monte Pisanino, reaching 1946 m or 6385 ft. They are not far from the sea. The warm and often wet weather patterns create a Mediterranean climate. The geology features the marble of the ancient Romans and Michelangelo who even hoped to carve a monument into the summit of M. Altissimo. Although common, the marble here is not particularly suitable for climbing. It is often slick, and where it is not slippery, it is loose. Grass and vegetation is often mixed with debris that interferes with climbing on the easier routes. The more solid routes, rated V and higher, occur in limestone. Limestone beds are scattered all over the range with concentrations at the two sides, roughly east-west. To the north-east is the huge north wall of Pizzo d' Uccello. It is a classic of the area with routes reaching to 700 m/2296 ft. To the south, near Monte Forato and Monte Nona, the free-standing tower of Procinto and its surrounding cliffs offer countless rock routes. The impressive big walls of marble or limestone in the central sector of the chain are not normally used for climbing due to loose rock. These cliffs of Monte Contrario, Roccandagia, and Penna di Sumbra do make for magnificent hiking. There is another variety of rock, a kind of schist, that makes for good climbing. It is hard and well supplied with holds. A local grass used for climbing holds in the absence of decent rock is an unusual feature of the local climbing scene. Routes can feature rock mixed with steep slopes covered with this long and very tough grass called *paleo*. It has a local reputation for being safe on precarious moves. You will want to make up your own mind when the opportunity presents itself. Winter in the Apuane Alps offers much interesting climbing over hard snow (that covers the grass), but that is another story.

The climbs described here are in both the north and the south of the range. You have the option of climbing from the valleys, or from the refuges (locally, *rifugio*) or huts. These are rustic hotels that offer dining and accommodations. Be forewarned that the food is often of such high quality that you would be missing a world class culinary event by returning late from climbing. You will need to reserve ahead for space and meals. Not to do so would be a criminal waste of a significant holiday experience.

The northern section is centered at Rifugio Donegani, an establishment with a formidable culinary reputation. In the area there are also two small huts, the Aronte and Garnerone. These are unmanned and locked. The keys may be obtained from the local chapter of the *Club Alpino Italiano* (CAI). The southern climbs are served by the Pietrapana and Forte dei Marmi refuges. Rifugio Pietrapana is reachable most conveniently from the towns of Pruno (trails #122 and #9), or Levigliani (trail #9). Rifugio Forte dei Marmi is reached from the town of Stazzema (trail #5).

In the northern sector

The recommended climbs start in the north. The first is a scramble-up a knife-edged ridge. It climbs up the Solco di Equi to Foce Siggioli, from Equi Terme to Rifugio Donegani. The scramble will give a flavor of the area that cannot be gained by driving to the refuge. A *Solco* is a little canyon or ravine. Other terms typical of the area are *Foce* for pass and *Via di Lizza*, or simply *Lizza,* for a steep marble ramp once used to lower heavy blocks of stone. A *Marmifera* is a gravel road graded for marble transport trucks. *Pizzo* is used for a sharp mountain top. A *Cava* is a marble or other stone quarry. *Tecchia* is an erosion cavity. *Tana* or *Buca* are used for caves. *Maestà* is a little chapel. Other local terms are given in the chapter "Before Starting Your Hike".

A first approach to climbing in the Apuane Alps
Hike 30 - Solco di Equi and Via Ferrata to Foce Siggioli

Difficulty	*Strenuous*
Length	*8 km*
Elevation gain	*1200 m, 350 m on cable*
Walking time	*5 ½ h*
Highest elevation	*1417 m (Costiera di Capradossa)*
Trailhead	*Equi Terme 250 m/820 ft*
Trails	*#192 from Solco di Equi up to the marmifera from Ugliancaldo;*
	along the marmifera up to the Casa dei Vecchi Macchinari (a small hut);
	continue on trail #190 and #187.
Points of interest	*Solco di Equi*
	View of the north wall of Pizzo d' Uccello
	Climbing the Via Ferrata
	The valley of Serenaia and the Orto di Donna (ladies' garden)
Equipment	*Strong boots or climbing shoes, climbing harness, nylon sling with carabiner for self-belay on the cable and a helmet. Lunch and water, it can be hot here so make sure you have plenty of water in summer.*

Equi Terme, a pleasant spa town on the Lunigiana side of the range, has an old center. Go by car or take the train (Lucca - Aulla) to Equi Terme. Accommodations are available at the Hotel *La Posta*. There are two large caves, *La Buca* and *La Tecchia*, with prehistoric remains. You should spend the night at the Rifugio Donegani (tel. 0583 610085). You will need to call the Rifugio to reserve accommodations and meals there.

How to reach the trailhead

From the center of Equi Terme a narrow road enters the Solco di Equi, after a kilometer the road becomes a dirt road. Follow the road for a further 1.5 km along the bottom of a wild canyon. After two short tunnels you

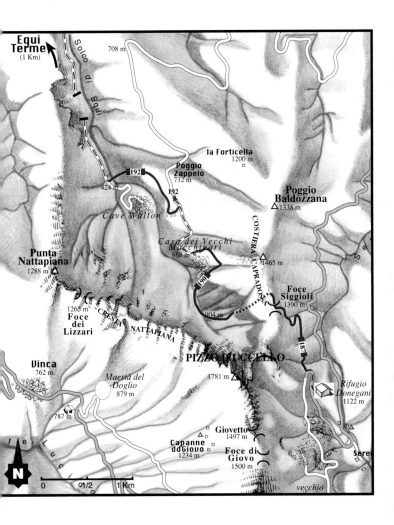

Equi Terme
(1 Km)

Solco di Equi

708 m

192

424 m

192

Cave Wallon

la Forticella
1200 m

Poggio
Zappelo
732 m

Poggio
Baldozzana
△ 1338 m

Casa dei Vecchi
Macchinari
868 m

COSTIERA CAPRADOSSA

△ 1465 m

Punta
Nattapiana
1288 m △

190

904 m

Foce
Siggioli
1390 m

187

1265 m

Foce
dei
Lizzari

CRESTA

NATTAPIANA

PIZZO D'UCCELLO

Rifugio
Donegani
1122 m

Vinca
762 m

Maestà del
Doglio
879 m

1781 m △

787 m

Giovetto
1497 m △

Capanne
ddGiovo
1234 m

Foce di
Giovo
1500 m

Sere

t e

L u c i

N

0   1/2   1 Km

vecchio

get the first view of the wall of Pizzo d' Uccello. A little further (elevation 400 m/1312 ft) you reach the bottom of the first quarries. On your left a trail marked in red leads across a stream.

The hike

Leave the road and cross some large rocks. A small trail (#192) climbs through the trees along the other side of the valley and over an old *Via di Lizza*. The higher quarries are now reached on a marmifera, along which trucks carry the marble to the small town of Ugliancaldo about 4 km north. This town is nicely situated at 740 m, but there is no public transport or hotel. Once at the marmifera turn right along the uneven road up to a small hut (the *Casa dei Vecchi Macchinari*, the warehouse for old machinery) and to the higher little quarry. Follow trail #190 which crosses, on the right, a depression in the marble. Go up through sparse woods and after the trail bends left head up to the base of a well defined rocky ridge (about 3 h from the town). This has the *Via Ferrata*, a metal cable for a length of 550 meters without interruption. It is hard, with small steps in the marble for the feet. The ridge is knife-edged with a wonderful view of the north wall of Pizzo d' Uccello. At the end of the cable you are over the *Costiera di Capradossa* (Capradossa ridge) (1½ h from the base of the ridge), just above the Foce Siggioli (elevation 1390 m/4559 ft). Proceed down along easy rocks and follow trail #187 to reach the Rifugio Donegani (elevation 1122 m/ 3680 ft) (about 1 h from Capradossa).

Where to end the hike

The hike ends at Rifugio Donegani, where the food is excellent and the atmosphere very friendly and cosy. You can spend the night here too. The accommodation is spartan but it is a worthwhile cultural experience. Rifugio Donegani is open all summer, but in other seasons it is open on reservation only. Call before going climbing (0583 610085).

Climbing routes from Rifugio Donegani

Climb 1 - Pizzo d' Uccello along the South Diedro and/or the Tiziana Route

Up to V, but can be easier; good rock. The SSW side of Pizzo d' Uccello has several ridges and ours is the one on the extreme right.

Following the normal route to Pizzo d' Uccello up to the Giovetto Pass (a pass just after Foce di Giovo) at the junction between trails #37 and #181, go down along the Sentiero attrezzato (equipped path) Piotti, trail #191 (very panoramic, for expert hikers only), and immediately after, cross to the right towards the start of the climbing.

The climbing route is obvious and very good, almost 200 m/656 ft high, a short passage of grade V. Find an isolated fin, and then the large open book, the South Diedro. Begin an ascending traverse and an inclined (oblique) chimney on the left and through debris to the top of the ridge. From the left join the *Tiziana* route, a less difficult one. The upper part of the slope could be avoided by joining the normal route to the right. If you follow the debris on the left instead, you can do a more challenging route along the second stretch of the Tiziana route, IV: dark dihedral, then on the left along the wall, fissure and dihedral, vertical face and small final jumps.

Climb 2 - Cresta Garnerone (Garnerone ridge)

From Foce di Giovo, elevation 1500 m/4920 ft; which you reach by trail #37, the fractured top ridge goes south, up to the last Peak of the Garnerone Ridge, and continues South-East to the top of Monte Grondilice (1805 m/5920 ft) and from here to Foce di Grondilice (1750 m/ 5740 ft). The distance from Foce di Giovo to Foce di Grondilice along the ridge is about 1.5 km. It is a traverse of traditional Alpinists. There are alternating difficulties, never more than III, and nice stretches mainly in the first part. Others are on less difficult rock. But the panorama and the feeling of altitude are noteworthy.

Beyond the beautiful meadows of the Foce di Giovo, climb the two small *Denti di* (Teeth of) *Giovo*, then the two *Guglie di Vinca* (needles of Vinca), the *Gobbo* (humpback), the three tops of Monte Garnerone.

Good luck blesses those who touch all the tops. From the following pass to the Foce di Grondilice it is easy. In total it takes about 4 h.

From the West side downwards, you can sight the *Guglie della Vacchereccia,* our next target, and at its feet, the Capanna Garnerone. From Foce di Grondilice follow trail #186 to the left to the *Cava* (quarry) *27.* Following the gravel road (*marmifera*) you will reach the Rifugio Donegani.

Climb 3 - Guglie della Vacchereccia (Vacchereccia Needles)

From Foce di Giovo near the town of Vinca follow trail #37. Go down about 200 m/656 ft and then almost flat along the base of the Cresta Garnerone-Grondilice and reach conifers where the Capanna Garnerone, a hut, is located at an elevation of 1260 m/4132 ft. It is unmanned and locked with keys available from the CAI Section of Carrara. Above a number of small limestone needles of good rock, there is a rock-climbing training spot. On your left are three needles close together. They are called *Biforca* (Bifurcate), *Cartuccia* (hunting projectile) and *Torracca*. To their right is an inclined wall 120 m/400 ft high, along which runs the *Via degli allievi* (the route of the trainees). It is suggested to climb it since it is easy, grade III, and the rock is good.

Climbing routes from Rifugio Aronte

The small rifugio-bivouac, Aronte, is unmanned (keys from the CAI Section of Massa). It is also ancient, about 100 years old, and is the highest in the area. The elevation is 1642 m/5385 ft.

From Rifugio Donegani to Rifugio Aronte

From Rifugio Donegani it takes 2½ h, along a wonderful hike that crosses Foce di Cardeto (1680 m/5510 ft). Take trail #180 and at the junction follow trail #178 up to the Foce di Cardeto. From here follow, on the other side of the pass, trail #179 leading to Passo della Focolaccia. Passo della Focolaccia (Focolaccia Pass), elevation 1650 m, has been badly damaged by the excavation of marble, but it partially retains the fascinating appeal of a high altitude pass over precipitous valleys to the sea. It is located between the huge grey massif of Monte Tambura and the recumbent Monte Cavallo (M. Horse), with its knobbed profile. The southern side of M. Cavallo, with a funny appendix, provides some short climbing routes. The rock is excellent dark schist. Directly in front of the rifugio Aronte on the sea side is the elegant profile of *Punta Carina* (Pretty Peak).

Climb 4 - Punta Carina (Pretty Peak)

Start through a grassy chimney to a small fork (pass) and then to the pointed cusp after having gained a short overhanging face. Elevation gain 50 m/164 ft, III+. To hungry climbers, this peak looks very much like a cut block of Parmesan cheese.

Climb 5 - Cresta Botto (Botto Ridge)

At the right of Punta Carina, hike up along the south ridge of M. Cavallo and climb the short stretch, called *Cresta Botto* (Botto Ridge). It is a beautiful short II - III climb.

Climb 6 - SE Wall of M. Cavallo

Just after the Botto Ridge, arrive at a small pass, called *Forcella di Porta* (door or "gate pass"). At the pass is the triangular SE wall of Monte Cavallo, 150 m/500 ft high. Climb almost in the middle, choosing between two clearly recognizable routes. The two routes cross each other at a terrace inside a break: maximum difficulty IV+. The climb ends at the top of the southern hump of M. Cavallo, elevation 1851 m/6071 ft.

Climb 7 - East Ridge of M. Cavallo

You can climb directly from Passo della Focolaccia to the top of this hump of M. Cavallo along the easier East Ridge, II and III. To descend from the top of the humps of Monte Cavallo, start on the left where the grassy slope looks less steep. Scramble down to a bench, which leads left to Forcella di Porta and then to rifugio Aronte.

If you do not sleep at the rifugio Aronte, either go back to Rifugio Donegani following the ascent route, or go down to the Garfagnana side along the gravel road to the town of Gorfigliano, elevation 700 m/2296 ft. In town you will find hotels and restaurants. Less easily, on the sea side, you could descend down to the town of Resceto, elevation 485 m/1591 ft, along a very steep *Via di Lizza*; the route from Resceto to Passo della Focolaccia is described in the "Hike 10 - Monte Tambura loop, from Resceto".

In the southern sector

Climbing routes from Rifugio Pietrapana

Rifugio Pietrapana at Foce di Mosceta, elevation 1180 m/3870 ft, is in front of Pania della Croce, the most climbed mountain of the chain.

Note on linking up by foot between the northern and southern sector

From rifugio Aronte a strong and skilled hiker can reach Rifugio Pietrapana in two days, with a stop for the night in the town of Arni-Campagrina (Hotel Aronte, Via Gobbie 14, 0584 77917). The route is via Monte Tambura and *via ferrata Vecchiacchi,* or Campocatino and *Cava Formignacola;* both are wonderful routes and have high interest from the environmental point of view.

Climb 8 - Campanile Francesca (Francesca Bell-tower)

At one side of Foce di Mosceta are the huge western slopes of Pania della Croce and Pizzo delle Saette. At the bottom of Pizzo delle Saette the slope is steep and rugged, with a rocky triangular massif. The higher summit is called *Punta Lenzi* (Lenzi Peak), while the lower on the left is *Campanile Francesca.* Among the several rock-climbing routes, the least difficult is classified IV and is 120 m/400 ft high. It runs along the NW ridge. The limestone rock is good here. You can reach the base from trail #9 from Foce di Mosceta continuing by the houses of Col di Favilla.

Climb 9 - North Crest of Pizzo delle Saette

Continue along the above trail #9. Just after a *Maestà*, go right along trail #127 and reach the base of the ponderous North Crest of Pizzo delle Saette, about 600 m/1968 ft high. Even if it is not more than IV in a few stretches, it is hard because of its length and the spots where the rock is loose. This route is only for climbers familiar with the less solid rock of the area. The route goes almost anywhere along the sharp ridge or close to it on the left. Once at the top, go along the crest until you reach the normal route to Pania della Croce (Hikes 22 and 2).

Climbing routes from Rifugio Forte dei Marmi

The approach

Most people start by driving past Stazzema to the start of trail #5. It takes off on the right of the road. See the description of "Hike 1 - Procinto and Monte Nona loop"

From the other side, you can reach the "Rifugio Forte dei Marmi" from the Foce di Mosceta in a half day walk (trail #121). This is a good crossing with panoramic views of the *Alta Versilia* (High Versilia). A large expanse of trees covers all of the valleys converging on the town of Ponte Stazzemese (damaged in the flood of 1996). Old towns are scattered on the top of the ridges. Vertical walls follow the route from Costa Pulita to Monte Matanna. Pania della Croce dominates one side of these mountains. In the center of these mountains is the peculiar tower of Procinto, a plug shaped, free standing tower. Its neighbours are its "Bimbi" (children). The Rifugio Forte dei Marmi is located in the trees at the foot of the overhanging smooth wall of Monte Nona near Procinto. Downhill are their small children including "La Bimba" (the baby girl), a monolith overhanging the valley.

Climb 10 - The "Bimbi" (the Children) traverse

Passages of III+, average time 3 h. Between Procinto and the Bimba appears *Piccolo Procinto* (Small Procinto), through which this traverse runs. Of the many high standard routes here, this is the only one suitable for the intermediate climber. There is a "Via Ferrata" up Procinto, see "Hike 1- Procinto and Monte Nona loop". From the West side of the

Cintura del Procinto (see Hike 1) go down along rocks, II, to the *Foce dei Bimbi*.

Start along an elegant ridge. In two aerial rope lengths you reach the top of an almost flat ridge with three small peaks. Go down steeply to the narrow break which separates these from Piccolo Procinto. Climb up the Piccolo Procinto in two beautiful lengths and go down, through a stony couloir-chimney, to the *Foce della Bimba*, with a lot of trees around. To get down from the foot of the rocks, go down northwards through a steep wood and then rappel either a deep and narrow chimney, or you could descend just on the left along an opened wall, reaching trail #121.

Illustration 31 - Piccolo Procinto (about 1100 m) and Bimba, from the west

Suggestions on climbing equipment

The routes in this guide book are well used. Fixed protection in the form of pitons and bolts, or the availability of rock horns and trees, is the norm. The use of removable pieces of protection, chocks and the like, is used for hard new routes. Hard sport climbing routes will be bolted. A sport climbing guide is listed in the climbing references.

Loose rock necessitates the use of a helmet. Harness, your customary belay and rappel (abseil) devices, rappel rings, rappel slings, and quick draws round out the selection. Local climbers use two 50 m half-ropes for rappels. Be prepared to execute your contingency plan "B" if you only have a single rope. Rappel anchors are often well placed and can feature chains and other secure mountings.

There are sports shops selling climbing gear in several of the towns - there is a good one near the railway station in Pietrasanta. *Politecnica Sport* in Pisa, Corso Italia 36, *Marcosport* in Carrara, Via Roma 16, and many other sports shops in the area offer discounts - usually from 10% to 20%, to CAI members (another good reason to become a member of the Club Alpino Italiano).

Climbing references

For detailed information about climbing and hiking in the Apuane Alps, see the guidebook *Alpi Apuane* by A. Nerli, A. Sabbadini and E. Montagna, in the series "Monti d' Italia" of CAI and TCI (Italian Touring Club), updated in 1978.

Mainly for sport climbing see *Alpi Apuane - Salite Scelte* (Apuane Alps - Selected Climbs), by S. Funck, ed. Pezzini, 1993.

For the northern area, a large scale (1:12500) Map is available: *Carta dei Sentieri delle Apuane settentrionali*, edited by the CAI Section of Pisa in 1988.

The Flora of the Apuane Alps

Introduction

Dave Coder

Apart from the unusual microclimates of the Apuane Alps, visitors should consider the history of Italy and its location in the center of the Mediterranean when viewing the plants that grow there today. The geographical position of the area on the coast of the Tyrrhenian Sea - the *central lake* of the Mediterranean - has provided a gateway to virtually all the countries that line the shores of the greater sea. One need not think long to imagine how differently the area may have appeared to early visitors. Think of Greek colonists from Sicily, or contemporaries of the mythical Aeneas. What plants might they have seen prior to the expansion of Rome and the later developments of the 20th Century? Today's visitor might also think of the flora on the mountains from which Michelangelo chose marble blocks, or on the mountains that inspired the Divine Comedy of Dante. During the last two millennia, economic and military activities as well as natural accidents have added exotic plants that found hospitable climates in the mountains or valleys of the Apuane Alps.

The varied flora of the Apuane Alps of today reflects the different habitats that result from both altitude and weather exposure. Although many foreign species have replaced indigenous plants, many native species unique to the area remain. On the other hand, there are plants from the area that have found homes in foreign lands - some may be familiar to the reader. The alert viewer can enjoy the variety of plants among the landscapes that range from maritime slopes to alpine peaks. The interaction of geography, climate and human activity that has resulted in today's landscape will continue to vary as the years pass.

The Flowers of the Apuane Alps

Bruno Barsella

The Apuane Alps are situated in a curious geographical position: neither north nor south and quite near to the Tyrrhenian Sea. They run North to South for about 60 kilometers at a distance of about 15 kilometers from the sea. This location and the temperate geographical position have given strange habits to the vegetation of the Apuane Alps. The tree maximum elevation is lower than in the Alps - Castanea sativa can be found at 800 m on the seaside and at 1200 m on the east side - facing the Apennines, and Fagus silvatica grows up to 1500 m on the east side). The situation is the same for herbaceous plants so that the alpine flora starts at really low elevations in our mountains. The tops of the most important mountains (Monte Pisanino 1946 m, Monte Cavallo 1895 m, Pania della Croce 1859 m) have no trees, and the alpine flora is the queen of these zones. The sea winds and the north winds arrive unshielded to this region and the flowering of the vegetation is more dependent on the wind exposure than on the elevation (this is true also for the southern parts of the Apuane Alps, *I Monti Pisani*).

The vegetation of the Apuane Alps is a large subset of the Italian one. Giuseppe Martinoli, in his preface on the *Flora e Vegetazione* to the Guide of 1958, writes: "The compiler who likes to describe the flora of Apuane Alps should insert such a number of species that his table should contain about two thirds of the Italian Flora". Another singular characteristic of Apuane Alps is that these mountains have had a separate evolution during the last glaciation leading to the formation of endemic species found only in the Apuane Alps or in the Apennines. Recently, botanists have been much more careful in deciding what is a new species, but in any case, about ten species are surely truly endemic to the Apuane Alps. Among these are:

Polygala carueliana	*Santolina pinnata*
Cerastium apuanum	*Hieracium anchusaefolium*
Rubus lucanescens	*Veronica longstyla*
Bunium rigidulum	*Salix crataegifoli*
	Alyssum bertolonii

Many of these plants are quite localized on a few tops in the mountain chain. The Apuane Alps have been included in a Natural Park, the *Parco Naturale delle Alpi Apuane*, and the writer hopes that the staff of the Park will start a World Wide Web page on the Natural History of this zone containing images of the most interesting species of the Park. For the moment, the web site at

\<URL:http://astr17pi.difi.unipi.it/Orchids/

contains at least the Orchidaceae family of the flora.

This family is extremely well represented in Italy and Apuane Alps contain a large subset of the complete list. In particular the rare *Dactylorhiza incarnata*, which lives in peat-bogs, is present in the Park. Near Monte Freddone there was an extremely beautiful peat-bog, the largest of Apuane Alps. Many years ago, on a sunny Saturday morning in June, I visited this zone and I found a place of incredible beauty. The damp meadow was full of Narcissus, Miosotis, and Pinguicola, and in many of the wet areas you could find the violet flowers of the Dactylorhiza. Now things have changed - during the construction of a road to the marble quarries, another road was started in the direction of Puntato. Although it was possible to stop this road construction, the work that had already been done cut the water supply and now the peat-bog is nearly dry. Last year it was possible to find some specimens of Dactylorhiza in the central area, but I fear that this beautiful zone will not live much longer.

Which is the best time to come to Apuane Alps to find the flowers? Luckily, the blossom period is long due to the fact that the vegetation spans the Mediterranean flora as well as the Alpine. Flowers begin to appear at low elevations from the beginning of March and, as time passes, the blossoming zone grows towards the tops. In April you begin to find many species in blossom at an elevation of 800 - 1000 meters. May brings new species and the first week of June is the most spectacular: you may find, in this period, *Narcissus poeticus, Pinguicola vulgaris, Soldanella alpina, Primula auricola,* and many of the endemic species cited before. You may also find many orchids. *Orchis mascula, Dactylorhiza sambucina, Orchis militaris, Corallorhiza trifida,* and *Cephalanthera rubra*. Near Pizzo d' Uccello you may be lucky enough to find the splendid purple-pink flowers of *Poeonia officinalis.*

In the alpine zone over 1400 m, you may find *Gentiana kochiana, Pulsatilla alpina, Cerastium apuanum,* and *Globularia incanescens.* In July flowering continues at higher elevations. In some places you may find another orchid, *Epipactis rubiginosa,* and, among the rocks many specimens of the genus Saxifraga including *Saxifraga azoides* var. *atropurpurea.* In August and September you may find, if you do not mind the high temperature of the hottest hours of the day, many other species, and until the beginning of October you may find in the woods, the long spikes of *Gentiana asclepiadea.* At this point the weather moves towards its winter state, the snow may begin to fall and the visitor to the Apuane Alps discovers that these Alps are quite similar to the true northern Alps. For three or four months, look at the tops, at the snowy sides of the mountains - the vegetation is sleeping!

Primula auricola

Habitats, Shrubs and Trees

Carlo Jacob

Habitat and history in Italy

To better understand the Italian Flora and landscape while visiting
Italy, you should realize that the Peninsula, after thousands of years of
human modifications, is more an artificial garden than a pristine land with
its own luxuriant vegetation. The main consequence of gradual human
modification of the landscape is that the endemic species in some areas
of the country, mainly in the North, are now almost rare, or at least less
common than the species introduced from both the old and new worlds
in the last centuries that have settled successfully in our climate.

For example, if a pre-Roman Italian farmer returned today, he could
not recognize 4 of 5 tree species. These would include Old World
species such as the **Cypress** (Cipresso) (*Cupressus sempervirens*)
introduced by the Etruscans from Greece and the Near East, the
Stone and **Maritime Pine** (Pino) (*Pinus Pinea* and *Pinus pinaster*)
probably introduced by the Romans from North Africa, the **Citrus**
(Agrumi) introduced by the Arabs from Greece and the near East.
Certainly he would not recognize any of the plant species
imported from the American Continent and Far East since the XVI
century, like the **Cedars** (Tuie) (*Thuja occidentalis*, *Thuja plicata*,
and *Thuja orientalis*), the **Lawson Cypress** (Falso Cipresso)
(*Chamaecyparis lawsoniana*), American **Firs**, **Spruces** and **Pines**
(*Abies concolor*, *Abies grandis*, *Picea
brewerana*, *Picea sitchensis*, *Pinus ponde-
rosa*, *Pinus strobus*), **Hemlocks** (Tsughe) and
Douglas Fir (Pseudotsughe) (*Tsuga
mertensiana*, *Tsuga heterophylla*, *Tsuga
canadensis*, *Pseudotsuga menziesii*
(Douglasia)), big **Yew** (Tasso) and **Redwood**
(Sequoia) (*Taxodium dysticum*, *Sequoia
sempervirens*), **Locust** (Robinia), **Tree of
Heaven** (Ailanto) (*Ailanthus*) and **Eucalyptus**
(Eucalipto) (*Robinia pseudoacacia*,
Ailanthus altissima, *Eucalyptus globulus*).
Although most of these species never

*Cupressus
sempervirens*

became wild in Italy, they are only common in botanical gardens, private and public gardens, roadsides, parks and agricultural areas, cultivated as ornamentals or for wood. On the contrary, locust and tree of Heaven are sometimes so well adapted and widespread to be considered pests.

Human modifications and land management

When viewing the Italian landscape, one should realize that what seem natural woods are nothing more than man-made formations, cultivated for wood or simply for reforestation. These human plantings sometimes are so mixed with natural ones in complex ways that, when describing the composition of Italian landscapes, occasionally included among native plants are the **Olives** (Ulivi) (*Olea europaea*), the **Chestnut** trees (Castagno) (*Castanea sativa*) and the **Poplar** (Pioppo) (*Populus x euroamericana*, (hybrid poplar)), not to mention the widespread **Vineyards** (vigneti), all human formations for several centuries, if not for thousands of years.

Vice versa, natural wood formations are only rarely found. Once spread along the Apennine slopes, the stands of **Christmas Tree** (Abete Bianco) (*Abies alba*) were reduced drastically after centuries of use by Roman navy yards followed by the four Italian Maritime Republics (Amalfi, Genova, Pisa and Venice) (mainly the Venetian arsenal). They grow now only in protected areas, surviving thanks to the patient preservation work of the monasteries (mainly Benedictines, the oldest order of monks), fortunately common in Italy.

The intensive exploitation of the soil for thousands of years has definitively marked the forest panorama of the entire Peninsula. The reduction of forest coverage seems to have been stopped only recently, thanks to a more decisive action of reforestation, on the wave of an increased pressure of public opinion. Popular movements have also led to more severe laws against arson, the acquisition of new land for cattle raising or for speculative development.

It should be noted in the last decades, there has been a natural reforestation of the mountains regions of the Italian peninsula. Paradoxically, the massive migration away from the countryside during the last fifty years has helped with the rehabilitation of the land especially

Abies alba

in mountainous areas subject to landslides - like the Apuane Alps - where endemic native species contribute to the consolidation of the soil.

The Apuane Alps

Also the flora of the Apuane Alps fits the above scenario, mainly due to the history of Tuscany and importantly its being a seaside territory.

The chain of the Apuane Alps, which runs from NW to SE, between the Apennines and the Tyrrhenian sea, defines two different microclimates: the one of the Mediterranean side, towards the sea in direction SW, and the other of the continental side, towards the Apennine massif (Tuscany - Emilia) and the Po valley to the NE. These two microclimates create different floristic habitats.

The Mediterranean side

Here we find a progression of plant habitats typical of peninsular Italy. From the coast going towards the peaks of the Apuane Alps, we find vegetation zones, which we may define approximately as:

1) Mediterranean bush, up to 300 - 400 m

2) oak caducifolia, up to 700 - 800 m

3) chestnut stands, up to 900 - 1000 m

4) meadows and rock formations, over 1000 m

The Mediterranean bush

The flora of the Mediterranean zone is perhaps the richest in historical and mythological references. In this habitat, hardly any species exist which are not tied in some way to the life and mythology of the ancient Italian populations - Etruscans, Romans and Greeks. These coastal plant species play a role - from sacred to profane - as do the conifers, birch and ash for the populations of Northern Europe. The vegetation of the Mediterranean zone should be divided between the real Mediterranean bush, typically shrubs, and the trees.

Some shrub species of the Mediterranean zone

- **Gorse** (Ginestrone) (*Ulex europaeus*): evergreen; spined, very sweet smelling and with legumes which crack when they are suddenly opened; loves a certain amount of humidity, even in summer; typical shrub of the sea slope of the Apuane Alps; flowers brilliant yellow, almost all year round.

- **Mastic Tree** or **Lentisc** (Lentisco) (*Pistacia lentiscus*): evergreen; leaves with a resinous smell; together with myrtle, strawberry tree and Mediterranean oak forms a consortium; it fights intensive deforestation by colonizing meadows; the trunk produces a resin, called "Chio's mastic", used in ancient times as a base for perfumes and for chewing, progenitor of the modern chewing gum; black ovoid fruits of about 5 mm;

- **Turpentine Tree** or **Terebinth** (Terebinto) (*Pistacia terebinthus*): deciduous; leaves with a strong smell of resin; similar to mastic tree, grows at relatively high elevations; red ovoid fruits of about 7 mm;

- **Fillirea** (*Phillyrea latifolia*): evergreen; wild throughout the Mediterranean basin, resistant to sea winds and to air pollution; black globose fruits of 5 - 7 mm;

- **Myrtle** (Mirto) (*Myrtus communis*): evergreen; it grows mainly close to the coast; in ancient times it was sacred to Venus, used for decorations at wedding ceremonies or to produce crowns for poets and heroes; blue-black elliptical fruits up to 1 cm;

- **Strawberry Tree** (Corbezzolo) (*Arbutus unedo*): evergreen; commonly in association with pine and oak trees; spherical fruits of about 2 cm, red and edible, although not very tasty;

- **Laurustinus** (Laurotino) (*Viburnum tinus*): evergreen; particularly suitable for decorative purposes; flowers particularly fragrant; small metallic-blue spherical fruits, poisonous;

- **Laurel** (Alloro)(*Laurus nobilis*): evergreen; famous for its use as a symbol of glory and success by the Romans; this practice probably led to the development of the classic crown with precious metals and stones used by medieval kings. Very aromatic leaves, which are used in Italy to flavor the meat; black spherical fruits of 1 - 2 cm, look like black olives;

- **Mediterranean Buckthorn** (Alaterno) (*Rhamnus alaternus*): evergreen; dark red spherical fruits of 4 mm, not edible, from which a dye called "vegetal green" is extracted.

Some tree species of the Mediterranean zone

- **Stone** or **Umbrella Pine** (Pino Domestico) (*Pinus pinea*): evergreen conifer with needles; it is the classic pine producing pine nuts (pinoli); it prefers sandy soil, grows mainly along the Versilia coast, where the pine stands of Migliarino and San Rossore - both very close to Pisa - are famous; large and flat crown (umbrella shaped); resinous trunk up to 25 m tall, no bottom branches; light brown, furrowed and scaly bark; cones (strobilus): the classic pine cone, 10 -15 cm long and up to 10 cm large, with edible seeds (pine nuts) up to 2 cm long.

- **Maritime Pine** (Pino Marittimo) (*Pinus pinaster*): evergreen conifer with needles up to 23 cm long; similar to the stone pine; up to 30 m tall; more grayish bark than the domestic pine and deeply fissured; not as common as wild stands, mainly planted along the coast for protection from the wind and cultivated for its turpentine oil; despite the name it hardly reaches the seaside and prefers the low maritime hills; the shape of the crown immediately distinguishes it from the stone pine; the maritime pine is not a regular umbrella shape, like the stone pine, but is shaped by the prevailing winds which result in a distinct flag-shaped crown; unlike the stone pine it retains old cones (up to 18 cm long) on the branches.

- **Aleppo Pine** (Pino d' Aleppo) (*Pinus halepensis*): evergreen conifer with short needles up to 6 - 10 cm long; up to 20 m tall; twisted trunk; grey and smooth bark in young trees, reddish brown and scaly with age; irregular, cone or umbrella shaped crown; very resistant in arid zones; in ancient times used by Roman naval yards, and is still used for ship building.

- the classical **Holm** or **Holly** or **Evergreen Oak** (Leccio) (*Quercus* *ilex*): evergreen oak; up to 20 m tall; broad, round and typically bushy crown; leaves hard and rough which are similar to the cork oak, a character which distinguishes these two from all the other oak species; leaves are elliptical, egg shaped, dark green on top and covered by very fine hairs beneath; acorns up to 3 cm long; commonly used for the forestation of the Mediterranean bush, for thousands of years these were the most common forests in the Mediterranean area; main source of tannins for ancient Greeks and Romans for tanning leather.

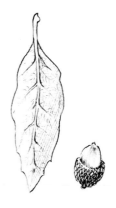

Quercus ilex

The oak caducifolia zone

In Italy, the typical tree formations in the lower mountain zone are the oak caducifolia, the plane-tree woods (mainly in the North), and chestnut stands. In oak stands, usually the dominant oaks grow in association with trees, like the **hop hornbeam** (carpino nero) (*Ostrya carpinifolia*) and the **manna ash** (orniello) (*Fraxinus ornus*), which in some cases and at lower elevations, may form isolated mixed stands. On the sea-facing slopes of the Apuane Alps, oak stands grow in the warmer and sunnier areas (thermophile oak stands), while the hornbeam and ash stands in the colder areas. Because of the climate and a favorable location, the oak caducifolia zone is the most exploited for farming, and when farming was abandoned the land reverted to brush where the conditions were no longer suitable for the growth of oak.

Some species of the oak caducifolia zone

- **Roverella** (*Quercus pubescens*): deciduous oak: up to 20 m tall; sinuous trunk; brown-grayish tough bark; lobed pubescent downy leaves; globe shaped (round) crown; resistant and irregular wood; grows in pure stands or forms mixed stands with Turkey oak, manna ash and maple; survives in rocky and dry locations.

- **Durmast** or **Sessile Oak** (Rovere) (*Quercus petraea*): majestic deciduous oak; up to 40 m tall; straight trunk; grey fissured and furrowed bark; pure stands or in association with sweet chestnut, hornbeam and beech; replaces the roverella in more moist sites; valuable wood; found up to 1300 m elevation.

- **Turkey** or **Manna Oak** (Cerro) (*Quercus cerris*): deciduous oak; up to 35 m tall; straight-sinuous trunk; deeply lobed (up to 10 cm) and toothed leaves; up to 2.5 cm long acorn, with the bottom a characteristic dome made of long and fibrous scales; lives up to 200 years.

- **Black Hornbeam** (Carpino Nero) (*Ostrya carpinifolia*): up to 15 m tall; crown

Quercus cerris

is conical oval often irregular; straight trunk; dark, brown grayish bark; deciduous regular egg shaped leaves, spine tipped, double toothed, regularly veined, very similar to that of the European hornbeam (Carpinus betulus); characteristic whitish fruits, similar to those of luppolos, thick and open bracts, like a shell (*ostreion*, in Greek); grows up to 1200 m elevation; often in association with roverella and manna ash.

-**Manna** or **Flowering Ash** (Frassino Minore or Orniello)(*Fraxinus ornus*): up to 15 m tall; flat-hemispheric crown; deciduous leaves, opposite and up to 25 cm long, characteristically pinnate, i.e. with 5 - 9 round-oval leaflets of about 7 cm; thin furrowed bark and grey branchlets; fruits are winged samaras; more common than the related species of common ash (*Fraxinus excelsior*); the wood is particularly suitable for producing sticks; (ash, a sacred tree for the Scandinavians, was used to make lances, spears, and staves by the Vikings); it is the tree of the biblical manna, which is obtained by cutting the bark and collecting the sweetish sap which dries in the air.

- **Hazel** (Nocciolo)(*Corylus avellana*): shrub up to 7 m tall, forms large stands; it is the most widely distributed naturally spread shrub in all regions of the Italian peninsula; leaves: wide, mucronate and toothed, of unique appearance; fruits are the famous hazelnuts, massively used in the manufacturing of candies, enclosed in a leafy (membranous) involucre, shaped like a helmet (koris in Greek: the Corinthian helmets were the most famous in classic Greece); the wood is very good for producing charcoal.

- **Dogwood** (Corniolo) (*Cornus mas*): up to 8 m tall; globe and not dense crown; leaves: deciduous, elliptical oval, acuminate, of 4 - 10 cm long, with evident veins; fruits are reddish stone fruits (drupes), from which a ruby red jam is produced (it is not very sweet; it is also used as a sauce for roast meat); the wood is yellowish and very resistant, and was used by the Romans for the wood part of the pilum, the Legionnaire's javelin (dogwood was also used to make the sacred lance which was thrown on the field of an enemy as a declaration of war).

- **Service Tree** (Sorbo Domestico) (*Sorbus domestica*): very similar to the mountain ash (sorbo degli uccellatori) (Sorbus aucuparia); very elegant, up to 20 m tall; straight trunk; ragged bark; leaves: deciduous, pinnate, 10 - 20 cm long, with 9 -19 leaflets; apple or pear shaped fruits of 2 - 4 cm, used by the Romans, together with wheat, to produce a drink similar to cider (*cerevisia*, mentioned by Virgil in his poem the Georgics); wood is valued in carpentry for its clear grain.

- **Black Alder** and **Green Alder** (Ontano Nero and Ontano Verde) (*Alnus glutinosa* and *Alnus viridis*): as indicated by the name (*ontano* comes from a Celtic route which means "by the shore") is a species which loves streams and swamps; the black ontano is up to 20 m tall, while the green ontano is always a shrub; not very common in the Apuane Alps, both species are grown almost exclusively close to water.

The Chestnut stands

The sweet chestnut is the king of the Mediterranean slopes of the Apuane Alps, where it forms wide stands, usually of human origin. The beech, also in the family, Fagaceae, is found on the eastern continental slopes.

- **Sweet** or **Spanish Chestnut** (Castagno) (*Castanea sativa*): very long-lived tree up to 20 m tall; tall and wide crown; straight trunk, branched at the higher part; leaves: deciduous, linear, lanceolate, serrate and mucronate, up to 20 cm long; flowers particularly suited for bee culture, from which bees produce a honey, aromatic and precious; fruits are the famous chestnuts, enclosed by a husk of 5 - 6 cm in diameter, with sharp and very stinging spines; grows up to 900 - 1000 m elevation; frequently forms pure stands, grown for sawn wood or lumber; imported by the Romans from Asia Minor, it immediately spread throughout Europe; the wood, brownish to blackish and very similar to the oak, is widely used for the construction of barrels, furniture and in past centuries for house building; its soil is particularly suitable for growing flowers.

Castanea sativa

Subalpine meadows

At high elevations, meadows lack trees and shrubs, but, isolated and at the border of the wood you may enjoy the view of a tree characteristic for the color of the bark, for the silver of the leaves and for the beauty of the fruits:

- **Whitebeam** (Sorbo Montano or Farinaccio) (*Sorbus aria*): up to 10 m tall; irregularly oval crown; straight trunk, often divided; grey and hairy apical branches; smooth gray-reddish bark; leaves: deciduous, elliptical egg shaped of 10x5 cm, shiny on top and white and tomentose (hairy) on the bottom side, double toothed along the margin; its look is unique and attractive since its crown, waving in the wind, flashes the large silver spot on the bottom part of each leaf; fruits: edible, apple egg shaped, 1.5 cm, orange-red when ripe, used to prepare sauces for game; the wood is very hard and was used to build the gears of wood machines.

The continental slope

The colder and harsher continental slope, is covered with beech stands from the lower elevation up. On this side of the mountain chain, beech competes for supremacy against scattered chestnut trees upwards to the tree line:

- **Common** or **European Beech** (Faggio)(*Fagus sylvatica*): majestic look, it can be 30 m tall; globe and dense crown; straight and branched trunk; typically grey and smooth bark; leaves: deciduous, elliptical egg shaped, 5 - 10 cm long and ciliated along the margin; fruits are made of two nuts (achenes) of 1.5 - 2 cm, enclosed in 4 valves; it forms stands managed for coppice and lumber; the reddish-white wood is widely used in carpentry and valued for the ease with wich it may be bent using steam; there are several different ornamental variations - **Copper Beech** (*Fagus purpurea*), *Fagus laciniata* (or heterophylla), *Fagus roseo-marginata*, **Weeping Beech** (*Fagus pendula*) - found here and there in the most human-influenced parts of the Apuane Alps.

Conclusion

The species we have described are only some of the trees and shrubs typical of the large area of the Apuane Alps. In the most human-influenced areas, close to towns, in the gardens, along the roads and around the farms, it is possible to find species which have nothing to do with the native and characteristic species of this area. The garden-like aspect of this region predominates on the Mediterranean slope; with its milder maritime climate it is mainly a residential and tourist area. Here we can enjoy the view of even the **Araucaria** (*Araucaria araucana*), **White Fir** (*Abies concolor*), **Sweet Gum** (Liquidambar) (*Liquidambar styraciflua*), **Japanese Maple** (*Acer palmatum* or *japonicum*), **Honey Locust** (Judah spines) (*Gleditsia triacanthos*), **False Cypress** (*Chamaecyparis lawsoniana*) and other imported species. Some imported trees, such as the **Douglas Fir** (*Pseudotsuga menziesii*), have become very well adapted to the climate of the Apuane Alps and have proved particularly suitable for reforestation of the mountains.

Flora References (in Italian)

1 - Aas G., Riedmiller A., *Alberi*, Editoriale Giorgio Mondadori, ISBN 88-374-1166-9

2 - Baldaccini N.E. et al., *Guida d'Italia, Natura Ambiente Paesagio*, Ed. Touring Club Italiano, 1991, ISBN 88-365-0486-8

3 - Goldstein M., Simonetti G., Watschinger M., *Guida al riconoscimeto degli alberi d'Europa*, Mondadori, IV ed.1990, ISBN 88-04-22448-7

4 - *Guida pratica agli alberi e arbusti in Italia,* Reader's Digest Selection, 1981-1989, Original Title "Nature lover's library field guide to trees and shrubs", ISBN 88-7045-037-6

5 - *Guida alle piante d'Italia e d'Europa*, Ed. Touring Club , Code G33

6 - Schauer T., Caspari C., *Guida alla identificazione delle piante*, Zanichelli,1987, ISBN 88-08-03780-0

7 - Barsella B., *Orchidaceae*, http://astr17pi.difi.unipi.it/Orchids/ (Internet)

Tree Dictionary

English	Italian	Latin
Aleppo Pine	Pino d' Aleppo	Pinus alepensis
Araucaria	Araucaria	Araucaria araucana
Ash	Frassino	Fraxinus ornus
Bald Cypress	Cipresso calvo di palude	Taxodium dysticum
Beech	Faggio	Fagus sylvatica
Birch	Betulla	Betula
Black Alder	Ontano Nero	Alnus glutinosa
Brewer Spruce	Abete di Brewer	Picea brewerana
Cedar	Cedro	Cedrus
Chestnut. see Sweet Chestnut		
Christmas Tree, Silver Fir	Abete bianco	Abies alba
Citrus	Agrume	Citrus
Common, European Ash	Frassino maggiore	Fraxinus excelsior
Common, European Beech	Faggio	Fagus sylvatica
Copper Beech	Faggio (variante purpurea)	Fagus purpurea
Cypress	Cipresso	Cupressus sempervirens
Dogwood	Corniolo	Cornus mas
Douglas Fir	Douglasia	Pseudotsuga menziesii

209

Durmast, Sessile Oak	Rovere	Quercus petraea
Eastern, Canada Hemlock	Abete o tsuga canadese	Tsuga canadensis
Eucalyptus	Eucalipto	Eucalyptus
European Hornbeam	Carpino bianco	Carpinus betulus
False Acacia	Robinia	Robinia pseudacacia
Fir	Abete	Abies
Flowering Ash	Orniello	Fraxinus ornus
Giant Fir	Abete di Vancouver	Abies grandis
Gorse	Ginestrone	Ulex europaeus
Green Alder	Ontano verde	Alnus viridis
Hazel	Nocciolo	Corylus avellana
Hemlock	Tsuga	Tsuga
Holm, Holly, Evergreen Oak	Leccio	Quercus ilex
Honey Locust	Spino di giuda	Gleditsia triacanthos
Hop Hornbeam	Carpino nero	Ostrya carpinifolia
Japanese Maple	Acero giapponese	Acer palmatum or japonicum
Larch	Larice	Larix
Laurel	Lauro	Laurus nobilis
Laurustinus	Laurotino	Viburnum tinus
Lawson Cypress	Falso Cipresso	Chamaecyparis lawsoniana
Locust	Robinia	Robinia pseudacacia

Manna Ash	Orniello	Fraxinus ornus
Maple	Acero	Acer
Maritime Pine	Pino marittimo	Pinus pinaster
Mastic Tree	Lentisco	Pistacia lentiscus
Mediterranean Buckthorn	Alaterno	Rhamnus alaternus
Mountain Ash	Sorbo degli uccellatori	Sorbus aucuparia
Mountain Hemlock	Tsuga mertensiana	Tsuga mertensiana
Myrtle	Mirto	Myrtus communis
Olive	Ulivo	Olea europaea
Oregon Cedar	Falso Cipresso	Chamaecyparis lawsoniana
Pine	Pino	Pinus
Poplar	Pioppo	Populus
Redwood	Sequoia	Sequoia sempervirens
Scotch Broom	Ginestra	Cytisus scoparius
Service Tree	Sorbo	Sorbus
Sitka Spruce	Abete di Sitka	Picea sitchensis
Southern Cypress	Cipresso calvo di palude	Taxodium dysticum
Spruce	Picea	Picea
Stone Pine	Pino domestico	Pinus pinea
Strawberry Tree	Corbezzolo	Arbutus unedo
Swamp Cypress	Cipresso calvo di palude	Taxodium dysticum
Sweet or Spanish Chestnut	Castagno	Castanea sativa

Sweet Gum	Liquidambar	Liquidambar styraciflua
Terebinth	Terebinto	Pistacia terebinthus
Tree of Heaven	Ailanto	Ailanthus altissima
Turkey, Manna Oak	Cerro	Quercus cerris
Turpentine Tree	Terebinto	Pistacia terebinthus
Umbrella Pine	Pino domestico	Pinus pinea
Weeping Beech	Faggio (variante pendula)	Fagus pendula
Western Hemlock	Abete o tsuga del Pacifico	Tsuga heterophylla
Western Red Cedar	Tuia gigante	Thuja plicata
Western White Cedar	Tuia occidentale	Thuja occidentalis
Western Yellow Pine	Pino giallo dell'Ovest	Pinus ponderosa
Whitebeam	Sorbo Montano	Farinaccio Sorbus aria
White Fir	Abete del Colorado	Abies concolor
Willow	Salice	Salix
Yew	Tasso	Taxus baccata
	Tuia orientale, Albero della vita	Thuja orientalis
	Pino strobo	Pinus strobus

Where to stay, What to eat, Where to eat, Rifugio

Where to stay

If you are planning a week or more walking in the Apuane Alps it is suggested that you should stay in two places - one on the west (Versilia) side and one on the east (Garfagnana) side.

During the visit of the Mountaineers, mentioned in the chapter "Hiking in the Apuane Alps: The Mountaineers - CAI program", the hotels used were:

- **Albergo Raffaello** in the center of Levigliani on the Versilia side. It is an inexpensive hotel. You can have room only, full pension (room, breakfast and 2 meals) or half pension (room, breakfast and one meal). The rooms are comfortable and all have a private bathroom. The rooms overlooking the valley are more spacious than those over the road. But all are quiet, since there is almost no traffic during the night. The very good restaurant serves generous portions. The speciality is *Spalla di capretto*, which is a delicious roast shoulder of kid. If you have more than 3-4 people in your party, you may ask them to prepare it over a wood-fire. It will be even tastier. This speciality is well known to the *Accademia della Cucina Italiana* (Italian Cuisine Academy); every year the Versilia branch of the Academy organizes a dinner here in order to enjoy "spalla di capretto". The hotel serves only continental breakfast, but if you ask in advance they may also provide cereal or fresh fruit.

The hotel is a very suitable base-camp for several hikes. You can start "Hike 2 - Pania della Croce" walking directly from the hotel, while it takes a few minutes by car to reach the trailhead of "Hike 23 - Monte Corchia loop", of "Hike 3 - Monte Altissimo loop", of "Hike 1 - Procinto and Monte Nona loop", of "Hike 21 - Monte Gabberi loop", and a little longer to reach the trailhead of the "Hike 4 - Penna di Sumbra", of "Hike 10 - Monte Tambura loop, from Resceto", of "Hike 11 - Monte Sella", of "Hike 16 - Monte Sagro loop, from Colonnata", of "Hike 17 - Monte Cavallo loop" and of "Hike 18 - Passo degli Uncini - Monte Carchio". And from Levigliani you can easily go to Cinque Terre or Portofino. In this case either drive to the railway station of Pietrasanta, ½ h driving, and from there take the train to La Spezia first, and then to Monterosso, or drive directly to the railway station of La Spezia, which takes about 1 h, and from there take the train to Monterosso; the best way to hike the Cinque Terre or Portofino is to use the train one way.

- **Albergo Da Carlino**, in Castelnuovo on the Garfagnana side, is upside-down, i.e. from the road you enter the hall of the hotel, but the rooms are at lower levels facing the river. The rooms are comfortable and quiet; the food is also excellent, but the portions are more Italian than American, as far as the quantity is concerned. Breakfast is continental. It is a little more expensive than the Hotel Raffaello. The hotel was our base-camp for the hikes to Monte Tambura from Arnetola (Hike 7) and Monte Forato from Fornovolasco (Hike 8). It is the ideal base-camp also for many other hikes: "Hike 20 - Monte Croce loop" from Palagnana, "Hike 13 - Pizzo d'Uccello" and "Hike 14 - Monte Pisanino" from Rifugio Donegani, and "Hike 22 - Pizzo delle Saette and Pania della Croce loop" from Piglionico.

Those who enjoy the somewhat more spartan accommodation of a rifugio, with dormitories and bunk beds but also sometimes with rooms for groups of two, three, four or six people, need not make any sacrifices in the area of food. Meals at the **rifugio Donegani** for example are excellent. This rifugio is highly recommended for the hikes in the north east of the Apuane - "Hike 6 - Pizzo d'Uccello", "Hike 13 - Pizzo di Uccello loop" and "Hike 14 - Monte Pisanino" leave directly from the rifugio, as well as the climbs - "Climb 1", "Climb 2" and "Climb 3". A complete list of the telephone numbers of the rifugio in the Apuane Alps is given below.

If there are some people in your party or family group for whom the beach and the warm sea hold a greater attraction than walking in the mountains, then **the Apuane Alps are a perfect destination**. There is a long beach stretching from Carrara to Viareggio with countless hotels, guest houses and campsites. From any point of this stretch of beach you can be in the mountains in 30 minutes.

214

Hotels around the Apuane Alps and Cinque Terre

Arni-Campagrina	*Aronte*, Via Gobbie 14, 0584 77917
Barga	*Alpino*, Via Mordini 16, 0583 723336
	Villa Libano, Via del Sasso 6, 0583 723059
Borgo a Mozzano	*Il Pescatore*, Via I maggio, 0583 88071
Castelnuovo G.	*Da Carlino,* Via Garibaldi 15, 0583 644270
	Vittoria, Piazza Umberto I, 0583 62165
Equi Terme	*Hotel la Posta,* Via Provinciale, 0585 97937
	Hotel Terme, 0585 97831
Fornovolasco	*Rifugio La Buca* (Mori Vito), 0583 722013
Framura (Cinque Terre)	*Pensione Ristorante Meri*, Costa di Framura, 0187 823059
Gallicano	*Campia*, Gallicano, 0583 766142
	Eliseo, Gallicano, 0583 74031
	Mediavalle, Gallicano, 0583 730074
Gorfigliano	*Acqua Bianca*, Via Rimesa 7, 0583 610047
	La Nina, Gorfigliano, 0583 610046
Gramolazzo	*Minihotel*, Gramolazzo, 0583 610153
Levigliani	*Raffaello*, Levigliani, 0584 778063
	Vallechiara, Levigliani, 0584 778054
Lucca	*Diana*, Via del Molinetto 11, 0583 492202
Manarola (Cinque Terre)	*Marina Piccola*, Manarola, 0187 920103
Molazzana	*Il Falco*, Molazzana, 0583 760030
Piazza al Serchio	*Bertolini*, Via Roma 42, 0583 60003
	Il Pisanino, P.za Giov. XXIII, 0583 696208
Pietrasanta	*Da Piero*, Via Traversagna 3, 0584 790031
	Stipino, Via Provinciale 50, 0584 71448
Vagli di Sotto	*La Guardia*, Fraz. Roggio, 0583 663001
	Le Alpi, Via Vandelli 8, 0583 664057

Should you prefer luxurious and memorable accommodations, you can try:

Pisa	*Villa di Corliano*, in an old villa in Rigoli 3 km from San Giuliano Terme along the old road toward Lucca, 050 818193. Annexed to the hotel is *Da Sergio*, one of the best restaurants in Tuscany
Lucca	*Villa La Principessa* , Massa Pisana, 4 km south of Lucca, on the State road "Del Brennero" 1600, 0583 370037
Barga	*il Ciocco*, 6 km from Barga, 55020 Castelvecchio Pascoli, 0583 7191
Camogli	*il Cenobio dei Dogi*, via Cuneo 34, 0185 770041

What to eat

Tuscany is well known for its medieval towns, the art treasures in its museums, ancient palaces and monuments, Medici villas, beautiful rolling landscapes with old farm houses and tall cypresses. It is famous also for its succulent, simple and tasty, Mediterranean cuisine, highlighted by dry Chianti wine. In addition to the well known Tuscan recipes described in almost all Italian cookery books, we would like to tell you about some of the more unusual dishes, which may not be known even to people from elsewhere in Tuscany. The specialities are very typical of Garfagnana, Lunigiana and Versilia, and you can enjoy them while in the area of the Alps of Tuscany. It is a unique cultural experience that you should not miss. Food in this area is fresh and homemade, traditionally prepared and served, and usually inexpensive.

Buon Appetito!

First courses

- *Farinata*: a special soup common in Lucca and Garfagnana. It is made of beans, maize flour, *lardo* and a special kind of cabbage, called in Italian *cavolo nero*, i.e. black cabbage. In Versilia this is called *Intruglia*.

- *Garmugia*: a soup of fresh vegetables: peas, broad beans (*fave* in Italian), artichokes (cut in small pieces) and asparagus. Enjoy the soup with toasted bread placed in the bottom of your soup plate.

- *Minestra di farro*: this is a local traditional soup made with a particular grain, called "Triticum spelta" and "borlotti", or better "lucchesi", beans. "Triticum spelta" is a wheat native to southern Europe and western Asia.

- *Panigacci*: flat, round bread "cakes", cooked between two *testi*, flat, terracotta plates, heated on a wood fire. They are piled one on top of the other with the bread dough in between. Panigacci are served with salami (*pancetta, coppa, lardo, prosciutto, salame toscano*) and a particularly creamy cheese, called *stracchino*.

- *Ravioli di ricotta*: small squares of pasta filled with ricotta cheese and spinach. They are served with a sauce of butter and sage, and grated cheese. "Raviolo" (singular of ravioli) means a little turnip.

- *Tagliatelle ai funghi:* long flat egg noodles seasoned with a mushroom sauce. The name "tagliatelle" comes from "taliare" (Latin) which means to cut. Here tagliatelle are usually homemade and in season the mushrooms are wild and fresh. In other seasons the mushrooms are usually dried.

- *Tagliarini con i fagioli*: a soup with long, flat, slender pieces of pasta, narrower than "tagliatelle", and beans.

- *Testaroli al pesto*: panigacci, either whole or in pieces, are boiled in water and served with pesto sauce. It may also be dressed with a tomato sauce.

If you hike this part of the Apuane Alps, you may enjoy Panigacci and Testaroli al Pesto at the *Ristorante La Gavarina d'Oro*, on the Via Castello, Podenzana, Aulla (0187 410021, closed on Wednesday). To find the restaurant, once you are in Aulla, follow the road signs to Podenzana. It is on the other side of the Magra River, which flows through Aulla. Cross the bridge and drive on the road going upward. You will pass under a bridge of the motorway Parma-La Spezia, and continue for about 5 km. At the junction with the road to the Castle (blue road sign to Casalina, Castello and Caviana), turn right on the road to the Ristorante La Gavarina d'Oro (you see the brown sign at the junction). There are several restaurants along the way, all good, but at La Gavarina d'Oro you can see panigacci cooking on a special hearth. You may also enjoy Panigacci and Testaroli at the *Rifugio Forte dei Marmi*. They are very good and homemade.

- *Testaroli alla Palagnina*: this is a slightly different version of the usual "testaroli". The dough is made of a mixture of wheat and maize flour. That is all. "Alla Palagnina" means that this way of preparing testaroli is found in Palagnana (on the Garfagnana side of the Apuane Alps).

- *Tordelli di* (or *alla*) *carne*: "tordelli" is the local spelling for "tortelli", which are small twisted wrappings of fresh egg pasta filled with meat (*carne* in Italian) and cheese.

Main courses

- *Coniglio* or *cervo alla cacciatora*: rabbit or deer stewed at length in a sauce of vegetables, dried mushrooms and wine.

- *Polenta e funghi*: polenta is a kind of porridge of maize and is served in this case with mushrooms. In Autumn the more frequently used mushrooms are wild "porcini" (*Boletus edulis*, Cep or Penny Bun in English), while in the other seasons they usually use dried porcini.

- *Spalla di capretto*: roast shoulder of kid. At the *Hotel Raffaello*, in Levigliani the food is excellent and "spalla di capretto" is their main speciality. Every year the Versilia members of the *Accademia della Cucina Italiana* schedule their annual meeting here at the Hotel Raffaello to enjoy the "spalla di capretto".

Snacks

- *Castagnaccio*: a cake made of chestnut flour, water and a little olive oil, with pine nuts and rosemary on top.

- *Cecina*: a flat layer of fresh chick-pea dough with a little olive oil on top, baked in a wood fired oven. It is served in small sections.

- *Focaccia con lardo di Colonnata*: *focaccia* is a flat homemade bread, which in this case is filled with the special lardo from Colonnata and toasted. Colonnata is a town on the Versilia side, very close to Carrara.

It is just the right snack after a long hiking day: enjoy it with a glass of local wine. On Sunday you can find a tasty focaccia and lardo at the *Trattoria La Romana* (0584 789023), a couple of km past the tunnel *Galleria del Cipollaio* on the Garfagnana side, on your right on the main road toward Castelnuovo Garfagnana.

- *Schiacciata*: a flat layer of wheat dough, baked in a wood fired oven, with or without a little olive oil on top. It is served in small or large sections, according to your instructions.

In Tuscany, in almost every Pizzeria you can find "schiacciata", "cecina" and "castagnaccio", but a place you should not miss is the *Bar Pasticceria Pizzeria Ghimenti*, in Pietrasanta, Piazza Statuto 12/13, 0584 70664, where the stone pizza oven is all fired up and ready to go at any time and the schiacciata, cecina, "cinque più cinque" and castagnaccio are really exceptional. Do you know what "cinque più cinque" stands for? In Italian you read "cinque più cinque", literally five plus five (5 + 5), which simply means the cents which were necessary a long time ago to buy a piece of schiacciata (five cents) with inside it a piece of cecina (another five cents). It is a tradition of the Alpine Club of Pisa to never pass by the town of Pietrasanta without stopping at Ghimenti for schiacciata.

Special side courses

- *Panzanella* or *Pasta fritta*: is a round piece of wheat dough fried in olive oil; "pasta fritta" or "panzanelle" (plural of panzanella) are served with salami and/or cheese. There may be ambiguity in the name, since in Firenze and in Napoli "panzanella" is based on hard bread softened in water and vinegar, and slices of cucumber, onions, tomatoes, basil, olives and olive oil.

- *Polenta fritta*: polenta is a kind of maize porridge; when hard, it is cut in slices and fried in olive oil. It is used mainly as a side course or it is served while waiting for the first course.

Special Pastries

- *Bomboloni* and *Frati*: are like doughnuts, "bomboloni" are sphere-shaped sometimes with jam or cream inside, while "frati" are round with a hole in the middle. Both are fried in olive oil and sprinkled with sugar.

- *Budino di riso*: is another kind of pastry filled with rice.

- *Sfoglia alla mela* and *sfoglia di riso*: "sfoglia" is a flacky pastry which is filled with fresh apple or rice respectively; very good with a cappuccino in the morning.

Other specialities in Tuscany

- *Bistecca alla Fiorentina*: a thick T-bone beef steak, part sirloin and part fillet, usually served rare. The name "bistecca" comes from the English "beef steak"; misspelling or/and mispronunciation? In Firenze you can find a delicious bistecca at the typical Florentine restaurant *Latini*, in via dei Palchetti 6, 055 210916, or at *Buca Lapi*, in via del Trebbio 1, 055 213768.

- *Bordatino*: is a soup made of maize flour, beans and vegetables, and is typical of Livorno and Pisa. It seems that this speciality was used by Pisan sailors while on board, in order to vary their normal diet based on fish. On board is *a bordo* in Italian, from which comes the name of the dish.

- *Brigidini di Lamporecchio*: aniseed flavored cookies as thin as a leaf, made in Lamporecchio, a town close to Pistoia in Tuscany.

- *Bruschetta*: a piece of bread, first toasted and then rubbed with garlic, and with olive oil, salt, pepper and sometimes with small pieces of tomato on top.

- *Cacciucco*: is a fish soup, typical of Livorno. It reminds one of the French *bouillabaisse*.

- *Cantuccini di Prato* (and *Vin Santo*): hard cookies from Prato (a town close to Firenze), which are softened by dipping them in a strong sweet Tuscan wine called "Vin Santo".

- *Cee alla salvia*: "cee" is the Tuscan pronunciation for "cieche" in Italian, they are baby eels less than half a centimeter long. They are fished at the mouth of the Arno river in January and February. They are sautéd in olive oil, garlic and sage leaves, and, once cooked, covered with bread crumbs, Parmesan cheese and fresh lemon juice.

- *Fagioli al forno*: literally they are beans which are baked. You find them at the restaurant of the Hotel Carignano in Lucca.

- *Panforte di Siena*: is a hard cake with almonds, dried and candied fruits and spices. It is typical of Siena, hence the name.

- *Panini Tartufati*: a small delicate sandwich filled with truffle patè, which you can find at *Procacci*, in via de' Tornabuoni 64, Firenze.

- *Pappa al pomodoro*: is a soup of tomatoes with basil, pepper, garlic and olive oil. Very common in Firenze.

- *Pecorino con baccelli* or *pere*: simply a piece of "pecorino" cheese served with fresh broad beans or a pear.

- *Prosciutto alla crosta*: is a whole ham, crusted and baked. It is served hot in slices. You can find it at the *Hotel Carignano*, Via per S. Alessio 3680, located at about 5 - 6 km from the center of Lucca.

- *Ricciarelli di Siena*, diamond shaped cookies made with a paste of pounded almonds and vanilla. Like the panforte, "ricciarelli" are typical of Siena.

- *Seppie con le bietole*: literally cuttlefish and bok-choy; it is mainly a stew of cuttlefish, tomatoes and bok-choy.

- *Torbone*: it is coffee with rum usually served after dinner. It seems that you can find the best torbone at the *Bar Civili*, Via D.Vigna, 55 in Livorno.

- *Triglie alla livornese*: red mullet sautéd in a fresh tomato sauce. Typical of Livorno.

- *Verdure in pinzimonio*: a mixture of fresh vegetables, including celery, fennel, artichoke, carrot, which you dip in a blend of olive oil, salt and pepper. It is very common as an appetizer.

When hiking in Liguria, you can find these specialities

- *Focaccia al formaggio*: flat bread with cheese inside,

- *Gianchet*: very small fish, sometimes baby sardines, coated with egg and bread crumbs and deep-fried,

- *Mesciua*: a soup with chick-peas, beans and wheat grains,

- *Pansotti*: a kind of ravioli stuffed with cheese and chard, and served with a creamy walnut sauce,

- *Sciacchetrà*: a local strong and sweet dessert wine,

- *Trenette al pesto*: a special kind of pasta with pesto sauce,

- *Trofie al pesto*: small dumplings with pesto sauce,

- *Vino delle Cinque Terre*: local dry white wine,

- *Zuppa di tartufi*: local shell fish soup, very difficult to find, expensive, but worth the price.

Where to eat

Restaurants in Garfagnana

Arni	*Trattoria La Romana*, Tre Fiumi, 0584 789023
Aulla, Podenzana	*La Gavarina d'Oro*, Via Castello, Podenzana, 0187 410021
Capanne di Careggine	*La Ceragetta*, Via Ceragetta 5, 0583 667065
Castelnuovo G.	*Da Carlino*, Via Garibaldi 13, 0583 644270
Equi Terme	*Hotel Posta*, Via Provinciale, 0585 97937
Gallicano	*Eliseo*, Gallicano, 0583 74031
Gombitelli	*Cerù*, Gombitelli, 0584 971901
Isola Santa	*Ristorante Giaccò,* 0583 667048
Lucca	*Giulio in Pelleria*, Via delle Conce 45, 0583 55948
	Hotel Carignano, Via per S. Alessio 3680, 0583 329618
	Vecchia Trattoria Buralli, Piazza S. Agostino 10, 0583 950611
Palagnana	*Circolo Sant' Anna* (Pietro Tommasi), 0584 776004
	Locanda dalla Gè, 0584 776050
Vagli di Sopra	*Bar Pizzeria Coltelli*, Via Vandelli 2, (pizza only in summer), 0583 664058
Vagli di Sotto	*Trattoria del Pescatore*, Bivio Al Ponte, 0583 664052

Gelateria in Garfagnana which should not be missed

Castelnuovo G.	*Baiocchi*, Piazza Umberto I, try "Alexander" (vanilla, cream and rum)
Ponte a Moriano	*Sauro*, Via del Brennero (on the road from Lucca at the entrance of the town, on the left)

Restaurants in Versilia and Cinque Terre

Azzano	*Clara*, Via Cappella 81, 0584 773250
Campiglia	*La Luna*, Piazza della Chiesa 2, 0187 758220
Campo Cecina	*Bar Ristorante Il Belvedere*, 0585 841973
Colonnata	*Venanzio*, Piazza Palestro 3, 0585 73617
	Locanda Apuana, Via Comunale 1, 0585 768017
Casoli	*Domenici*, Località Tre Scogli, 0584 988019
Farnocchia	*Bar Trattoria Franca*, Piazza IV Novembre 1/2, 0584 777022
La Spezia	*Caran*, via Genova 1, 0187 703777, very old and typical restaurant, local food
Levanto	*La Giada del Mesco*, 0187 808705
Levigliani	*Raffaello*, Levigliani, 0584 778063
Livorno	*Antico Moro*, Via di Franco 59, 0586 884659
Mulina di Stazzema	*Trattoria Luciana*, Via Provinciale 33, 0584 777008
Pasquilio (Massa)	*La Gotica*, Via E. Pea 28, 0585 819230
Pietrasanta	*Da Piero*, Via Traversagna 3, 0584 790031
	Da Beppino, Via Valdicastello Carducci 34, 0584 790400
Pisa	*Trattoria S. Omobono*, Piazza Santomobono
	La Cereria, via P.Gori 33, 050 20336
	I Quattro Venti, Molina di Quosa, 050 850109
Portovenere	*Taverna del Corsaro*, calata Doria 102, 0187 900622, very nice but expensive
Riomaggiore	*Da Natale*, Telegrafo, 0187 920792
Resceto	*Circolo Arci*, Resceto, 0585 315182
Seravezza	*Giardino dei Medici*, 0584 757339
Terrinca	*da Tassilone*, 0584 778140

And for a snack, a Bar which should not be missed

Pietrasanta	*Bar Pasticceria Pizzeria Ghimenti*, Piazza Statuto, 12/13, 0584 70664 (schiacciata, cecina, "cinque più' cinque", castagnaccio)

Rifugio

CAI Rifugio in the Apuane Alps

Rifugio Aronte (1642 m), Passo Focolaccia, unmanned
Capanna Garnerone (1300 m), unmanned
Rifugio Carrara (1100 m), Campo Cecina   0585 841972
Rifugio Città di Massa (900 m), Pian della Fioba   0585 319923
Rifugio Rossi alla Pania (1609 m)   0583 710386
Rifugio Forte dei Marmi (865 m), Alpe della Grotta   0584 777051
Rifugio Del Freo or Pietrapana (1180 m), Mosceta   0584 778007
Rifugio Donegani (1122 m), Orto di Donna   0583 610085

Private Rifugio

Albergo Alto Matanna (1030 m), Pian d'Orsina   0584 776005
                drinks & food only
Rifugio Nello Conti (1400 m), Via Vandelli   0585 793059

Warning: A rifugio may not always be open, therefore please call before going. It could be very disappointing to find a rifugio closed, especially after a very strenuous hike, when you are tired, hungry and thirsty. In general, rifugio are open every day from the middle of June to the middle of September (for example Rifugio Forte dei Marmi and Rifugio Del Freo), some are open in July and August only (for example Rifugio Rossi). Rifugio Città di Massa is open from May to September. Almost all are open on holidays only for the rest of the year. On request they may open even for quite small groups.

The Alpine Club of Italy (CAI)

Fabio Salomoni

The Alpine Club of Italy (CAI) was founded on August 12, 1863 by Quintino Sella, a scientist and a statesman from Biella (close to Turin). After climbing M. Monviso, the mountain in which the river Po rises, Quintino Sella had the idea of forming a club for Italian mountaineers similar to the ones started in the previous year in Great Britain and in Austria, and only few months earlier in Switzerland. At first CAI had its only location in Turin. Later branches were opened in Aosta, Agordo, Firenze, Napoli, Sondrio, Bergamo, Roma, Milano, Cuneo, Lecco, and eventually in many other places, from big cities to small towns, from the Alps to the South - it almost immediately became a nationwide organisation. After the first World War two main Associations, rich in history and experience, the *Societa' degli Alpinisti Tridentini* (Association of the Tridentine mountaineers) and *Societa' Alpina delle Giulie* (Alpine Association of Julian Alps) became sections of CAI. The success of CAI is based on the enthusiasm of its members and on their voluntary activities. This has been the driving force which has made possible the wide range of facilities CAI provides for mountain lovers:

- **719 rifugio** (manned or unmanned huts), bivouacs, shelters in the Alps, Apennines and Islands; included in these figures are the rifugio in the Apuane Alps listed in the chapter 'Where to stay, What to eat, Where to eat, Rifugio". All CAI rifugio are listed in Internet at: http://www.racine.ra.it/cailugo;

- **457 sections**, the Milano branch was founded in 1874, Florence in 1868, Pisa in 1926;
- **220 sections** of the National Alpine & Speleological Rescue Corps, with over 6,800 volunteers;
- a **National Alpine Library**, located in Torino;
- a **National Museum** (*Museo della Montagna*), located in Torino.

As for CAI people, at the end of 1995, there were :

- **563 National Instructors** of Alpinism;
- **1320 leaders** and assistants, in addition to national field experts, national alpine youth leaders, glacier surveyors, rangers charged with the protection of the mountain environment, national avalanche experts;
- more than **318,000 members** all over Italy (at the end of 1996).

All this makes CAI, including its Pisa section, a tremendously effective and influential organization in promoting all mountaineering activities, including research and exploration in the mountains and the preservation of their environment.

Amongst the 500 members of the Pisa section are two national instructors of Alpinism, four instructors of Alpinism, eighteen assistants of Alpinism, three ski-mountaineering instructors, three mountaineering leaders and many volunteer hike leaders. The Pisa section is divided into several groups: Alpinism, Speleological, Hiking, Cross-country Skiing, Ski mountaineering, Alpine Skiing. Each group has available gear to rent (ropes, crampons, ice-axes, helmets, skis, harness). A library with a large choice of mountaineering books and a complete *Monti d' Italia* (Mountains of Italy) book collection is available to the members. Through its courses on rock-climbing and winter alpinism the Pisa section encourages a new generation to enjoy the world of the mountains, so rich in history and traditions, by improving their technical skills and general knowledge of hiking and climbing.

The Mountaineers

Dianne Hoff

The Mountaineers, founded in 1906, is a non-profit outdoor activity and conservation club, whose mission is "to explore, study, preserve and enjoy the natural beauty of the outdoors...." Based in Seattle, Washington, the club is now the third largest such organization in the United States, with 15,000 members, five branches throughout Washington State, and members throughout the world.

The Mountaineers sponsors both classes and year-round outdoor activities in the Pacific Northwest, which include hiking, mountain climbing, ski-touring, snow shoeing, bicycling, camping, kayaking and canoeing, nature study, sailing, and adventure travel. The club's conservation division supports environmental causes through educational activities, sponsoring legislation, and presenting informational programs. All club activities are led by skilled, experienced volunteers, who are dedicated to promoting safe and responsible enjoyment and preservation of the outdoors.

The club's International Exchange activities were begun in 1993 to enhance our mountaineering, environmental, recreational and organizational skills; to encourage personal relationships, common initiatives and interests, and share skills with members of similar clubs in other countries and cultures; and to extend to the world the purposes of The Mountaineers.

The Mountaineers Books, an active, non-profit publishing program of the club, produces guidebooks, instructional texts, historical works, natural history guides, and works on environmental conservation.

Mountaineering: The Freedom of the Hills, written and published by The Mountaineers, has been the "bible" of the climbing world for over 30 years; it is used by the U.S. Military and by mountaineering clubs in the United States and many countries of the world as a comprehensive guide to the sport of mountaineering. All books produced by The Mountaineers are aimed at fulfilling the club's mission.

The ten essentials

Just how much and what kind of gear to take on a trip into the mountains is a subject for considerable debate. But The Mountaineers and a majority of climbers and hikers agree that the Ten Essentials are the best insurance for a safe and comfortable trip:

1. Map
2. Compass
3. Flashlight/headlamp with spare bulbs and batteries
4. Extra food
5. Extra clothing
6. Sunglasses, sunscreen
7. First aid supplies
8. Pocket knife
9. Matches in waterproof container
10. Fire starter

Group Size Limits: It is the policy of The Mountaineers to promote a "wilderness experience" through limiting the size of our trips to 12 people. Most American land management agencies and the national and state park systems have similar requirements.

The CAI/Mountaineer International Exchange

Italy, 1995; Washington, USA, 1996

We believe you will enjoy the beauty of the Apuane Alps as we did and invite you to try the hikes listed here. And, although strikingly different from Apuane, the beauty of the Pacific Northwest is unique in the world. If you love majestic mountains, glaciers, vast forests, wildlife, rugged sea coasts, mountain lakes and wild rivers, you will love our home.

We found an astonishing compatibility between CAI and The Mountaineers, and among the members of the two clubs. In the belief that this compatibility will be found in many other people and organizations in the world, we invite you who read this guide to contact

CAI or The Mountaineers. We would like to explore an exchange relationship with your similarly minded organization.

"We are eager for clean, blue skies, long reaches of sea and plain, great spreading forests and the romance and inspiration of our country that is in the mountains and the sea. As we spend our days occupied with the tasks of tilling, making, buying and selling, our hearts long for the summits, the seas and the green slopes. We escape when we can, never to return as we were." (Henry Suzzallo, President of the University of Washington, 1920's, and Mountaineer).

Hiking in the Apuane Alps:
The Mountaineers-CAI program

October 17 - November 1, 1995

THE MOUNTAINEERS - CAI

HIKING IN THE APUANE ALPS
October 17 - November 1, 1995

(Classifications: E = Easy, M = Moderate, S = Strenuous)

October 17 - Arrival in Milano (Malpensa, Linate)

Tuesday   Milano- Pisa , by car and Van
           Lunch at the
           Ristorante La Garavina D'Oro (Panigacci), Podenzana
           CAI Section : Pisa Hosts and Guests Get Together
           Dinner at the *Trattoria S. Omobono*, Pisa
           Night in Pisa

October 18 - Visit to Pisa and Lucca
Wednesday   Calci, *Museo di Storia Naturale* of the University of Pisa
            Dinner at the *Agriturismo Omberaldi* Calci
            Night in Pisa

October 19 - Monte Nona loop (M: 6 h, 10 Km, 850 m gain)
Thursday   -Stazzema (439 m)
            -Rifugio Forte dei Marmi (868 m)
            -Callare Procinto
            -Callare Matanna (1130 m)
            -Monte Nona (1279 m)
            -Foce delle Porchette (982 m)
            -Stazzema
            Visit to Stazzema
            Night in Levigliani: Hotel Raffaello

October 20 - Pania della Croce (S: 9 h, 16 Km, 1250 m gain)
Friday   -Levigliani (600 m)
            -Rifugio del Freo (1180 m)
            -Monte Pania della Croce (1859 m)
            -Levigliani
            Night in Levigliani: Hotel Raffaello

October 21- Saturday	Monte Altissimo loop (M: 6.5 h, 10 Km, 700 m gain)

October 21-   Monte Altissimo loop (M: 6.5 h, 10 Km, 700 m gain)
Saturday   -Colle del Cipollaio (990 m)
               -Foce Falcovaia (1194 m), marble quarry (Le Cervaiole)
               -Monte Altissimo (1589 m)
               -Colle del Cipollaio
               Castagnata at Le Piane Alte (Giuliano's home)
               Night in Levigliani: Hotel Raffaello

October 22 -   Penna di Sumbra (S: 8 h, 15 Km, 900 m gain)
Sunday   -Arni (916 m)
               -Passo Fiocca (1550 m)
               -Penna di Sumbra (1765 m)
               -Capanne di Careggine (840 m)
               Night in Levigliani: Hotel Raffaello

October 23 -   5 Terre (E: 5 h, 10 Km, 500 m gain)
Monday   -Monterosso, Vernazza, Corniglia, Manarola and
               Riomaggiore
               Dinner at the *Trattoria Pozzo di Bugia*, Querceta (Lucca)
               Night in Pisa

October 24 -   Visit to Volterra and San Gimignano
Tuesday   Dinner at the *Vecchia Cantina Formichi*, Cascina
               CAI section of Pisa: slide projection by Dianne Hoff
               Night in Pisa

October 25 -   Monte Sagro (E: 5 h, 7 Km, 500 m gain)
Wednesday   -Foce di Pianza (1279 m)
               -Foce della Faggiola (1426 m)
               -Monte Sagro (1749 m)
               -Foce di Pianza
               -Night in Levigliani: Hotel Raffaello
               Dancing with *Dome'* and *Vitto'* (fisarmonica)

October 26 -   Pizzo d' Uccello (M: scrambling, 6 h, 6 Km, 650 m gain)
Thursday   -Rifugio Donegani (1200 m)
               -Foce di Giovo (1500 m)
               -Pizzo d'Uccello (1781 m)
               Lunch at the Rifugio Donegani
               Night in Levigliani: Hotel Raffaello
               Music with *Dome'* (fisarmonica) and *Leslie* (guitar)

October 27 - Friday
Monte Tambura (S: 6.5 h, 10 Km, 1000 m gain)
-Arnetola (900 m)
-Passo Tambura (1620 m)
-Monte Tambura (1890 m)
-Arnetola - from Arnetola to Castelnuovo Garfagnana, by car
Meeting at the CAI section of Castelnuovo Garfagnana
Night in Castelnuovo Garfagnana: Hotel Carlino

October 28 - Saturday
Monte Forato loop (M: 6 h, 8 Km, 800 m gain)
-Fornovolasco (480 m)
-Foce di Petrosciana (961 m)
-Monte Forato (1223 m)
-Foce di Valli (1266 m)
-Fornovolasco
Dinner with the Pisa Hosts and Night in Pisa

October 29 - Sunday
Tradizionale Castagnata CAI: Monte Pisano (E: 3 h,5 Km, 450 m gain)
-Montemagno (150 m), by car
-Verruca (537 m)
-Capanna *Le Mandrie* (395 m)
-Vico Pisano (Visit to the town)
Dinner at the *Ristorante Gimmy*, S. Giovanni alla Vena
Night in Pisa

October 30 - Monday
Departure for Milano,
Lunch at the *Ristorante La Garavina* D'Oro (Panigacci), Podenzana
Milano Hosts and Guests Get Together and Dinner at the *Clubino Rossini*
Night in Milano

October 31 - Tuesday
Visit to Milano
Dinner at the *Pizza Pazza*, Piazza S. Stefano
Meeting at the CAI section of Milano: slide projection by Dianne Hoff
Night in Milano

November 1 - Wednesday
End

CLIMBING AND CAVING

CLIMBING

Rock-climbing Instructors of the CAI section of Pisa are available to offer you their assistance for the following climbs during the weekends.
Climbs are classified according to the UIAA rating system.

M. Procinto: I Bimbi, 200 m gain, 3
                      East wall, 200 m gain, different routes from 5 to 8
                      North Wall, 100 m gain, from 4 to 6

Pania Group: Torrioni del Corchia, 300 m gain, from 3 to 7

5 Terre: Muzzerone, 200 m gain, from 5 to 9

Vinca- Donegani area
                      M. Garnerone - South Wall, 200 m gain,
                        from 4 to 8+
                      Torre di Monzone, 300 m gain, from 5 to 7+
                      Pizzo d'Uccello, North Wall, 700 m gain,
                      from 4 to 7+

CAVING

In the Apuane Alps there are more than 600 caves. Very close to Levigliani there is one of the most interesting caves of Europe, An-tro del Corchia, a little more than 1200 m deep.
Exploration of the *Antro del Corchia* or of other caves can be arranged for you by the Speleological Group of the CAI section of Pisa.

Welcome to Italy !

Arriving in Italy you may find a lot of differences, some good, others not, but it is useful to know about all of them in advance.

About People: In Italy you do not see people calm and relaxed as you can see in other countries. People here seem to be running as if they had urgent appointments or urgent matters to attend to. Sometimes they seem arrogant, rude, serious, unsmiling like VIP people too busy to smile. This is especially true in Milano, maybe less in Pisa or in other small towns. But everywhere there will be a lot of people, a crowd all around you (does it seem more crowded because of the lack of order?). When they are in groups, they are usually very loud. Are they really like they seem? They do not seem happy, do not smile at you, they seem even unkind, but after a few words with them, they may change completely. They are gentle, smiling, willing to help you and maybe even shy.

About Public Transportation: Public transportation is provided by the local public organization, in Milano for example by ATM (which is not the acronym for Automatic Teller Machine, but for *Azienda Trasporti Milanese*). There are busses in almost every town, in some big cities there are colorful trams, and only in Rome and Milano are there Metropolitana (Underground). In Milano, the underground stations are indicated by MM , and there are 3 routes: 1 - the red; 2 - the green; and 3 - the yellow.

No busses or trams have wheelchair lifts, and there are no Free Ride Areas.

About Bus Tickets: You enter the bus or tram, but where to buy the ticket? Here is a funny rule. You cannot buy tickets on board. You have to buy them outside in shops like *Giornali* (newspapers) or *Tabacchi* or other shops. So you have to go down and try to find one of the above shops open. Fortunately, tickets do not cost too much. You can use them on all routes in town, but only once in the underground.

When you succeed in finding a ticket distributor, please buy as many tickets as you may need while in town, and even more. When you enter the bus, you have to obliterate the ticket. Do you know such a word? In Italian we say *obliterare*, a very uncommon word surely unknown to many Italians. Nevertheless the ATM as well as the similar organizations throughout Italy, adopted such an archaic word. According to the Microsoft Bookshelf 1994 - Dictionary, *obliterate* means "to wipe out, rub off or erase (writing or other markings)"; it comes from the Latin "ob litteras scribere". For us it means that you have to insert the ticket in a machine which prints on it the time and is located in the Bus or in the MM station at the entrance.

There are different kind of tickets, some can be used only once, others may last 60, 75, 120 minutes, others half a day and even longer. Ask before buying tickets. If your ticket lasts for a period of time, when that time is over and you are still in the bus, you have to obliterate another ticket! Very far from the normal understanding, this is the rule! Unfortunately just recently the Railway Company (*Ferrovie dello Stato*) has adopted the same system for the train tickets. So, when you buy a train ticket before taking the train you have to obliterate your ticket. Do not forget to do it: the fine for not obliterating your ticket is very high!

About Traffic: When the Bus starts the ride, do not panic! Cars, taxis, busses all frenetically passing close to the Bus, in front of it or beside it. Along the road towards Milano you can see painted lanes on the pavement; but they disappear once you enter the town. Do not worry, the Bus driver is used to it and, despite the visible chaos, there are rules and traffic guards. For the main driving differences between USA and Italy see the chapter *Driving in Italy*.

About "Bar", "Caffè": Usually you stand while ordering, paying and enjoying your "cappuccino" or whatever you asked for. Unless you are terribly tired, do not sit down at the tables around, if any, for the price may suddenly double!

Cappuccini (plural of cappuccino) are wonderful. The coffee here is much stronger and served in a very small quantity. It is like a drug and not a hot drink like in other countries. Together with cappuccino try the *brioche*, plain or with either jam or cream. In Pisa, or in Tuscany in general, you should not miss the *sfoglia alla mela* or simply *mela* (apple), a unique wonderful local brioche, or *budino di riso*.

Unfortunately *Bar* or *Caffe'* do not serve American or English breakfast, and nor do the Restaurants. But around noon in Bar and Caffe' you'll find a variegated display of nuts, chips, bruschette, black or green ripe olives, and many other things, ready to be enjoyed with your *aperitivo*. Very common in Milano, less so in Pisa. Aperitivo can be a glass of wine (usually dry white sparkling wine), vermouth (either Martini or Cinzano), Bitter Campari, Campari soda, or the *aperitivo della casa*, either sweet or dry, but almost always alcoholic. If you do not want alcoholic aperitivo you should explicitly ask for it. The cost of an aperitivo should be around 3500-4000 lire, and it is worth having.

About Restaurants: Restaurants may be very expensive, especially in big towns. To the price of the courses you usually have to add the *"coperto"* plus the service charge. The service does not mean the tip the waiter is expecting from you; in Italy you may leave 5 % of the bill, and not the exaggerated percentage used in the States, and the waiter is still very happy.

In Italy the structure of a meal is different from the structure you may be used to. Here a meal may start with *antipasti* (appetizers), almost everybody, unless they have weight problems, is going to have a *primo piatto*, which means the first course. It could be a soup as well as *spaghetti* or other kind of pasta. Usually this course is not so generous as in the States, nor is it submerged in a mountain of tomato and meat sauce. Sauces here are meant to dress the pasta not to provide the eater with all the proteins he/she needs for a week. Then the main course follows, *secondo piatto* as called in Italy. Here is another big difference, the main course does not come with fixed side dishes, called *contorni*. You have to choose them from the list (and the cost of the contorni will be added to the cost of the main course). You may see this also as an advantage for you, since you can design your main course as you like and in detail.

The last but not the least difference is that for dinner the main course does not come with a soup or salad and dessert included.

You design the entire meal, from the appetizers to the dessert, or cheese, to conclude.

Restaurants are not open all the day. They are open only during lunch and dinner time: i.e. from noon to 2:00-2:30 pm and at the earliest from 7:00 to 10:00-12:00 pm. Restaurants do not serve breakfast nor Tea or coffee during the day or at tea-time.

About Walking in Town: As soon as you walk along the streets of a big, or recently even small town, a multitude of beggars, cigarette smugglers, people wanting to sell you counterfeited products, and, if you drive, window-cleaners will be all around you. You may wonder why the Italian Authorities allow this. So do I. To survive you have to resist the assault without talking with these people, without answering their questions, without caring for them. It seems cruel, but it is the only thing to do to survive. And be careful, watch for thieves. They are around, especially in busses, undergrounds, railway stations or wherever people are. In particular watch for young people, sometime young Gypsies (Italian law does not permit young people to be kept in prison; if caught, they will be released immediately, and so they start again the endless loop).

Walking in town you may have a claustrophobic feeling: you are suffocated by cars, some parked in single or double file and others running along the road; and in addition the parking spots are not marked.

You may see one of the most unusual records in the Guiness book: the smallest possible space, if any, between parked cars. Cars are parked everywhere, on the sidewalks and even in the driveway for the wheelchairs. Probably this is one of the reasons that you do not see wheelchairs in the streets. Another reason may be that busses do not have wheelchair lifts. Or maybe there are no disabled people in town!

About Alcohol: Except for the usual limitations about the Blood Alcohol Concentration (BAC, which by the way are the initial letters of Bacchus, the God of wine) while driving, there are no other restrictions: you may have your bottle of wine in the car, unsealed I mean, without infringing any rule, or in a National Park or wherever you are.

About Trains: The railway system in Italy is good. Trains are very frequent for short and long distances. They are cheap and people use them very often, but not so frequently as they should. Even in Italy the lobby of the car companies is very powerful. And not everything is perfect: trains may be late and may be very crowded, and both things may happen together and frequently. Almost every town has a train station; Milano has several, Pisa only 2. In any town, the main station is called *Stazione Centrale.*

To take a train you need a train ticket, which you may buy at the train station or at almost any Travel Agency. And **remember to obliterate** the ticket as soon as you enter the station or anywhere before taking the train. But as usual, in Italy things should not be very simple: the Authorities try desperately to not let Italians be ever relaxed. The price of the train tickets depend not only on the distance of the trip, but also on the kind of train you are going to take. So, if your train is an *Intercity* you must pay a *supplemento*, in other words an additional fare. At other times, for special trains, you are required to pay a fee for booking your seat (*prenotazione obbligatoria*). So, when you buy a ticket, tell the ticket agent which train you are going to take, and be sure that your ticket includes everything (supplemento and prenotazione obbligatoria, if any). It seems that just recently almost all trains have become Intercity. By this means the cost of the train ticket has been doubled but the inflation rate has remained unchanged.

About Shops: In Italy shops are more often closed than open. No shops are open on Sunday, nor during the night. You never see 24 h/day and 7 days/week shops in Italy! Only recently, despite Vatican objections, a few shops in the center of Milano are staying open for a few hours on Sunday.

Therefore you should plan well in advance what to buy and mainly when to buy. You may find yourself starving, if forget to plan your shopping well in advance. To plan your shopping you need to know the Retail Shop hours. The most usual hours are:

from	9:00 am	to	12:30-1:00 pm
from	3:00-4:30 pm	to	7:00- 8:00 pm

A few shops in the Center may be open from 9:00 am or earlier up to 7:30 pm, without any lunch break. Very few shops are open after

7:30 pm and sometimes after dinner, like *Rinascente* in Milano (the Bon Marche-like shop in Italy). *Supermercati* (supermarkets) hours usually are from 8:00-8:30 am up to 7:30-8:00 pm, with only 1 hour break and sometimes no break at all.

Shops for food: You can buy food at Supermercati, or at many other Retail Shops, like:

Frutta e Verdura	for	Fruit and vegetables
Latteria	for	Dairy products
Pane, or Forno	for	Bread, or Bakery
Alimentari	for	all other kinds of food
Pasticceria	for	Pastry
Gelateria	for	Ice cream

All shops have another ½ day off, which may differ from shop to shop and from town to town.

Forget the common fantastic policy "satisfied or reimbursed" adopted by almost all USA stores. With this policy shops give you back the money you spent buying any product which you are not happy about for any reason. The policy is completely unknown in Italy.

About Banks: They open in the morning between 8:00 and 9:00 am up to 1:15 pm, and in the afternoon from around 3:00 to 4:30 pm. The ATM (Automatic Teller Machine) is called here BANCOMAT .

About Stamps: Finally something smart and consumer-friendly in Italy. You can buy stamps at the Post office as well as in any "Tabacchi" shop. You may find stamps also wherever you buy a postcard.

About Medical Emergencies: In case of emergency, whether due to accident or natural causes, go immediately to the *Pronto Soccorso* (First Aid) of the nearest Public Hospital. They will perform all the necessary tests, like X-ray, MRI, TAC, blood tests, and if there is a problem they will admit you and operate. All for completely no-charge; all the expenses will be covered by the Italian Health Service. You may find stingy patients from around the world there but the service is nice.

Driving in Italy: differences from the USA

What you may not know while driving in Italy

Measurement Units

Liquids are in liters (l): 1 l = .264 gallons, 1 gallon = 3.785 l

Distances are in kilometers (km) or meters (m) and speed is measured in kilometers per hour (km/h).

Conversion of mph to km/h

1	mph	=	1.609	km/h
20	mph	=	32.18	km/h
25	mph	=	40.23	km/h
50	mph	=	80.45	km/h
55	mph	=	88.50	km/h
65	mph	=	104.59	km/h

Conversion of km/h to mph

1	km/h	=	.62	mph
50	km/h	=	31.07	mph
90	km/h	=	55.93	mph
100	km/h	=	62.15	mph
110	km/h	=	68.36	mph
130	km/h	=	80.79	mph

Speed Limits

For passenger vehicles, and unless otherwise posted:

-in town	50	km/h
-in town, on designated roads	70	km/h
-out of town, on secondary roads	90	km/h
-out of town, on main roads (highways)	110	km/h
-freeways (autostrade)	130	km/h

Right-of-Way

When roads cross and none has stop or yield signs, the general rule is to give the right-of-way to any vehicle coming on your right. **Trams have the right-of-way** whichever direction they are coming from. There are roads which have the right-of-way. In this case you see the relevant signs posted along the road either:

- *road with right-of-way sign* (diamond shaped with white edges and yellow background);

or close to an intersection, the

- *intersection with right-of-way sign* (triangular shaped with red edges, white background and a drawing of the intersection). The road with the right-of-way is larger than the other. There is a sign for every kind of intersection. Be careful: Italian drivers with the right-of-way **demand the right-of-way** at any cost.

The *all way stop sign* does not exist.

Roadway Markings

In Italy **white lines** are used
- to separate traffic moving in opposite directions (yellow lines in the US),
- to separate lanes,
- as edge lines.

Solid white lines should not be crossed, except for entering either an emergency lane or a shoulder for an emergency.

Two solid white lines are used as center lines for 2-way roads with two or more lanes for traffic flow. They should never be crossed.

Edge lines are solid white lines. They may be broken at the intersections with roads (in this case such roads do not have the right-of-way). Solid edge lines should not be crossed, unless you have an emergency.

There are no *two-way turn lanes.*

Overtaking and passing vehicles

Passing a vehicle on the right is illegal, even in a road with 2 or more lanes in your direction. It is possible to pass on the right when the traffic is slow or when traffic guards allow you to do so.

There are no *Diamond* or *Car-pool lanes.*

Turning right at an Intersection with Signal Lights

In Italy there is *no right turn on red*. You should never turn right on red unless a steady green arrow to the right is on.

Turning left

Two-way turn lanes do not exist in Italy. You can turn left only if you do not have to cross one solid or two solid white lines and the *no left turn sign* is not posted there.

Parking

Unless otherwise posted, parking in town is allowed everywhere with almost the same restrictions as in the USA. But in Italy unfortunately it is very difficult to find a place to park. For this reason Traffic Guards are very tolerant (see Welcome to Italy: About Walking in Town).

Alcohol

There is no *Open Container Law* in Italy, but there are almost the same limitations about the Blood Alcohol Content (BAC) for the driver.

Traffic Signs

In Europe because of the different languages spoken in the different countries, signs are more pictorial than written (as they are in the States, perhaps because of the one language?). In addition, and probably because of it, the signs in Europe are much more numerous than in USA.

The **Standard Shape and Color** of the
- *Regulatory Signs* are **circular** shaped and may be either
    - red circles with white or blue background: they tell the driver what is not allowed; or
    - blue circle with white arrows, pictures, or numbers: they are the *must do* signs.
- *Warning Signs* have a **triangular** shape with red edges and white background. They may have yellow background for temporary warnings, like the construction and maintenance signs.
- *Guide Signs* are mostly **rectangular** with different colors, like:
    - green, for signs related to Freeways,
    - blue, for signs related to out-of-town main roads,

- white, for town/city roads,
- yellow, for temporary warnings,
- brown (like in USA), for recreational, touristic signs,
- red, for SOS or accident signs,
- orange, for School Bus or Taxi signs.

Crosswalks

Crosswalks are usually marked (they are called also *zebre*). Pedestrians have the right of way; but **you have to claim** it otherwise vehicles do not stop. On the other hand, if you cross the road not in a crosswalk, surprisingly vehicles may stop.

Freeway Driving

In Italy there are no"freeways". There are instead *autostrade* (plural of au-tostrada), where you have to pay a toll either at the entrance, exit, or at several places along the way. Autostrade are very expensive (e.g., from Milano to Pisa, the cost is more than 100 lire/km, which is 10 cents/mile at the current change rate).

Autostrade are divided highways with at least two lanes per direction. Each side has an emergency lane on the right. There are no intersections or private accesses, but there are service stations (gas stations, restrooms, picnic areas, bars and restaurants) within the autostrade, so you do not have to pay your toll to stop for a coffee. Entering an autostrada sooner or later you'll find a toll gate, where you either collect a card (usually unmanned gate) or pay the toll. If you lose your toll card, you'll be asked to pay for the longest itinerary along the autostrada to your exit, unless you can prove you came a shorter distance.

Very seldom do autostrade pass through towns. Usually they pass by and may have one or more exits for that town. Together with the name of the town you may see other information, like *Centro, Est* (East), *Ovest* (West), *Nord* (North), *Sud* (South). You do not find exits labeled to specific streets.

Exit from an Autostrada: 500 m (½ km) ahead, when possible, you will see the sign with the name of your exit. Before the exit the solid white line of the emergency lane becomes a broken line and the emergency lane becomes a deceleration lane.

It does not happen that a lane becomes an exit lane and you must exit.

Have a nice and safe drive in Italy!

The most common measurement units

Length

cm = centimeter (centimetro); m = meter (metro); km = kilometer (chilometro)

1 inch	=	2.54	cm	1 cm	=	.3937	inches
1 foot	=	30.48	cm	1 m	=	39.37	inches
1 yard	=	.914	m	1 m	=	3.28	feet
1 mile	=	1.609	km	1 km	=	.621	miles

Speed

km/h, for the conversion table from km/h to mi/h see the chapter "Driving in Italy"

Capacity

l = liter (litro)

1 gallon	=	3.785 l	1 liter (litro)	= 2.1	pints
1 quart	=	.946 l	1 l	= 1.056	quarts
			1 l	= .264	gallons

Weight

g = gram (grammo); hg = hectogram (ettogrammo, or simply etto); kg = kilogram (chilogrammo, or simply chilo; in Italian "ch" is pronounced like"k")

1 ounce	= 28.35 g	1 hg	= 3.527 ounces
1 pound	= .4536 kg	1 hg	= 0.220 pounds
		1 kg	=2.2046 pounds

Temperature

Temperatures are in Italy measured according to the Celsius centigrade scale.
To convert Celsius (°C) in Fahrenheit grades (°F), apply the following formula:

Temperature in °F = Temperature in °C x 1.8 + 32°
i.e.   15 °C = (15 x 1.8 + 32) °F = 59 °F

Conversion table:

°Fahrenheit	°Celsius
14	-10
32	0
50	10
68	20
86	30
212	100

In Italy the decimal point becomes a comma, while the comma replaces the USA use of the point for separating units from thousands, etc.
Example: 3,567.89 in the USA becomes 3.567,89 in Italy.
In Italy and USA decimal point and comma have exactly opposite uses in the number system.

The local CAI Sections

Local CAI Sections around the Apuane Alps

Section	Telephone	Address	Days open	Hours open
55051 Barga	0583 724125	Piazza Angelio, 5	Friday	21:00-23:00
54033 Carrara	0585 776782	Via Giorgi, 1	from Monday to Saturday	19:00-20:00
			Thursday	21:00-23:00
55032 Castelnuovo G.	0583 74352	Via V. Emanuele	Saturday	18:00-19:00
50122 Firenze	055 2340580	Via dello Studio, 5	from Monday to Friday	17:00-19:00
55042 Forte dei Marmi	0584 80412	Via Michelangelo, 47	Friday	21:00-23:00
57123 Livorno	0586 897785	Via Santa Fortunata 31	from Monday to Friday	16:30-18:30
55100 Lucca	0583 582669	Cortile Carrara, 18	from Monday to Friday	19:00-20:30
54100 Massa	0585 488081	Piazza Mazzini, 13	Monday, Wednesday, Friday	19:00-20:00
55045 Pietrasanta	0584 70563	Via Mazzini, 105	Friday	21:00-23:00
56100 Pisa	050 578004	Via Cisanello, 2	Wednesday and Friday	21:00-23:00
			Friday	17:00-19:00
19038 Sarzana	0187 625154	Piazza Firmafede, 13	from Monday to Saturday	18:00-19:00
55049 Viareggio	0584 56226	Via S. Maria Goretti	Tuesday and Thursday	18:00-20:00
			Friday	21:00-23:00

Local CAI Sections around the Cinque Terre Riviera

Section	Telephone	Address	Days open	Hours open
16043 Chiavari	0185 311851	Via San Francesco, 27	Friday	20:30-23:00
16129 Genova	010 310584	Piazza Palermo, 11	from Tuesday to Friday on Thursday, also	17:00-19:00 21:00-23:00
16123 Genova	010 565564	Vico Parmigiani, 1/3	Tuesday and Friday	18:00-19:30
16100 Genova	010 466709	Via Agnese, 1	Tuesday and Friday	21:00-23:00
19100 La Spezia	0187 22873	Via Amendola, 196	Monday, Wednesday, Friday Thursday	17:00-18:00 21:00-23:00

The CAI trails in the Apuane Alps

#2   Casoli - Foce del Crocione - Pascoso

#3   Capezzano - Foce di S. Anna - Farnocchia - Foce di S. Rocchino - Foce di Grattaculo - Foce del Pallone - Matanna - Palagnana

#4   S. Anna di Stazzema - Case di Berna - Foce di Farnocchia - Farnocchia

#5   Stazzema - Rifugio "Forte dei Marmi"- Callare Matanna - Alto Matanna

#5bis Dirt road over Stazzema - Casa del Pittore - Rifugio Forte dei Marmi

#6   Stazzema - Fonte Moscoso - Foce di Petrosciana - Fornovolasco

#7   Cardoso Collemezzana - Foce di Valli - Passo degli Uomini della Neve Foce del Puntone - Rifugio Rossi - Piglionico

#8   Cardoso - Fonte Moscoso - Foce delle Porchette - Palagnana

#9   Levigliani - Passo dell' Alpino - Foce di Mosceta - Col di Favilla - Isola Santa

#10   Ponte Merletti - Passo dei Fordazzani - Passo Croce

#11   Passo Croce - Fociomboli - Puntato - Col di Favilla - Isola Santa

#12   Cardoso - Monte Forato - Casa Felice - Le Casette - Junction #6 - Fornovolasco

#31   Azzano - Cervaiole - marmifera to Cave Fondone - Arni - Cave del Tombaccio - marmifera to Passo Sella - Arnetola

#33   Pasquilio - Passo del Pitone - Passo della Greppia - Passo degli Uncini - Le Gobbie - Rifugio Puliti - Arni

#35   Reseceto - Via Vandelli - Passo Tambura - Arnetola

#36   Casa Biforco - Canal Cerignano - Vettolina - Piastrone - Cava della Piastra Marina - Passo della Focolaccia

#37   Canal Regolo (Forno) - Foce di Navola - Capanna Garnerone - Foce di Giovo - Rifugio Donegani

#38   Colonnata - Case Vergheto - Foce Luccica - Foce di Vinca - Vinca

#39   Ravaccione - Foce di Pianza - il Balzone - Vinca - Castellaccio - Aiola - Equi Terme

#40   Carrara - M. Darma - La Pianacca - Piscinicchi - Prati di Cardeto - Monzone

#41   Pian della Fioba (Rifugio "Città di Massa") - Colle della Tecchia - la Strega - Canal d' Angiola - Foce del Frate - Passo degli Uncini

#42   Foce del Frate junction to #33 towards Le Gobbie

#46	Ponte Storto - Passo Gabellaccia - Valsaliceto - Via del Sale - Maestà della Villa - Tenerano
#101	Foce Lucese - Mirabello - Campo all'Orzo - Foce del Crocione - Foce del Pallone - Alto Matanna
#102	S. Giuseppe in Trebbio - Ritrogoli - Campo all'Orzo
#103	Groppa - Prati del Piglione - Foce del Crocione
#104	Metato - Campo all'Orzo - Monte Prano
#106	Trescolli - Foce di S. Rocchino - Pomezzana - Rifugio Forte dei Marmi
#107	La Culla - Case i Lecci - Le Piastre - Monte Gabberi - Foce di S. Rocchino
#108	Foce delle Porchette - le Scalette - Foce del Pallino - il Termine
#109	Alto Matanna - Foce delle Porchette - Foce di Petrosciana
#112	Casoli - Campo all'Orzo
#121	Foce di S. Rocchino - Foce di Grattaculo - Rifugio Forte dei Marmi - Fonte Moscoso
#122	Pruno - Le Caselle - Passo dell'Alpino
#123	Retignano - le Scalette - Casa Guidi - Junction #122 - Passo dell'Alpino
#124	Foce di Mosceta - La Fania- Collemezzana - Penna Rossa - Foce di Petrosciana
#124bis	Junction #124 - Casa Colleoni - junction #6 (Fonte Moscoso)
#125	Foce Mosceta - Foce di Valli
#126	Foce Mosceta - Gorfigliette - Collo della Pania - Foce del Puntone - Rifugio Rossi
#127	Foce Mosceta - junction #139 to Borra di Canala - Piglionico
#128	Tre Fiumi - Puntato - Foce Mosceta
#129	Ponte Merletti - Campanice - Fociomboli - Foce Mosceta
#130	Fornovolasco - Foce di Valli
#131	Foce di Petrosciana - Casa del Monte - Foce di Valli
#132	Vergemoli - Le Rocchette
#133	Casa Riccio - Alpe di S. Antonio - Peritano - Pasquigliora - Colle Panestra
#134	Fornovolasco - Le Tese - Le Rocchette
#135	Trassilico - Il Termine - Pioppo (Palagnana)
#136	Cardoso - S. Luigi - Foce Palodina - Foce Pampanella (junction #135)
#137	Il Termine - Colle Maschio - Foce di Petrosciana
#138	Pizzorno - Colle Panestra - Piglionico

#139   Rifugio Rossi - Foce del Puntone - Borra di Canala - Junction #127

#140   Seravezza - La Canala - Cerreta S. Nicola - Pasquilio

#141   Passo dei Fordazzani - Colle Cipollaio - Junction #31

#142   Cervaiole - Passo del Vaso Tondo - Cave del Fondone

#143   Passo degli Uncini - Monte Altissimo - Passo del Vaso Tondo - Junction #142

#144   Arni - Malpasso - Fatonero - Passo Fiocca - Capanna di Romecchio - Passo Sella

#145   Capanne di Careggine - Colle delle Capanne - Penna di Sumbra - Sentiero "R. Malfatti"- Passo Fiocca

#146   Arnetola - Junction Ferrata "Vecchiacchi"

#147   Campocatino - San Viano - Cava Formignacola - Junction #35 (via Vandelli)

#148   Passo Tambura - Monte Tambura - Passo della Focolaccia

#150   Le Gobbie - Passo del Vestito - Sella di Macina - Passo Sella - Junction #31

#160   Junction #165 Canale della Neve - Focola del Vento - Cava Bagnoli - Monte Sella

#161   Resceto - Monte Castagnolo - Cave della Mandriola - Junction #36 - Cava della Sordola - Celia Caldia - Poggio della Greppa

#162   Renara - Casa Bonotti - Passo del Vestito - Le Gobbie

#163   Miniera della Vandelli - Junction #166 below Cave Magnani

#164   Canale della Neve - Fosso dei Campaniletti - Rifugio Conti - Focetta dell'Acqua Fredda

#165   Resceto - Canale dei Vernacchi - Ponte Pisciarotto - Canale della Neve - La Selvarella - Cave Cruze - Foce dell'Acqua Fredda

#166   Resceto - Casa del Fondo - Lizza Magnani - Cave Magnani - Rifugio Aronte - Passo della Focolaccia

#166bis Resceto - Casa del Fondo - Lizza Silvia - Junction #36 - Piastrone - Cava della Piastra Marina - Rifugio Aronte - Passo della Focolaccia

#167   Casa Biforco - Valle degli Alberghi - Case Carpano - Forcella di Porta - Rifugio Aronte

#168   Casa Biforco - Canal Fondone - Traversa - Cormeneto - Foce di Monte Rasori

#169   Forno - Road to Case Vergheto - La Lavagnina - Casette

#170   Resceto - Vettolina - Case Carpano

#171	Tenerano - Foce S. Antonio - Casa Cardeto - Acquasparta - Rifugio Carrara
#172	Foce Luccica - Foce della Faggiola - Foce di Pianza
#173	Rifugio Carrara - Foce di Pianza - Foce del Faneletto - Foce del Pollaro - Foce di Vinca - Foce di Navola - Capanna Garnerone
#174	Casa Cardeto - Foce Pozzi - Foce di Pianza
#175	Vinca - Capanne di Giovo - Foce di Giovo
#176	Equi Terme - Orti di Pozzola - Ugliancaldo
#177	Vagli di Sopra - Campocatino - Passo Tombaccia - Carcaraia - Passo della Focolaccia
#178	Serenaia - Foce di Cardeto - Passo della Focolaccia
#179	Foce di Giovo - Cava 27 - Foce di Cardeto - Passo della Focolaccia
#180	Rifugio Donegani - Orto di Donna - Junction #178
#181	Pieve S. Lorenza (FS Station) - Ugliancaldo - Poggio Baldozzana - Capradossa - Foce Siggioli - Foce di Giovo
#182	Piastra - Cave di Lorano - Piazzale dell'Uccelliera - Fontana Antica - Rifugio Carrara
#183	Case dei Monzonari - Casa Respettolo - Foce Pozzi - Rifugio Carrara
#184	Gragnana - La Pianaccia - Casa Cardeto - Foce Porcigliola- Casa Respettolo
#185	Castelpoggio - Gabellaccia - Acquasparta - Rifugio Carrara
#186	Foce Rasori - Finestra Grondilice - Cava 27
#187	Rifugio Donegani - Foce Siggioli
#188	Pian della Fioba (Rifugio "Città di Massa") - Colle della Tecchia - Passo della Greppia
#190	Vinca - Foce dei Lizzari - Ferrata Zaccagna - Cava del Cantonaccio
#191	Capanne di Giovo - Sentiero Piotti - Foce dei Lizzari
#192	Solco di Equi - Cave Walton - La Forticella - Poggio Baldozzana

The trails leading to the summit of the following mountains are not numbered but usually signed with blue (sometimes red) marks:

Monte Lieto	from	S. Anna di Stazzema
Monte Matanna	from	Foce del Pallone
Monte Nona	from	Callare Matanna
Monte Forato	from	Foce di Valli
Monte Palodina	from	Foce Palodina

Monte Freddone	from	Fociomboli
Monte Corchia	from	Foce di Mosceta
Pania della Croce	from	Colle della Pania
Pizzo delle Saette	from	Foce del Puntone
Pania Secca	from	Rifugio Rossi
Monte Sella	from	Passo Sella
Monte Pisanino	from	Foce di Cardeto
Monte Grondilice	from	Finestra del Grondilice
Pizzo d'Uccello	from	Giovetto
Monte Sagro	from	Foce della Faggiola

Main CAI trails along the Cinque Terre

1   Portovenere - Punta Mesco - Levanto, along the main divide
2   Riomaggiore - Monterosso, along the coast
3   Riomaggiore - Telegrafo - Biassa
4   Pegazzano - Biassa - Sant'Antonio - Schiara mare
5   San Benedetto - Quaratica - Marvede
7   Riccò del Golfo - Casella - Cigoletta - Vernazza
8   Vernazza - Foce Drignana
9   Monterosso - Santuario Madonna di Saviore
10   Punta Mesco - Monterosso
11   Marola - Campiglia - Tramonti - Persico mare

Main trails around Monte Portofino

bb   Camogli - San Rosso - San Fruttuoso - Base "0"- Prato - Olmi -
      San Sebastiano - Portofino
c   Camogli - Gaixella - Pietre Strette - San Fruttuoso
sq   Ruta - Portofino Vetta - Gaixella - Pietre Strette - Bocche - Crocetta
      - Olmi - Portofino
t t   Fornelli - Toca - Paradiso - Monte di Portofino - Pietre Strette
bbb   Toca - Pietre Strette - Base "0"

In Monte Portofino trails have no numbers, but symbols, precisely:

bb   stands for "two small red balls"
c   stands for "empty red circle"
sq   stands for a "small red square"
t t   stands for "two small empty red triangles"
bbb   stands for "a triangle of three small red balls in the vertices"

REFERENCES

1 - Amery L.S., *Scrambling in the Carrara Marbles*, Alpine Journal, February 1913

2 - Comunità Montana della Garfagnana, *GT-Garfagnana Trekking,* Tamari Montagna Edizioni, Bologna, 1986, Map 1:30000 attached (in Italian)

3 - Desio A., *Guida Naturalistica Tascabile del Monte di Portofino,* Stringa Editore, Genova, 1978

4 - Dickens Charles, *American Notes & Pictures from Italy*, Chapman Hall Ltd., London, pg. 347-349, July 1907

5 - Freshfield D.W., *Sketches from the Apennines*, Alpine Journal, February 1876

6 - Funck S., *Alpi Apuane - Salite Scelte*, ed. Pezzini, 1993

7 - Girani A., *Guida al Monte di Portofino*, Sagep Libri, Genova, 1997, Map 1:10000 attached

8 - Montagna E., Nerli A., Sabbadini A., *Alpi Apuane*, CAI - TCI, 1979

9 - *Home Emerges at Lake's Bottom,* National Geographic Magazine, Geographica, Vol.186, n. 6, December 1994

10 - Newman Cathy, *Carrara Marble: Touchstone of Eternity*, National Geographic Magazine, Vol. 162, n. 1, July 1982, pag. 42-59

11 - Suter K., *Die Apuanischen Alpen*, Die Alpen, 1946

12 - The Sierra Club National Traveler, *Wild Italy*, Sierra Club Books, 1994 (pag. 111-117 -Apuane Alps)

13 - Tuckett F.F., *The Pizzo d'Uccello and the Solco d'Equi*, Alpine Journal, November 1883

14 - Utterson Kelso W.E., *Les Alpes Apuanes*, Boll. CAI 1873, n. 21, 37

Internet

15 - CAI Lugo, *Tutti i rifugi del CAI* (a list of all the Mountain Huts), http://www.racine.ra.it/cailugo

16 - Prosperini G., *Alpi Apuane*, http:www.aspide.it/freeweb/ g.prosperini

Maps

1 - *Carta dei Sentieri delle Apuane Settentrionali*, 1:12500, edited by the CAI Section of Pisa, 1988

2 - *Alpi Apuane, Carta dei sentieri e rifugi,* 1:25000, Ed. Multigraphic, Firenze, 1993

3 - *Alpi Apuane,* Carta escursionistica 1:10,000, SELCA, Firenze, 1995

4 - *Toscana*, 1:200000, Touring Club Italiano, 1996

5 - *Carta dei sentieri delle Alpi Apuane*, Club Alpino Italiano Sezione di Lucca, 1996 (sketch map)

Comments, suggestions or corrections

If you have comments, suggestions or corrections, please send e-mail
to: **TuscanAlps@aol.com**

or address mail to:

The Alps of Tuscany
28426 16th Ave. S., Apt. 1
Federal Way, WA 98003, USA

Many thanks for your help!

INDEX